MISSING PIECES

Missing Pieces

MY LIFE AS A CHILD SURVIVOR
OF THE HOLOCAUST

Olga Verrall

UNIVERSITY OF
CALGARY
PRESS

University of Calgary Press
2500 University Drive NW
Calgary, Alberta
Canada T2N 1N4
www.uofcpress.com

LIBRARY AND ARCHIVES CANADA CATALOGUING IN PUBLICATION

Verrall, Olga, 1936-
    Missing pieces : my life as a child survivor of the Holocaust / Olga Verrall.

(Legacies shared ; 22)
ISBN 978-1-55238-220-2

    1. Verrall, Olga, 1936-. 2. Jews –Hungary–Biography. 3. Holocaust, Jewish (1939-1945)–Hungary–Personal narratives. 4. Jewish children in the Holocaust–Hungary–Biography. 5. Holocaust survivors–Canada–Biography. I. Title. II. Series.

DS135.H93B36 2007   940.53'18092   C2007-901732-0

The University of Calgary Press acknowledges the support of the Alberta Foundation for the Arts for our publications. We acknowledge the financial support of the Government of Canada through the Book Publishing Industry Development Program (BPIDP) for our publishing activities. We acknowledge the financial support of the Canada Council for the Arts for our publishing program. This book has been published with the aid of a grant from the Alberta Lottery Fund — Community Initiatives Program.

Printed and bound in Canada by AGMV Marquis
∞ This book is printed on Silva Enviro paper

Cover design, page design and typesetting by Melina Cusano

Dedication

For all those I hold dear in my heart and for those who are still suffering at the hands of brutal regimes

Author's Note

Upon publication of this book, all money due to Olga Verrall from book sales shall go directly to the Autism Spectrum Disorders Society of Ontario to help all the Michaels and Davids to overcome their difficulties.

Grief is better than gaiety — for through a sad countenance, the heart is improved. — Ecclesiastes

Table of Contents

FOREWORD

In the spring of 1944, Adolf Eichmann arrived in Hungary with the responsibility of deporting the 800,000 remaining Jews within the country. The atrocities committed by the Nazis were already well known, and the political pressure to cease the deportations was strong. Despite the warnings by American president Franklin Delano Roosevelt, the objections from within the political leadership of Hungary, and the fruitless efforts made by Hungarian Jewish community leaders Joel Brand and Rudolph Kasztner, 437,000 Jews were deported between May 15 and June 9 – the fastest deportation since Poland in 1941. Only the Swedish diplomat Raoul Wallenberg managed to save a significant number of Jews by providing them with Swedish passports and housing them in properties he either bought or rented. Dr. Kasztner's secret co-operation agreement with Eichmann – to exchange Jews for cash, goods, and Kasztner's promise to keep order in the camps – saved only a small group of Jews, many of whom were elitists, relatives, or residents from his village. It is reported that Eichmann transferred approximately 15,000 Jews to Vienna and Strasshof for labour to "put them on ice" (that is, not for extermination) as a sign of good faith. Kasztner was later accused in Israel of facilitating the Jewish Hungarian deportation. By the end of the war, one year after the Nazi invasion of Hungary, the Nazis had murdered 570,000 out of the 800,000 Hungarian Jews.

It was in late spring of 1944 when the deportation of my family began. The process of transportation from one holding area to another took approximately six weeks until they arrived at their final destination, a concentration camp called Strasshof. There is no explanation as to why their cattle train stopped in Strasshof rather than being delivered directly to Auschwitz as so many others were. Nevertheless, while at that camp, the gesture of one man changed the course of my family's life forever. This man, an acquaintance of my grandfather's, whispered into my grandfather's ear, "When the Germans ask if anyone has any skills, raise your hand." My grandfather obeyed this man's instruction, and subsequently, the entire family was sent to a little-known labour camp called Auspitz. That bit of luck on that fateful day was definitely responsible for prolonging the lives of my family until they were liberated on April 13, 1945 – my father's birthday. My father's parents and younger sister all managed to stay together and survived, each with his or her own version of the suffering and abuse they endured.

My father, Tibor (Tibi) Barsony, finally returned to the site of Auspitz in present-day Slovakia where most of his family had been held captive from 1944 to 1945. This was during the time when millions of Jews from all over Europe were being systematically slaughtered. In 1944, my father was eleven years old. Now, sixty years later, he was determined to find traces of his own grandfather, who had died during his internment.

When my father and I arrived at the town of Auspitz (now called Hustopece), we drove around aimlessly as if some memory of his would trigger our direction. Eventually, destiny and perseverance found a local historical society that has collected records from that dark period. With unexpected exuberance, two locals responsible for the town's museum greeted my father as if he were a hero and studied his face with a peculiar look of incredulity on their faces. They were genuinely excited about the prospects of learning more about the events that had occurred on their soil so they began to quiz my father for every detail. It turned out that the historians of this town have been trying desperately to prove the existence of the Auspitz labour camp since information became unearthed in 2001. After answering all their queries and providing them with additional details, my father was taken upstairs to a small, locally preserved museum in the same building. In one small room of this museum was a book, which the Germans had left, documenting local deaths during the Nazi occupation period. To our amazement, the glass-encased book

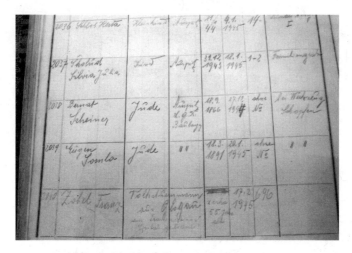

Page from a book in the Mestske Museum in Hustopece open to my grandfather's death notice.

was opened to the winter of 1944 to the only page where the names of two Jews stood. The first Jew on the list was my great-grandfather. It was like a miracle. It seemed this book was there waiting for my father to find it. He read over and over again: *Bernard Scheiner. Jude. Died: December 1944. Buried: On location.*

This unlikely event – finding documentation of his grandfather's death in the labour camp – was the culmination of years of uncertainty and the breakthrough my father had prayed for. It was also an emotional moment that none of us there that day will forget. This pilgrimage to Hustopece and our walk through the former labour camp was my father's way of confirming that the horrors he had experienced in this camp were real. These appalling events – the details of which he has held deep within him for the past sixty years – stole the innocence of his childhood, and yet nobody seemed to take notice. No one was ever told of the lesser-known labour camp called Auspitz. Even the local historical society didn't have many facts

MĚSTSKÉ MUZEUM A GALERIE HUSTOPEČE
organizační složka města Hustopeče
Dukelské náměstí 23, 693 01 Hustopeče
tel.: +420 519 413 849, 519 412 254
e-mail: muzeum@hustopece-city.cz
galerie@hustopece-city.cz

Hustopeče, 31. August, 2005

Dear Olga Verrall,

I thank You very much for Your (for us) so important letters. We found by this time nobody from the survivors.

It is sad that Your memories of Hustopeče are associated with the local concentration camp. This fact (then about KZ-Lager) knew in Hustopeče nobody.

In Hustopeče lived in the war time about 1800 Germans and 700 Czechs (about 1000 Czech was from Hustopeče expelled in October 1938 – before came the Hilter´s army to Hustopeče - and Hustopeče became a part of Nazi-empire). In 1945 (past the war) was the authentic Germans – citizen expelled.

Only one of the authentic Czechs – Mr. Šimša (Your brother meet him in Hustopeče, Mr. Šimša had to work near the labor camp, the Czechs was at that time the citizen of 2. category) gave evidence to all this reality.

Past 1989 („the velvet revolution") visit the authentic Germans citizen Hustopeče and they remember not the camp (maybe they will not remember).

I´m looking forward to Your visit (give me – pleace - the date in advance).

I´m looking forward to our co-operation.

Give – please – Your brother (his wife and son) my greatest regards.

Sincerely

Soňa Nezhodová
Městské muzeum a galerie
Dukelské náměstí 23
693 01 Hustopeče
Czech Republic

Letter from the Mestske Museum in Hustopece, 2005, validating the existence of the Auspitz labour camp.

about the camp. My father didn't want to return; he was compelled to return. It allowed him an opportunity to share a long-denied glimpse into his past with me, his son. It allowed him to pay his respects to his grandfather on his own terms. But most importantly, his return to Auspitz now stands as a testimonial to all those who seek the truth of this labour camp. Indeed, the members of my father's family are the last known survivors.

Infamous death camps throughout Europe received worldwide attention after the war whereas this lesser-known camp called Auspitz remained unnoticed, its prisoners never to return to confirm their experiences. Only after my father's pilgrimage did the historical society of Hustopece begin to collect and examine the corroborating facts pertaining to this Nazi-run Jewish labour camp. My aunt Olga has long wanted to share the horrendous events she experienced during the Nazi occupation and hopes to finally document the truth behind the existence of the Auspitz camp and the permanent effect the camp has had on her life. After sixty years, the truth and scope of the Holocaust continues to be revealed. For her family, for herself, and for humanity, this book recounts my aunt's story. It is the story of survival, and a tale of the hope and exceptional circumstances that shaped the life of one helplessly brave eight-year-old girl.

Robert Barsony
November 2005

Reflections

Yesterday is the past. Tomorrow is the future, but today is a Gift.
That is why it is called the present. – Anonymous

There is a beautiful tract of land near my Toronto home called G. Lord Ross Park, and every day for the last twenty-five years, I have been taking the same route through this park on my daily walk. As I walk, I am reminded of how my life has been shaped by nature and natural forces. I love the tranquility that nature inspires in me and how at critical times, it has helped me to heal. The West Don River runs through the park, and I often stop to watch the flowing water and wonder at the force with which the water changes every second. I watch, fascinated, as some small leaves and other debris get stuck in eddies in the river while others keep rolling along in the roiling water. I realize that I, too, have been compelled by life's forces to change direction and to keep moving. As I walk, I frequently run into the same people, and I greet them and look into their eyes and smile. How satisfying it is when my smile brings a smile in return.

Along the path I always stop to look at one particular old oak tree that I have grown very fond of over the years. This particular oak's solidity and special grace give me comfort somehow. I often think about how much that tree must have seen in its many years in this spot and how the world around it has changed since it first took root here. Silently, standing so sturdily among the other trees, it speaks to me almost as if it were trying to convey a message as I walk by, to encourage me with its strength.

We have been aging together these twenty-five years, this oak and I. Perhaps, I think as I look at the growths that have developed on its bark, it isn't as strong as it looks; perhaps the oak is being consumed by disease from within. What a sad day it would be for me if something should suddenly happen to this grand old tree that has somehow become a symbol to me of my own life and my own struggle to survive. I came here to Canada from a different life in Hungary where I witnessed and heard so many horrible, tragic things. Yet with all that I have seen and lived through, I am still here to bear witness to what I have experienced. I know I carry a knowledge that will fade away into the dark after I am gone. I think of these things as I pass the oak tree and sense the secrets he is also carrying. Sometimes I imagine him whispering to me. "I see you and care for you, too," he seems to be saying. "We have developed a pact, you and I, an understanding between us." We both may be aging, growing more vulnerable and fragile, but we have within us a power and strength that is born of survival.

I am writing this book as a legacy and a small contribution on my part in the struggle of all mankind to create a better world. This book has been building in me for a long time, and I cannot keep it inside any more. I want and I need to talk about it. I had never really thought of myself as a Holocaust survivor until I saw a film in 1983 at the Royal Ontario Museum during the exhibit "The Precious Legacy: Judaic Treasures from the Czechoslovak State Collection."

This film spoke of how few children of my age and younger lived through the Holocaust. I was moved emotionally by my overwhelming feeling of guilt at having survived and had to be ushered out of the theatre. Like other survivors, I felt that I had travelled a road unknown and sometimes disbelieved by everyone else. I saw my journey as one that was at times gruesome and dark, yet at other times amazingly colourful and precious. And I began to see that writing this book would be a form of needed validation for me and my memories. As with other child survivors, it is hard to believe I am still here after all we endured. Perhaps by writing it down I will be able to show ordinary people like me that by learning from all of life's extraordinary difficulties it is possible to move on and use everything as a great learning experience.

Some people have said that there are so many Holocaust survivor memoirs already. But will there ever be enough? The generation that provides the rest of the world with personal accounts of the Holocaust is slowly dying out. The Holocaust was one of the turning points in history of humanity, and it is crucial that each and every survivor be offered the opportunity to publish his or her experiences so that the rest of the world can become familiar with the survivors' analyses of the profound lessons of life and death they learned. To appreciate history means understanding the perception and observation of events by those who experienced those events first-hand. Factual events are historically meaningful, but a person's perception of those historical events brings the facts to life. Holocaust survivors are living historians who contribute their testimony to educate the world on the events of the past. *The American Heritage Dictionary* defines "history" as follows: "A narrative of events; a story. A chronological record of events, as of the life or development of a people or institution, often including an explanation or commentary on those events." I would find it hard to believe that historians would agree that there are just too many Holocaust memoirs available.

My hope is that this book will be available to students who should be prepared for life in unconditional love, understanding, and mutual respect for one another. I feel that in this way I will have fulfilled my promise to honour the memory of the murdered and to bear witness to the darkest period of history in my lifetime.

That way, when my time comes, I can leave this earth with some kind of closure.

Olga Verrall
April 2006

ACKNOWLEDGEMENTS

It is a difficult task for me to adequately express my gratitude to everyone who so willingly contributed to my project and made it possible for me to complete *Missing Pieces*, one more testimonial to the suffering endured by victims of the Holocaust and its aftermath. I've always had great admiration for people who fight for a human cause: people like June Callwood, Simon Wiesenthal, Elie Wiesel – they are my mentors. And I have taken the mortar for my story from some precious moments on my daily walks: moments when my Creator has guided me through tough times and showed me the right places, moments when strangers have returned my smiles.

My thanks go to the following wonderful people who encouraged me and helped me make *Missing Pieces* the book you now hold:

The late Janos Forrai for his encouragement and loving friendship; I wish he were here now.

The late Ibolya Szalai Groszman for reading my very first scribbles; she was my role model.

Myrna Riback, my first editor and writing coach, for laying down a solid foundation for this book; without her help, my memoirs might not have evolved into the book you are now holding.

Cheryl Freedman, my occasionally crabby but otherwise wonderful second editor, who reorganized and polished the first draft of the manuscript, deciphered my handwritten notes, and held my hand and forced me to finish the book when I was depressed and ready to give up; without her, this might not have evolved into a book at all.

John King, senior editor at University of Calgary Press, who became my soul mate throughout our many conversations with his soothing voice that I so needed.

David Carr, University of Manitoba Press, who referred me to John King. (Many kind and talented people hail from Manitoba).

The other staff at University of Calgary Press – Walter Hildebrandt, Karen Buttner, Melina Cusano, Kellie Moynihan, Peter Enman, Greg Madsen, and Geoffrey Simmins – for their knowledgeable touch in making my book a reality.

Librarian Steven M. Bergson for looking up material for me at the Jewish Public Library of Toronto.

Martin Goldman from the United States Holocaust Memorial Museum in Washington, DC, for reading the first draft of my manuscript, believing that it was good enough to be published, and helping me find a publisher; Martin, you are a *mensch*.

Editor John Parry for reading my manuscript and giving expert advice.

Author Sylvia Maultash Warsh for her valuable remarks and referral.

Philippa Daly for caring and valued advice.

My children for their help and support (even through their frustration) as they watched me relive my past.

Karen Vadasz for cheerfully helping out when she could.

Robert Barsony for his excellent contribution.

Dino, my hairdresser of 35 years at Fantasy Cuts. (As the saying goes, "Only her hairdresser knows.")

Last, but not least, my brothers – Peter, Paul, and Tibi – and sisters-in-law – Zsuzsi and Marika – for validating me and filling in some childhood stories my memory did not reach.

There are many other worthy people who came into my life during the writing of this book, and if my selective memory is forgetting anyone, I ask for forgiveness – we are human, after all.

Special thanks to Ira Levis and the team at Breakthrough Films and Television for including us in their "Stories of mothers and daughters," which made our trip to Hungary possible.

CHAPTER 1

Birth, Love, and Tradition

The greatest gift in life is life itself. – Anonymous

I came into this world on July 10, 1936, in the small town of Szarvas, Hungary. I was born at home on a street named after the famous nineteenth-century Hungarian novelist Jokai Mor. It was during the first seven wonderful years of my life in that house at Jokai Mor Utca 236 that I learned all the important things I still cherish in life, the most important of which is love.

My mother was thirty-five by the time I came along. My parents already had three sons – Peter, Pali, and Tibi – ranging in age from twelve to three and very much wanted a girl. Both my maternal (Olga Esther) and paternal (Paula Pearl) grandmothers had died by then, and I was named for both of them. How very happy she was, my mother often told me, when they told her it was a girl and cut the umbilical cord, a cord with which I think I am still somehow tied to her even now.

I can still feel the warmth of my mother's embrace as she sat beside me when I was a child and told me the story of my birth, a story I was delighted to hear over and over again. My grandparents came from noble stock and were well loved in the community so the townspeople, excited at the news that Mariska Berger had given birth to a baby girl, rang the church bells to announce my arrival. My parents and grandfather celebrated my birth with Jews and non-Jews alike, a testament both to their pride as highly assimilated Hungarians *and* to the absence of anti-Semitism in Szarvas at that time. My mother would also describe the white bunting she wrapped me in. It was called *polya* and was made of a white, embroidered pillow sham with a small pillow tucked into it to give the new mother a firm, easy way to hold her baby. Everyone came to see me and brought a gift, and proudly my mother handed me around from person to person so they could have a good look. All of them, she told me, said I was beautiful. Then she would smile and say that when people first saw me, they said, "After so many gorgeous boys, now you have a girl who has a mouth from ear to ear." It didn't seem like much of a compliment to me then, but in due time I discovered that a big mouth can be an asset.

I had arrived into a big, beautiful family, and everyone was ecstatic. We were an upper-middle-class, observant Jewish family, who lived a proper, modest life steeped in Jewish heritage. My mother was born Maria Scheiner on January 23, 1902, in Szarvas, in the same house where all her children would later be born and where we all lived with her father, Bernat, until the war. I don't remember my grandfather as a particularly lovable or happy person, but perhaps the loss of his wife to diabetes four years before my birth had something to do with that. My mother, who could never speak of her mother without her eyes welling up with tears, always said that whoever knew her had loved her. My grandfather certainly had loved her very dearly and must have missed her terribly. He was tall and straight and had a good, strong, lean body. He wasn't an overly tidy person, though, and his clothes were loose and ill-fitting. To me, he always looked very old, particularly when he sat in the yard smoking the pipe he always seemed to have between his teeth and watching me play with the newborn chicks and white rabbits my brother Peter was raising for their fur.

My grandfather owned and ran a bread-only bakery, which was also located on our property, and to this day the aroma of freshly baked bread brings back to me a flood of pleasant memories. I remember my grandfather would come home from the bakery for lunch. He was always absorbed in a book or newspaper and smoked his pipe constantly. Craving some affection, I would rub up against his leg, but rather than holding me, he would gently push my behind and say, "Run along and play, Olgicam."

My mother was an only child. I don't think she had been shown a great deal of physical affection as she was growing up so she was not particularly physical with us either. It was also a different world back then, and among the upper middle class, obvious signs of affection like hugging and kissing, even with children, were thought to be too demonstrative. Still, my mother, whom I called *Anyuka* (Mama), loved us all very much and showed us her love in many other ways: her elaborate meals, her emphasis on etiquette and bringing us up properly, and her constant attention to our well-being. She was a good-looking and gracious woman with heavy, chestnut-brown hair that she wore up plainly to frame her aristocratic face.

Anyuka was intelligent and could speak High German, which she had learned from a private tutor. She hadn't been able to go to university, something she had very much wanted to do, because the anti-Jewish laws, *Numerus Clausus* (restricted admission), barred Jews from attending. Instead she went to chef school and became a pastry chef, this being one of the options open to her. In the first years of the war, she owned a pastry shop on the main market square, but because the anti-Jewish laws also wouldn't allow her to own a business, the shop was managed by a non-Jew, a front man named Mr. Moldavanyi. However, she did have a Jewish baker, Mr. Weiss, supplying her with pastries.

She herself did not bake for the shop because she had her hands full running a kosher home and making sure her four children followed all the rules of Jewish modesty and tradition. My mother was an exceptionally good cook, and, oh my, how she could bake! The aromas coming from her kitchen always permeated our entire house, and the memory of them still fills my nostrils whenever I am preparing for Shabbat or the holidays: the fragrance of her golden chicken soup, fried liver with onions, freshly baked *challah*, the Sabbath one-pot meal of beans and meat called *cholent*, cheese buns, *kuglof* (yeast coffee cake filled with chocolate), and so much more. How grateful I am to have inherited some of her cooking and baking talent so I can continue her traditions.

My father, Laszlo Berger, was a very good-looking man with his soft, smiling face and dark, penetrating eyes. He had black wavy hair, which remained black until the day he died, and his only large feature was his Semitic nose, which nevertheless suited the rest of his face very well. He was of average built and somewhat shorter than my mother, but they looked good together. He was born August 8, 1893, in Torokszentmiklos, a town one-third of the way from Szarvas to Budapest, but he moved to Szarvas when he and my mother got married on November 15, 1922. After attending business school, which unlike university was still open to Jews, he opened a granary on our property.

An exceptionally loving person, my father, whom I called *Apuka* (Papa), was somehow able to control us without ever having to raise his voice, and I never once recall him yelling at any one of us. He travelled a lot, and each time he came home, he brought something back for me. If nothing else, he would save a little piece of bread and tell me that it was very special because "*Madar latta*" or "The birds saw it, but I saved it for you." I have many clear, sweet memories of him, especially of him telling me stories and singing to me. It was so good to be a child and have someone like my *Apuka* as a father. I truly believed that a kiss or a hug from him could make everything better, and I think of him to this day with a great deal of love.

My father was a very fastidious person, always neat and clean, and he liked to have things just so. I will always remember with a smile how he would walk into a room and adjust the pictures on the wall so that they hung perfectly straight, even if they were only a fraction off to the left or right, or how he would sit at the dinner table cleaning traces of bread from the tablecloth with a gentle, brushing movement of his hand as he spoke. He was a very observant Jew and put on his *tallit* (prayer shawl) and *tefillin* (phylacteries) every morning to pray. He went to synagogue regularly, and even later on during the Communist period when Jews were forbidden to practise our religion, he secretly attended Shabbat and High Holiday services. He was at his happiest on Shabbat and the holidays when all of us were together celebrating and eating my mother's delicious food, and he made every one of those occasions special for us.

Shabbat was strictly observed in our home. It was a day of rest, and we were not allowed to do anything that could be construed as work, not even turning on a light. I remember clearly how on Friday mornings in the summertime, my father would lower a cantaloupe or watermelon into our well so that it would be cold for dessert after Friday night dinner. Then just before the sun set and Shabbat began, he would go to the well to fetch the melon out with a bucket that he lowered into the water on a strong steel chain. Sometimes he would let me come and watch him, always cautioning me not to fall into the well. I don't know how I could have fallen in, though, since even just to peek over the wooden barrier, I had to stand on my tiptoes.

As I think back on those years, it feels as if every day and every special occasion is etched in my memory. But for me, *Erev* Shabbat, Friday evening, was the most joyous time of the week. I had my own small candlesticks so I could make the blessing over the candles with my mother, and I would peek at her as she lit the seven-candle candelabrum and said the Sabbath prayer, shedding a tear or two, probably remembering her own mother. When she finished the blessing, *Apuka* would bless all of us children. He would take the wine-filled *kiddush* cup from its special plate, say the prayer welcoming Shabbat, and make a blessing over the freshly baked braided *challah*. Then we would sit down to a delectable Shabbat meal. My father always complimented my mother lavishly on her outstanding cooking and after dinner led the family in singing Shabbat songs.

On Shabbat, particularly in the winter time, there was always something prepared on Friday and kept warm overnight on the stove for the afternoon meal. Since there were very few activities we could participate in on the Day of Rest, one of my favourite memories is of being allowed to take hot chickpeas, which had been warming in the pot on the stove, and sitting in the darkness with my brothers, eating the chickpeas and telling stories until the lights came on. It was so good to be together on those cozy winter evenings.

When he came home from synagogue Saturday evening, my father would take me on one knee and my youngest brother, Tibi, on the other, and we would all sing a special prayer, *Gott fun Avrohom*, composed by Rebbe Levi Yitzchak Berdichev, for the end of Shabbat. Its lovely melody and words will remain with me forever:

> God of Abraham, of Isaac, and of Jacob, protect Your people, Israel, from all evil. The holy Shabbat is departing, and may this week come to us with good health, *mazel* [good fortune], blessing, success, wealth, humour, honour, *naches* [great joy], reverence of God, and all that is good.

Then my father would make *havdalah*, the ceremony that bids farewell to Shabbat for another week. He would light the special braided *havdalah* candle and say the closing prayer over *schnapps* (liquor). My job, which I enjoyed very much, was to hold the *havdalah* candle, which I raised as high as I could as my father prayed because I had been told that the higher I held the candle, the taller my husband would be. Then my father would shake sweet spices in a special container reserved for that purpose and hand the container around so everyone could enjoy the lingering sweet scent of Shabbat. After we finished *havdalah*, he would dip the lit candle into the liquor, and I would watch wide-eyed as the flame lit the alcohol. When the flame died down, everyone would dip their little finger into the liquor, dab it on their forehead, and then put their hand in their pocket. Tradition

The last happy picture of my family, 1941.
L to R: Peter, Bernard Scheiner (my grandfather), Pali,
Mariska (my mother), me, Laszlo (my father), Tibi.

said that by doing this, one would be assured of having lots of money in their pocket for the week to come.

Those first seven and a half years from my birth till our deportation to the Nazi labour camps were punctuated by the many holidays we celebrated so whole-heartedly throughout the year and by the beautiful traditions bound up with each one of them. The holidays and their traditions are what I see in my mind's eye when I remember my childhood. These were the best of times: when our family was together, bright with excitement and joy, sitting around the dining room table, singing and giving thanks to God for the blessings and good fortune we had been given.

Our house was rather modest-looking from the road, and its five windows and large gate did not reveal any of the beauty of the inside. We had a magnificent sunroom with three glass walls overlooking our lush flower garden. We would usually dine in the sunroom during the summer, but in the winter and on special occasions, we used our dining room with its heavy table that could easily seat twenty-four people. During holidays, our beautiful dining room glowed in the light of our happiness as we all sat eating, singing, and talking, the aromas of my mother's cooking filling the air.

I think my love of nature began in my childhood when I saw the beauty of our lives reflected in the beauty of what was happening outside. This love took shape long before I could truly appreciate nature in every minute detail. It was certainly long before I came to know of nature's power to heal my mind and soul and before I could consciously savour just being alive and understand how the complex changes in human life are an echo of the ever-changing seasons. Each season brought its own wonders and delights, and each one its special holidays, which I spent playing with my brothers, basking in the warmth of their affection.

We followed the holidays according to the Jewish calendar. As the warm summer nights started to cool off and we could see the tips of the chestnut leaves beginning to turn colours, along came the first holiday of the year: Rosh Hashanah, the Jewish New Year. Rosh Hashanah is a solemn holiday, unlike the secular New Year, and we could always sense in our parents an atmosphere of holiness. On the first day of Rosh Hashanah in the late afternoon, we went to the river to perform *tashlich* (the ritual of throwing pieces of bread symbolizing our sins into the water), and I truly believed my sins would be taken away with every little piece of *challah* I cast away. We always had new clothes to wear for this holiday, and my father would place his hands on our heads and bless us one by one as we set off for synagogue on the first night.

Both my parents were very involved in the life of our synagogue, which was just a block and a half from our house. My mother often invited out-of-town guests to our home for Shabbat and holiday meals, and my father was among the leaders of the congregation. I also remember our rabbi and his wife with great fondness. The rabbi was middle-aged with a soft spot for children. The *rebbitzen* (rabbi's wife) organized plays for different social events and holidays, and I always felt that I was one of her favourites.

Men and women sat apart from each other in our synagogue. Sometimes during holiday services, I sat beside my mother or went outside with the other children to play in the courtyard. But as a child, I was allowed to sit with my father even though I was a girl. Neither of my parents spoke Yiddish, but they both could read Hebrew from the prayer book, and each time my father read a prayer, he would explain the beauty of the prayer to me. On Rosh Hashanah, I listened intently to him, sensing that these were very holy days when we were asking God to inscribe us in the heavenly Book of Life. I was transformed by what I heard, which pleased my father immensely. As a child, I believed in the power of prayer so much. This feeling has remained strong within me in spite of how first the Nazis and then the Communists tried to tear it from my heart, and I have tried to hand it down to my own children.

Rosh Hashanah is the beginning of the Ten Days of Penitence when we are supposed to contemplate all our wrong-doings and resolve to change for the better. Ten days after Rosh Hashanah comes Yom Kippur, the Day of Atonement, when we ask forgiveness for all our sins and when our fate for the year to come is tentatively sealed in heaven. On the day of the eve of the holiday, *Erev* Yom Kippur, we would get up very early in the morning to perform the ritual of *kapporot*. My mother or father would wave a live chicken over the head of each of my brothers and me in the symbolic act of offering the chickens up as a substitute for the sins we had accumulated over the year. Then the chickens would be taken to be slaughtered and given away to the poor.

We all went to synagogue for the chanting of *Kol Nidre*, the prayer where we beg God to annul the vows and promises we made to Him during the year. This prayer remains for me one of the most awe-inspiring of all. Even today when I hear the melody, I can see the men praying, their prayer shawls enveloping both their heads and bodies, and I can't stop my tears. The prayer shawls covered their pure white *kittels* (a caftan-like garment) that they would ultimately be buried in and that they wore on Yom Kippur to remind them of their mortality. As a child, I often wanted to fast on Yom Kippur, just like the grown-ups, but at lunch time I was always sent home from synagogue to eat. It was a tradition with us that the children bring back to the synagogue a quince apple stuck with cloves for our parents to smell. The smell, it was thought, would make people feel better if they were getting a headache from lack of food. I always walked proudly back to the synagogue, bringing quince apples for both my parents to help them through the fast.

If the afternoon prayers finished early, we would walk home for a little rest and then return to synagogue for *Ne'ilah*, the concluding prayer service. If the regular service took longer, we would just stay and wait until the end. I always sat beside my mother for the blowing of the *shofar* (ram's horn), and during *Ne'ilah* I would watch her as she said the prayers, repeating each one four times, once for each of us children. This ritual was something she continued as long as she lived.

After breaking the Yom Kippur fast, we began to build the *succah* for the upcoming eight-day festival of Succoth. As we built the *succah*, a hut-like structure made of wood panels and attached to one wall of our house, we rejoiced and gave thanks that we had survived another year and that we would be sealed into the Book of Life. We had a beautiful, large *succah*, and when it was fully erected, I was allowed to decorate it. A plate of sticky paste made from flour and water was prepared for me, and I had lots of coloured papers from which I made rings. We would paste these coloured rings together and hang them from one corner of our *succah* to the other. We also hung holiday drawings on the walls, those that my brothers had made when they were small and some that I drew myself. Because this festival comes at harvest time, it is also traditional to hang different fruits of the season like pears, apples, and grapes on the walls, so our *succah* was certainly bright and colourful. Lights were drawn from the end of our house to the *succah*, and since the weather is still pleasant at that time of year in Hungary, we all ate our meals together there during Succoth.

Succoth concludes with two very important days. Hoshanah Rabbah, the seventh day of Succoth, is the day when we are, we hope, sealed for the coming year into the heavenly Book of Life. The final day is Simchat Torah, the Celebration of the Torah. In the afternoon, there was always a special Simchat Torah dinner at our synagogue when we children were all sent into the courtyard and the adults threw apples, chocolates, candies, and nuts at us, a symbolic gesture meant to grant us a fruitful and sweet life. In the evening, the joy of this special day came to a peak when the Torah was taken out of the Holy Ark. Then, waving flags we had made and decorated ourselves for this special day, all of us children would march around the synagogue behind the man carrying the Torah.

As winter blanketed the earth with snow, we celebrated Hannukah, the Festival of Miracles that commemorates the liberation of the Second Temple from the Seleucid Greeks as well as the miracle that a single tiny flask of consecrated oil lasted not one but eight days. Every evening for eight days, we lit our traditional oil-burning *menorah*, my father, grandfather, and brothers in turn being given the honour of doing the lighting. After the traditional blessings, we would sing Hannukah songs and then sit down and play with wooden four-sided *dreidels* (tops), something we could do for hours. The *dreidel* game involves either giving or receiving small tokens depending on how the *dreidel* falls when it stops spinning. It was not our tradition to exchange presents on Hannukah, as is done today, but every day we were given a small amount of money, and we would use either this money or candies and peanuts to play the game. My mother would make piles of hot, crispy potato latkes and other special treats for the festival. At our school there was always a

Hannukah play, and for weeks we practised singing Hannukah songs in Hebrew and Hungarian, dancing and spinning like *dreidels* or standing like Hannukah candles ready to be "lit." Even though there were Christians living all around us, I never wondered why we had Hannukah and not Christmas.

Purim, which falls in March, signals the end of winter and the coming of spring, although you wouldn't have believed it from our street, which was usually still covered with freshly fallen snow. I remember peeking out through my bedroom window on Purim mornings, gently pulling back the beautifully crocheted lace curtains only to find lacy frost designs on the windows themselves. As I looked out onto the street, I saw very few people moving about, although here and there someone might be sweeping the snow or going out all bundled up. Once in a while, a sleigh might come by, pulled by a horse wearing around its neck a jingling bell, which tinkled delicately in the crisp morning air.

When *Anyuka* baked for Purim, our home always filled with sweet aromas. She loved to bake; you could see it in the way she moved around her kitchen. I never saw her tired or complaining, and I couldn't believe it when the delicacies came out of the oven that they were made by an ordinary person. My mother always baked at least seven different kinds of pastries, and after all the dough or creamed icing was scraped from the bowl, I was allowed to lick whatever was left over. Even though she would often joke that superstition said it would rain on my wedding day if I licked the cream, she still beamed as I polished off the scraps of her irresistible concoctions. I still remember many of those cookies, how they looked and tasted, especially the little hard, round cookies with white sugar glaze that just melted in your mouth when you bit into them. Of course, we always had poppy seed and walnut rolls (*kindli*), and she even made a special quince apple jelly with big pieces of walnut in it, which was moulded in special forms and cut with a knife. That was one of my favourites.

My parents always sent my middle brother, Pali, out to deliver great quantities of *shalach manot*, plates full of specially wrapped pastries to friends and the poor during Purim, and in the evening we would have a special Purim dinner, either at home with guests or at the synagogue, where the featured item was fish in aspic. This was accompanied by all sorts of other delicious foods, including, of course, my mother's baked goods and sweets. She always made so many different kinds of goodies that I cannot remember them all, but they always lasted until the last crumbs had to be cleared away as we began to prepare for Passover.

As the snow melted and spring finally settled in, the acacia trees outside our house started to bud. The sweet fragrance of their blossoms is one of my enduring loves. I still buy acacia honey for the holidays, and its smell takes me back to my childhood. Spring heralded Passover, and our house, too, came to life again. By that time, our lilac tree was in full bloom and everything outside had turned to green. With the rebirth of our surroundings, we began to get ready to celebrate the spring festival, shedding our winter garments and scouring winter out of our home. Everything was turned inside out to be made kosher for Passover. We had special china, which had to be taken out of the attic and washed outside. I remember the enormous pot set up in the yard over a fire where the big spoons and all the cutlery were boiled to make them kosher. Even the table was scrubbed with hard brushes to clean it thoroughly. The floors were often redone and the carpets taken out, hung on a very heavy rod, and beaten until all the dust came out of them. My mother would take down our gorgeous lace curtains to wash and starch them by hand. Even all our best holiday clothes were hung outside to air out. Not every year, but when the house needed painting, it was always done before Passover. Everything in our home sparkled because my mother took such pride in her home and everything she had.

Even I, young as I was, had my special preparations for Passover. I had to make sure my pockets were shaken out and that no bread or pastry crumbs remained. I made sure there were no crumbs in my school bag either and was not allowed to eat anywhere in the house except for a special place designated for *chometz* (leavened bread and other such food not permitted at Passover) until the last day before Passover.

When people today complain about preparing for Passover, having all the comforts and conveniences that we have now, it makes me smile to think back to the days when we did everything by hand. There was no dishwasher, no vacuum cleaner, no running water, and certainly no hot water for laundry and bathing. We even had to make arrangements with a local farmer to supervise the milking of the cows, and we'd take our own "kosher-for-Passover pail" with us to bring the milk home in. Then we would set about making butter, a very long and arduous job indeed. Even baking a cake was more difficult when we had to whip the cream by hand. It was all a long and tiring process, but it was also a very rewarding one. You felt, every day during those long preparations, that the house was being readied for something extraordinary, and when it was done, we felt such pride and such a sense of accomplishment.

The day before Passover, we would "sell" any remaining *chometz* that we didn't want to throw away to our rabbi for a token sum of money, and he, in turn, would sell it to a gentile from whom we would redeem it after Passover. Finally, the night before Passover, we all went in search of any remaining *chometz* with a wooden spoon, a candle, and a long feather. There was not much to find after the weeks of scrubbing and cleaning, but the last few tiny crumbs of *chometz* were collected, and after we recited the prayer, they were tied in a piece of cloth to be burned the next morning in the yard. The final symbolic gesture. Now both we and our house were ready for the holiday.

The next day, holiday smells and the holiday mood began to fill the air. With no commercial products readily available for Passover, everything was made at home and tasted very special. Even the potatoes tasted different from the potatoes we ate the rest of the year. My father and one of my brothers always went to pick up the *matzah* from the bakery, taking a big basket with a special white cloth liner to bring it home in. *Anyuka* bought the chickens and took them to be slaughtered. Sometimes she took me with her, but I hated that, especially when a chicken escaped from the butcher and ran around wildly for a few seconds with its head cut off. When she brought the chickens home, they still had the feathers on them and had to be opened and cleaned. As she cleaned them, my mother would collect the "unhatched" eggs (eggs that were just yolks, no whites or shells) from inside the chickens to be cooked in her soup. Those eggs were what made her chicken soup extra good, and we children always got our soup with those little egg yolks in it, served in bowls decorated with fairy tale designs. And every year, there was a *matzah* ball debate. Which year, this or the previous one, were the *matzah* balls more perfect? Were they better a little bit harder or a little bit softer? And who liked them this way or that? In the end, it didn't really matter. We just loved my mother's cooking, and whatever there was, we relished it.

As the sun set, my mother and I would usher in the Passover holiday, each of us lighting our own candles just as we did at Rosh Hashanah, and I have continued this tradition with my own daughters. We had two *seder* nights, and on each night, with the table beautifully set, my father would recite the Hagaddah from beginning to end, explaining everything to us. Our *seders* were mostly a family affair, but when I was older, I was usually allowed to invite a girlfriend. The two of us were permitted to have some wine and often ended up under the table (literally) where we fell asleep clutching our dolls. Since I was the youngest, I asked the Four Questions at the *seder*. I was so happy and proud when I could ask my father the Four Questions and

Me at three, March 1939.

Me, 1941.

have him answer me. I can still see my mother, as tired as she was, see her smiling, happy face as she looked around her magnificent table at her beloved family. Everything was so very difficult in those days, but it all had its own beauty. Many beautiful things come to us with difficulty, but the harder they come sometimes, the more we appreciate them. *Anyuka* did it all for her family, for all of us. God bless her. May she rest in peace.

After Passover, spring turned into summer and our garden filled with flowers and became more and more colourful. The first sign of Shavuot, the next holiday, was the appearance of the many coloured peony blooms. This holiday, one of rejoicing and giving, comes seven weeks after Passover and celebrates the giving of the Ten Commandments on Mount Sinai. Our synagogue was always decorated with beautiful flowers at Shavuot, and it was our custom to present our parents with flowers, both at home and in the synagogue. Shavuot is a very happy and beautiful holiday because it comes when hearts are light and summery. We rejoice in God's gifts and at our special place in His universe.

At Shavuot, I also got to bloom, wearing my best dress of the season. My mother ordered my dresses twice a year, at Rosh Hashanah and Shavuot, from a special children's designer in Budapest, and I was always dressed like a real princess. The clothes I wore as a child really spoiled me, and I can still feel the soft touch of their beautiful fabrics on my skin. I remember a white organdie dress with ribbons at the back that were longer than I was tall, a navy silk-velvet dress with pink silk ribbon hand embroidered around the skirt, a white and navy sailor suit with buttons at the waist, and a baby-blue dress with golden buttons. There were two winter coats that I remember: one made of imitation white fur and the other of black velvet with white fur trimming on the hood and a muff to match. I always had matching shoes and socks, and I wore my dark blond wavy hair in long ringlets tied together with a big ribbon. I feel very special about those early years when I was spoiled and given so many things by my parents.

I think that many things have remained with me from those years, especially the look of pride in *Anyuka*'s eyes when she looked at me. I hope she would still be proud of me even now in the way I carry on in her footsteps.

Year in and year out, this is how we celebrated the many Jewish holidays when I was a child, and I really don't know how to thank my parents for instilling in me all these beautiful traditions that I still cherish today. It is in this way that I remember our life before the war – through these celebrations and repetitions of the holidays as the seasons came and went peacefully and naturally.

But when the Germans invaded Hungary in 1944 and we were driven from our home and taken to concentration camps, then everything in this beautiful world that I loved came to an end. There were no more seasons or holidays after that, only greyness and suffering and loss.

CHAPTER 2

Playful Years End in Tears

Blessed is he who loves his wife and honors her and directs his children into paths of righteousness. – "The Jewish Home," *Sabbath and Festival Prayer Book*

We all have stories to tell, of people we love and loved and memories of glorious days that ended too soon. Somehow, though, when I think back to those first seven and a half years of my life from my birth in July 1936 until the Nazis deported us in the spring of 1944 – to that other world I inhabited as an innocent, sheltered child before the war had such an impact on my life – it seems too full, too rich to have lasted such a short time. Every detail, every person, takes up so much space in my mind that it seems impossible it was all wrenched from me before I even knew what I had. I savour each memory, each anecdote, each mishap, like a special treat before bedtime, taking tiny bites, willing it to last so I can stay up a little longer, so I can live there a moment more before the night enfolds me and the past is gone again.

Perhaps this image is not surprising since some of my dearest memories of childhood revolve around bedtime. In the evenings, a wooden bathtub in the kitchen would be filled with warm water, and the evening ritual would begin. My mother would scrub me while I splashed and played. She would dry me with a big, soft, white towel, and it was a special moment for me to feel her closeness. Before being tucked into bed, I would be given a snack, perhaps a glass of warm milk and a cookie or pastry. Then one of my brothers or my father (if he was home from one of his frequent business trips) would be given the honour of reading me one of my favourite stories – "Bambi" (which was written by Austrian Felix Salten in 1923), "Snow White and the Seven Dwarfs," "Cinderella," "Jancsi es Juliska," and other Hungarian fairy tales – all of which I knew by heart. Every night, I would say my Hebrew and Hungarian evening prayers with my father or mother sitting beside me on my bed. That childish Hungarian prayer still rings in my ears as I imagine myself snug in my warm, cozy bed, saying the words I believed completely:

Hungarian Evening Prayer for Children

En Istenem, Jo Istenem	My God, my good God
Becsukodik Mar a Szemem	My eyes are closing
De a Tied Nyitva Atyam	But Your eyes, Almighty,
Amig alszom	Remain open while I sleep
Vigyazz Ream	Take care of me
Vigyazz az en Szüleimre	Look after my parents
Vigyazz az en Testvereimre	Watch over my brothers
Hogyha a nap Ujra felkel	Should the sun rise again
Csokolhassuk Egymast reggel	We can kiss again in the morning

Once we had exchanged kisses, my parents would lovingly tuck me into bed. I still recall how secure I felt, nuzzled into my luxuriantly soft down comforter. Like all the houses in Europe at that time, we did not have central heating in our home, just a big stove in the kitchen. But the kitchen door was always kept open at night so that the warmth from the stove could spread through the whole house. I was safe in this world with the people I loved most all around me. Before long, I would usually fall into a delicious, deep sleep.

There were nights, however, that I, like any other child, couldn't get to sleep, and I would get out of bed for any number of excuses. The most successful excuse, I found, was to say that I needed to go make "pee-pee." Immediately, one of my brothers would be summoned to take me to the outhouse since we had no indoor bathroom. Our outhouse, though, was as clean as any indoor toilet in the most modern home today, with a higher seat for the adults and a lower seat for children. There were always comic books and newspapers supplied for reading material, and these became toilet paper when we were done reading them. One of my brothers would walk with me to the edge of the house while I ran through the dark yard. He would stand leaning against the house, whistling so that I could hear him and wouldn't be afraid of the dark. We even came up with a tune that we whistled to each other. One of us would begin and the other would reply, communicating through the evening air. Later on, my brothers and I used this special tune as a signal if we wanted to find each other in a crowded place. Even later, after the war began, my brothers recently told me, they and their Jewish friends would use this responsive whistling to signal for help when a fight broke out at school where they were challenged for being Jewish.

My three brothers played a huge part in my life in my early years. Having them around when I was a child was wonderful, and being the baby sister, I had it made. They protected me, always included me in their activities, and if they could, took me with them when they went out in search of adventure. Peter, the eldest, is twelve years older than I am. He was, and still is, very good-looking. He is of medium height and has an elegantly lithe, sportsman's body. He is soft-spoken, always well-dressed, and has inherited my father's habit for exceptional cleanliness. When I think of Peter in those early years, I have an image of him standing in front of the mirror singing or whistling his favourite song, *"Vagyom egy no utan"* ("You are my heart's delight") from Franz Lehar's *Mosoly Orszaga (The Land of Smiles)*, as he brushed his beautiful, light brown, curly hair. I would stand and watch him, fascinated, because he could stand in front of that mirror looking at himself for hours. He seemed so grown up to me, so confident and strong. Someone on the verge of adulthood.

My middle brother, Pali, is ten years older than I am and a person of great sensitivity and kindness. He is a little taller than Peter but stockier with a good body. He has always been active in sports like

Peter, and he has a heart of gold, always pleasant, obliging, and soft-spoken. He is very much like my father, except with respect to cleanliness. We have always called him "a Scheiner" (my mother's family) because he was less interested in cleanliness than my father and Peter. He radiates love and has always been very good to me. I loved him and counted on him as a child and still love him very, very dearly today. It was Pali who just recently told me an interesting story of something that happened when I was a baby. As my older brother, now a mature man, sat and told me this story, my mind went back to when we were children, and I saw him in my mind's eye as the adolescent boy he was during my early childhood.

When I was about a year old, Pali told me, I became very ill, so ill in fact that my parents feared I might die. Our family doctor was summoned, and after examining me, he told my parents there was nothing he could do, that someone could have given me the evil eye. Desperate, my father sent for a very celebrated old Jewish woman, who was said to have special powers, in the hope that she could help me. Pali was in the room when she arrived, and he told me what he saw. The woman came into my room with a tall glass of warm water in one hand and four or five pieces of charcoal in the other. She put the glass on the table next to my head and solemnly dropped the pieces of charcoal into it. "If the charcoal sinks during the night," she explained to my parents, "your child, too, will sink and go back to where she came from when she was born." In short, I would die. If, however, the charcoal was floating on top of the water in the morning, then I would live. My mother, Pali told me, spent a sleepless night sitting by my bed. Morning broke, and she was greatly relieved to find me breathing and sleeping peacefully. I was still alive. When she glanced at the charcoal in the glass, all the pieces were floating.

My youngest brother, Tibi, is three years older than me and the brains in the family. He is the tallest of the four of us children, very outspoken, a good organizer, and a hard worker. Even though he is the go-getter of the family, he is very soft-hearted and has always been the one to keep the family together. He is a giver, like my mother. Being closest to me in age, he was the one around the most. Although I loved to play with him, he often got me into trouble. One of the clearest memories I have of him is from when I was five and he asked me to pull down my panties so he could show a friend of his – for a fee, of course – what a girl looked like. Later when I told my mother what happened, I got my first sex education lecture and a good spanking. Tibi, for his part, ran away, and by the time he got back, my parents had forgotten the entire incident.

My childhood was full of the joyful things I did with my big brothers, my teachers and sometime partners in crime. In winter, they would take me skating and push me around on the ice on a special skating chair, or we would go sledding and they would pull me around and around, at times turning me over onto the crisp, white snow just for mischief. I was always bundled up very warmly, and they were careful not to hurt me, but afterwards in pretend anger, we would have big snowball fights. My brothers always ran away, and by the time they returned, all was forgotten. We would also build the most wonderful snowmen, and I can see them now with their carrot noses and black coal eyes, pipes in their mouths, wearing hats and carrying large sticks in their hands.

The greatest fun my brothers and I had, though, was going for horse-drawn sleigh rides when I was a little older. Although forbidden to do so by our parents, we would run after the horses, jumping onto the sleigh and riding till the driver noticed and ordered us off. Such antics could come at a price, however. Once I broke my wrist in the process, but I didn't care and the fun continued on.

In the summertime, we spent the endless warm days playing ball in our yard. I can still see my favourite red ball with the large white polka dots flying through the air into the bright blue sky. The Koros River ran through our town, and we spent a lot of time on the water. Perhaps, though, I shouldn't say that the river "ran." This branch of the Koros was called the *holt Koros* (the lazy branch), and the water was almost always still and reflective. I loved swimming and going fishing and boating with my brothers, and I was always so excited to be on the river in their company. How I must have driven them crazy, carrying on boisterously and jumping around in the boat. But God bless them, they let me.

These were my brothers: Peter who was very handsome and intelligent, Pali who was very caring and had all the sensitivity in the world, and Tibi who was very clever and good-hearted. I remember looking up to them and wanting to hurry and grow up so I, too, would have some special privileges like going to movies and staying out late. But their love and companionship meant and still means everything to me. I want to thank all my brothers for being so loving and being such wonderful role models for me. I even want to thank them for their pranks, like pulling my long braids that reached below my waist every time they passed by and jokingly twisting my arm so hard it would make me cry out. I loved all of it – climbing trees and singing, swimming and running carelessly through my early childhood. Every moment of that childhood was bliss because of them.

There were others in my life who meant a great deal to me, particularly my dog, a small terrier named Pengo, named after the Hungarian currency at the time. I remember so fondly how the two of us would run around, splashing in and out of the ditches in the street, getting my lovely outfits so dirty that I knew I would be scolded later but not caring because we were having so much fun.

And I had a best friend, Kati, a little Jewish girl, who would often sleep over at my house. There weren't many little girls who lived close by for me to play with, and I did not have many toys (at least, compared to my own grandchildren's collection): a ball, a pail and shovel for the sand, a jumping rope, picture books, push-out cardboard dolls, and a small table with two seats attached where I could draw with coloured pencils or give pretend tea parties in the afternoons using my tiny cups and saucers. I loved those wonderful carefree days when Kati and I and our dolls would throw our famous

Me with my doll, Pani, and Tibi with the family dog, Pengo, March 1939.

tea parties, copying my mother and setting the table as if for a queen, serving coloured water for tea and real pastries cut into miniature pieces. When we tired of playing grown-up, we would chase after the chickens and white rabbits in our yard. Once Tibi made us crawl up on top of the granary and hop over above the wooden boxes where the rabbits were kept. We both fell down into the feces of hundreds of rabbits and had to get tetanus shots.

When I was two, my parents bought me a doll for my birthday. She was almost fifteen inches tall from head to toe and had a plastic head and face and light brown painted hair. She came all dressed with underwear, shoes and socks, and a lovely dress. She even had a coat and hat. I named her Annie but decided that this name was too serious. All of us children had nicknames – I was called Gica, for Olgica – so why not my dolly, I thought. And that's how Annie mostly went by the nickname Pani. Pani was my soul mate. If I was sad, she would make me laugh, and if I told her my secrets, she never told anyone. When I was very little, she slept in bed with me. When I got older, someone made a crib for her out of a cardboard box, and I lovingly put together some bedding for her so she could sleep beside me in my room. Before we went to bed, I would always kiss her and tuck her in.

I loved Pani the way a real mommy loves her baby. She had a pram, and when we went out together for long walks to the backyard swings and the sandbox, I would talk to her, mimicking the way my mother talked to me as we walked. She was a good baby who very seldom cried, and I would praise her a lot. Occasionally, though, she needed to be punished, and then she would cry and I would hug her and love her again. Sometimes, however, I was a bad mother, not paying much attention to her when I was occupied with other friends or bored with taking her everywhere with me. But I always came back to her and knew she would never leave me because she loved me as much as I loved her. I think I loved and needed her so much because she was the little sister my age I so wanted. I knew my family loved me, but I think they were happy if I was occupied and keeping out of their way as they went about their busy schedules, particularly as the war started taking hold of our lives. Pani belonged to me alone, and she comforted me. She was the most important possession I had.

In spite of the rambunctious influence of my three older brothers and my own tomboy nature, my mother tried to bring me up to be a very prim and proper young lady. Whenever I went out, even if it was just to play with Pengo, I looked like a new doll just taken out of the box in my starched dress and pinafore, white shoes, and ribbons in my dark blond ringlets. *Anyuka* taught me to walk straight, to sit with my legs crossed, and to eat properly with a knife and fork, elbows off the table. I remember having to walk around the house holding a broom across my back threaded through my elbows so that I wouldn't walk bent over. There were also piano lessons, which I actually enjoyed, and I learned to play Hungarian nursery rhyme tunes and light Hungarian folk music. All of these lessons were meant to make a lady of me, but I saw them only as minor irritants in my otherwise untroubled existence.

When I was around four or five years old, my parents took me to Budapest. Since this was my first visit, they promised to take me to Hauer, one of the most elegant pastry shops in the city, where just looking in the window would make your mouth water. There were two great pastry shop/cafés in Budapest at the time, Hauer and Gerbeaud (both of which are still there to this day), and there was no greater treat than to be taken to one of them. As we stood on the busy street where Hauer was located, my father sternly told me, "You know, this is not Szarvas. You are not to run across the street because you will be killed by the cars." Of course, I was impatient, and being brought up with three brothers, I wasn't exactly a demure little girl who listened carefully to her father. When I thought he wasn't looking, I bolted across the street, streetcars clanging and cars screeching to a halt behind me. I was very lucky not to have been killed. All I remember after that is that my usually gentle and loving father, who had been terrified at my stupid antic, came after me, took me into the inner court of an apartment building, and spanked me until I peed my pants. Not before and not afterward for as long as he lived did he ever lay a hand on me. I must have scared him half to death.

On that same trip, I contracted measles. At first, my parents thought that the sardines I had been eating the night before had given me a rash, but a doctor soon confirmed it was measles. We were staying at a very small, affordable hotel, but because measles was such a communicable disease, the hotel wanted to throw me out. My parents had to bribe the owner to let me stay there until I was well again.

Far too soon, however, the dream that was my childhood became a nightmare, and looking back, I realize how small and vulnerable I was when I had to discover that there was evil in the world. The world was at war, and one day, men marched into my yard and ripped the child out of my body and the joy out of my heart. After that day, there were no more songs, no more stories, no more toys, no more carefree days of laughter and fun. My world would never be the same again.

In the early years of the war, though, it seemed that we were living an almost normal life. In September 1942, I started first grade at the Jewish school located on the grounds of our synagogue, about a block and a half from our house, and went there every morning with my brother Tibi who was then in fourth grade. Even though I loved school and my teacher, I also liked sleeping in and usually woke up so late that I had to scramble to get ready. I have vivid memories of the days I forgot my lunch or my snow shoes at home because our maid would appear at my classroom door holding my missing lunch or shoes, fully embarrassing me although obviously not enough to make me wake up earlier or learn to bring my things with me in the rush of the morning. I was so spoiled and so well taken care of then.

I played with my friend Kati as usual, and I continued to love the things I had always loved, like skating and climbing trees, while I never stopped hating spinach and having my hair washed and combed. My family was still all around me, and my home was solid and intact. How could I know that my life was about to change forever?

Luckily for me, during those first years of the war before Hungary was invaded by the Germans, a young Jewish woman, Zsofi Markus, came into my life. Zsofi and her sister, Ilonka, had fled to Budapest from Kormend, another town in Hungary, in 1942 when their parents committed suicide. In Budapest, Ilonka and Zsofi were taken in by a wonderful couple who owned a restaurant at the corner of Mester Utca and Ulloi Ut. It so happened that my father's younger brother, Miklos, also worked at that restaurant. Soon Miklos and the very slight, elegantly beautiful Ilonka were in love. When Miklos and Ilonka got married and decided to stay in Budapest, my family took Zsofi in and she came to live with us and look after me. Zsofi, then in her early thirties, was outwardly less beautiful than her sister, huskier and rather stern-looking when she was angry or sad, but she had a heart of gold and she grew to be everything to me. She must have been so lonely and unhappy when she came to us, and I hope it gave her solace to be with me.

Now, as an adult, when I try to recall the beginning of the war, I first see the grown-ups in our house clustered around the Blaupunkt radio, listening intently. I was too young to remember whether they started listening as early as 1939 when Hitler invaded Poland, but I think they must have. I do recall them listening in 1942, though, because they would always make sure the children were out of sight before they turned the radio on. They would listen and whisper together, and whenever we would appear, they would use the expression "*Zsindej van a haz teton*" to alert everyone to the fact that there were children in the room and that the adults needed to keep quiet. But whenever I heard that expression, I knew that there was something strange and possibly scary going on and that my parents were trying to keep it a secret from me. I shared my concerns and fears with Pani and Zsofi, but Zsofi would take me to another room and tell me stories and calm my fears.

Apart from the strange behaviour of the adults listening to the radio, I remember that we went about in our small town as smug as bugs in a rug while the Germans were advancing and killing their own Jews and the Jews of Poland. I know now that as news of what was happening in other parts of Europe began to trickle in, my parents and their friends were in denial. As the Germans invaded the countries around us and began clearing out groups like Gypsies and Jews whom they liked to call "inferior peoples," whoever could do so escaped and slipped into Hungary. These people told their stories of horror, but my parents still called it hysteria. They just could not believe it. "It will never come to Hungary," they, especially my father, would say. Even though it would not have been easy for us, there was still plenty of time then, during the early years of the war, to get out, to run. But nobody made a move. It seems tragically comical now that we should have been so totally stupefied and taken by such complete surprise when the Germans started rounding up Hungarian Jews when they took over Hungary in spring of 1944.

By late 1943, even though they still didn't believe that they as good Hungarians, albeit Jews, would be taken away, the grown-ups were worried most of the time at the news of the advancing German armies. They were so preoccupied that they had little time for me. I have learned from watching my own grandchildren that no matter how young they are, children instinctively sense and react strongly to what the adults around them are feeling. Certainly, during that terrifying time in 1943, I could only judge what was happening around me through my parents' behaviour. How does a child cope or feel safe when his or her parents are frightened and don't know what to do themselves? I honestly think a numbness set in then in me, and the realization of what was happening didn't come to me until later, much later.

Zsofi was the only grown-up who had time to play. I remember fondly how we would spend hours playing together with Pani. Zsofi would help me bathe Pani, and she sewed tiny doll-sized dresses and bedding as I sat beside her, watching in fascination. The three of us became a tiny perfect family inside our larger one. In addition, Zsofi was gentle and very affectionate and loved me very much. But as soft as she was on the inside, she was equally strong on the outside. I have to smile when I remember the battles we had every time she had to wash my hair. I careened around the house, putting up a great fight, as she came chasing after me.

I am grateful to Zsofi, who was so kind and loving to me at a time when the rest of the world was becoming more and more brutal and confused. She loved me as if I were her own child, and I basked in her warmth and caring devotion. She, in turn, was grateful to my family for adopting her and for allowing her to come and live with us, and she remained with us until we were deported and separated in the Strasshof labour camp. After the war, Zsofi returned to us, although

Zsofi Markus, my "surrogate" mother, aged 74.

I don't remember how or exactly when that was. Her sister, Ilonka, had been killed in Auschwitz, and Zsofi would never talk about her or the horrors she herself had lived through during the war. In due course, she married my uncle Miklos, Ilonka's widower, and they lived in Budapest until both of their deaths. I loved her dearly and will always think of her as my surrogate mother.

By the time I started my second year at school in September 1943, even the children knew that something horrible was going on and that even harder times were coming. By then, we had already been singled out as Jews. Until that time, I had never felt any different from anyone else who lived around us. We had always been very well liked by all of our Christian neighbours and friends, but suddenly everybody began to pull away, to draw their blinds or simply turn their heads when we passed by. I didn't understand their behaviour then, but now I realize that it was a combination of being afraid for themselves combined with the latent anti-Semitism that was now becoming acceptable to express. My teacher, whom I loved, was taken away to a labour camp very soon after we started the school-year. Before he was taken, he made a little speech telling us that he had to leave. He told us that "something was wrong," that we had to be strong and listen to the very nice woman who would be our substitute teacher. All the kids cried when he left. Why, I wondered, were we so different from all the other people in our town? Why were we so hated?

But as frightening and difficult as it was then, it became far worse when the Germans invaded Szarvas in spring of 1944. Our school had closed down the month before; now we were made to wear yellow stars sewn to our clothing, and these stars had to be visible whenever we left our homes. There was a strictly enforced curfew at night. People who had been so peaceful and friendly, people who I thought were just like my parents, suddenly wouldn't even say hello to us. Soon they were even coming out to watch Jews being kicked and beaten down the street, and I was sure they were already planning

My family wearing yellow stars and standing in front of our house, 1944.
L to R (back row): Pali, my mother, my father, Peter;
(front row): me, Tibi.

how to steal from our beautiful home. Peter and Pali were taken away to forced labour camps. My family was ripped apart, and life took on a new bizarre and monstrous face. By the time we were marched to the newly created Szarvas ghetto sometime in April, people we had known all our lives were just spitting at us. "Look at these pigs," they would say as we passed by.

When the soldiers came to take us, they just marched through our gate and shouted at us to gather our things together. We were allowed to take only what we could carry in our hands, just some clothing, a few shirts or sweaters. We barely had time to say good-bye to our home, to everything we had held dear for generations. I have a photograph of myself at about this time, at the age of seven and a half, and in my eyes I see reflected the disbelief and numbness I must have been feeling at the time. Why? Why? Why? It took me a long time to understand. I did not know about history then, about the teaching of religious hatred, about ethnic cleansing. I was just terrified of all the frightening changes I saw and did not understand. Why? What was wrong with me? What did my parents do? To this day, I have unresolved fears and mental scars.

I did something then, at that moment when they were taking us away, that I am convinced was the outward manifestation of all the inner turmoil I was feeling. All I could think about was my doll, Pani. She was going with me, and I had to make sure I had her and all her belongings, too. I remember bringing Pani to the gate with me and clutching her to myself as I carried her. I remember that it was a rather cool day and that Pani was wearing a light brown corduroy coat and hat. I was cold, my whole body was shivering, and my mother must have said that it was too cold and I should put on an extra sweater. If I needed a sweater, then Pani was also cold and needed her blanket. But where was her blanket? At the gate to our house was the little table where I usually played with friends, and I put Pani down on the table so I could run back to the house where my parents were still packing up and find her blanket.

When I got back to the gate, I looked around frantically, but Pani wasn't there. There were two officers standing by the gate, turned away from me. "Where is my doll?" I screamed hysterically. "I want my doll!" Nobody answered me. I think I pulled at one of the officers and started to cry. "I just put down my doll. I want my doll." They just brushed me off when I begged them to help me find her. I don't remember if they said anything to me, but I threw myself on the ground, screaming, "Please, if you have to take somebody away or kill someone, then kill me. I want to die. But give me back my doll." Nothing – no reply. My heart broke as my childhood was taken away.

By this time, I remember that my parents were there, too. I remember seeing my mother turn the key in the lock and hand it to an officer. I remember the officers telling me to gather up my things and go along with the rest of my family. It was at this point, I think, that I realized I had lost Pani, and the trauma of what was happening took me over. I decided that this was too much, and I just turned off. I don't remember myself ever crying after that or feeling anything at all. I don't remember hunger, thirst, dirt – anything except fear. I don't know why nothing after that felt quite as shocking or why that incident left such a deep scar on me for the rest of my life. But I grew up that day, grew up in a grotesque way that has nothing to do with years. I made up my mind there and then that I would never be a burden to my parents again and would never add to their pain. I could take anything. I was almost eight now – a big girl. I knew that whatever I asked of my mother, whatever I wanted, was impossible for her to give now. And I wanted to take care of myself, to carry my own belongings, my own weight, in what was to come.

Then my mother, my father, my grandfather, Tibi, Zsofi, and I were marched through our gate and away from the only home I had ever known towards the ghetto that was only a block and a half from our house, the ghetto that had once been my school and our beautiful synagogue. Other Jews joined us and I walked along, watching the tears streaming down the grown-ups' faces. I felt my hand slip from the strong grip of whoever was holding it, and from that moment on, I felt completely alone. I didn't really know where I would end up. Much later, I realized that the grown-ups did not know either, that they only knew that Hitler had a final solution for the Jews. He was going to wipe us off the face of the earth altogether.

CHAPTER 3

Rude Awakening

> *The traditional idea of the Chosen People involves obligation rather than privileges.* —Sabbath and Festival Prayer Book

It is true that the Hungarian Jews were relatively safe and almost too comfortable until March 1944 when German troops occupied Hungary. Except for some men who were deported to labour camps, we lived the first few years of the war hearing horror stories from elsewhere and pretending the atrocities we heard about wouldn't reach us. We were deeply assimilated, loyal *Magyars* and lived in total denial, confident that Hungarians were different – cultured, nice people. Then we were rounded up with lightning speed. By the time the Nazis got to us, to the small towns and villages like Szarvas all over Hungary, they had perfected their brutal art and were making up for lost time. And the Hungarians were good partners. They were eager and, if possible, over-anxious to get on with the work. Sometimes it is hard for me to say who was worse, the German SS or the Hungarian Iron Cross. To this day, I feel more hatred in my heart for the Hungarians, those sly foxes who betrayed us to the Nazis, than I do for the German SS, who to me were simply savages carrying out the final solution decreed by their sick-minded leaders.

The Iron Cross rounded us up in the early spring of 1944. I don't recall the actual weather that day, but in my mind now, I'd like to think that it started as a clear, sunny morning but that in no time at all, grey clouds began to gather in the blue sky and the sun disappeared as if too ashamed to be a witness to what was happening. The soldiers marched us to my former school on the grounds of our synagogue that they were using as the local ghetto, and I remember passing by my favourite pastry shop where, only a short time earlier, I had spent my allowance on ice cream.

When we got to the school, they told everyone to hand over all their precious gold jewellery, even the smallest wedding rings. People were hiding gold and other things in different places – the linings of their coats, inside their shoes, in their body cavities – and the guards didn't hesitate to feel around in our bodies to make sure we had given everything up. If someone was caught with anything on his or her body that they hadn't given up voluntarily, that person was severely punished. I remember people running to the outhouses in the garden to get their treasures out. It was a pitiful sight. My parents hadn't hidden anything, but the guards examined me anyway to make sure there wasn't any gold or other precious jewellery on my body. I will never forget my tremendous shame when I felt their fingers going up my anal canal and into my vagina. Total humiliation – the first of many that would follow. My childhood stripped away in just a few moments.

The Jewish population of Szarvas at that time was around 650 people, and we were all crowded into a small space. Those three weeks or so we spent in the Szarvas ghetto were chaos all around, with people crying or too quiet and the elderly completely confused. I don't remember much of my parents at that time, and I don't think anyone spoke to me once we got there. No one ever explained what we were doing there or tried to tell me what was going on. I don't remember what we ate in the ghetto other than bread or potatoes. I think in the beginning we were still given some privileges to go out or to have people bring food in. My family had always been well off and well liked, so I couldn't understand why so little was being brought or given to us. But soon it became very dangerous for anyone from the outside to be seen giving us food or even talking to us, with both those on the outside and the prisoners inside being severely punished.

I remember some people showing up with food and being turned away very harshly. I learned very early that whatever the guards told us to do, we had to do quickly and efficiently or we would be brutally beaten.

At first, we felt only shock and numbness, but then we began to take it in. It was anarchy in the school building. The only routine was the guards ordering us to line up every morning or any time at all at their whim, or someone dying, either killed by the guards or dying of sickness. Otherwise, I just remember sitting in a corner, looking at the faces of the grown-ups or listening to their hushed conversations. I had come from a loving home straight into this hell, and suddenly, in a moment, I was having this other life. I kept trying to make believe that it was just a cruel dream. I know that I felt very vulnerable all the time. Why were we being punished? I was positive that we were all going to die, but what I did not know at the time was how it would happen or how much we would be forced to endure until then.

After three weeks, they moved us to the Szolnok ghetto. I remember being marched to the railway station, but I don't recall how they transported us to Szolnok. We were still not so many then. Did they load us into trains? Trucks? Szolnok was not far from Szarvas, only about an hour or so away, but it was already a much more organized camp. I remember sprawling buildings there with large rooms that were crammed with people. The Hungarians had been in charge in Szarvas, but in Szolnok, the Germans ran the ghetto. I can still see their big boots and hear their large, scary dogs in front of me. I remember the searchlights and the orders being "barked" at us from loudspeakers. If someone tried to escape or went missing, we would hear the sirens go off even in the middle of the night, and they would start shouting at us to hurry up and get in line so they could count us. "*Schnell! Schnell!*" they would snap as we stumbled out of the buildings to line up in the dead of night. This was something the Germans and the Russians had in common. They were always rushing us, screaming at us to hurry up.

When we arrived at the Szolnok ghetto, we were shoe-horned into a large sugar factory, which had been owned by a Jewish family before the war. I learned a lot of things there that I was not prepared for at my age. You had to grow up fast if you wanted to survive in that place. I'm not sure I wanted to survive, but I just went along, and it was some kind of faith which kept me going. Here I saw death for the first time. I saw people dying – people being shot, people being beaten to death in front of me. All the time I would be thinking, "How would I be killed? Would it be like the man who died when he was shot in the head or like the baby that was thrown against the wall and smashed to a pulp? How would it happen to me? And where would I be? Would my family be with me or would I be alone?" Eerily, I never felt sorry for anyone who died. I felt they were much better off than I was. For them it was over. I wouldn't turn eight till July, but I felt as if an invisible hangman's noose had been slipped over my head. Every so often as the days and months of our ordeal piled up, I would feel the noose being pulled tighter and tighter as my fear grew, and I would come to believe that it was only a matter of time until the final jerk would bring the so often prayed for redeeming end.

Of all the horrors and inhumanity that I saw for the first time in Szolnok, the latrines were the most appalling. They were open ditches dug into the courtyard, about six to eight feet wide and very long, with a plank thrown across them. It was unthinkable to me that everyone had to carry out this very private human function in full view of everyone else. Coming from my prim and overly-protected upbringing where I was not even allowed to sit on a strange toilet seat, I found the sight of people sitting on the planks, their private parts exposed and their feces dropping into the pit below them, extremely repulsive. Even more ghastly was the plight of the children my age and younger. When a small child stood on the edge of the ditch, he or she couldn't possibly reach the plank to sit down. I saw children fall in and choke to death and others being fished out covered in feces for days because they had no way of washing it off. It was an incredibly horrifying experience, and the stink was so strong that even today if I am depressed, have a headache, or am nauseous, I can still smell the stench of those latrines. I am still haunted by the memory of those children, and in my nightmares, I still see their floating bodies and bobbing heads. Why did that not happen to me? The haunting never quite ends.

One of the families among us whom we knew quite well from our town consisted of a young doctor, his wife, and their two children. The older girl was a schoolmate of mine, and her baby sister was just two or three years old. We had been in Szolnok for a week or less, all huddled together on the floor, when the doctor approached my father and told him that he was going to give his family fatal injections. I never knew where he had hidden the drug or the needles – perhaps in the lining of his jacket – but he asked if we wanted him to do the same to us. Of course, my father, a religious man and a great optimist, said no. In the morning when I woke up, the doctor, the mother, and the baby were dead, their bodies lying practically on top of us, we were so crammed in together. I still remember looking at the small, lifeless body of the baby, so innocent and cold. My friend, barely alive and unconscious, was taken away. It seems her father had not given her quite enough of the deadly drug. I could never understand why the Germans wanted to save her or where they took her. Death was fast becoming part of my "normal" daily life. I was barely eight then, but I began to question the value of life. I might even have been angry in my own little heart that my father had not agreed to let us die. I envied the doctor's family. For them, it was over. To just go to sleep and never wake up again, that was something to envy. Wouldn't it be easier to die than to endure all this? To this day, I think of death as a release and it doesn't frighten me.

None of us did much of anything at Szolnok. Everyone just sat around, waiting and talking, telling their shocking stories, constantly speculating about what was going to happen next. By this time, everyone was lethargic, and I slowly began to believe we had all just silently given in to our fate. But my family's fate was not sealed yet.

We had been in the ghetto for a few weeks when the soldiers crammed us into cattle cars to be deported. Counting off a hundred of us at a time, they herded us into the boxcars. People were in a panic because we didn't know where they were taking us, and there was no place to sit, stand, or breathe. There were four little windows in each boxcar, two on either end, with bars across them. My grandfather sat down in the corner across from the door, and we all kind of snuggled together around him there. Ironically, I felt closer to my family in the cattle car than in the ghetto because in our misery, we all huddled close together, and that gave me some comfort. But everyone was either completely drained or praying, and I don't remember anyone, my parents included, talking to me any more than was absolutely necessary. On top of everything else that was happening to me, I found this "silent treatment" unsettling and very painful.

If a person died in the cattle car, which happened all around us, he or she was not removed from the car. It didn't matter how much we hammered on the locked door or screamed, the dead bodies simply remained where they dropped. Finally, exhausted, we just lay down beside them and slept, holding each other for comfort. We couldn't help it – corpses were all around us and we were lucky to be able to find a spot to sit down. Once or twice a day, we got some water to drink, but of course there was no water for washing. There was some sawdust at each end of the car and a little pot for excrement, which we emptied by throwing it against the windows. As often as not, the contents would come back at us, whipped by the wind. But in the end, it made little difference because many people either could not or did not even bother trying to get to the pot. We were like beasts. The stench inside the car in the summer heat was unbearable with the dead bodies, the excrement, the vomit, and the unwashed, terrified humanity inside. The noise was deafening with people crying, screaming, and shouting all kinds of craziness. Some women had to be slapped to quiet them down. I don't think any of us were sane by this time. If we had been sane, we couldn't have lived through it. Thinking back to that time, with the sensibilities and knowledge I have today, I don't understand how we survived it. I didn't and still don't understand a lot of things.

On the third night, the train stopped. The next morning, we were ordered out very early to be counted. It was still dark. I saw the Nazi soldiers in their high black boots, their pistols at their sides, their terrifying dogs beside them. I felt hardly as tall as their boots or their dogs. As in Szolnok, they began counting us, a hundred to a car, and pushing people back in, passing the children around, throwing them like footballs. My family was already on the train when they got to me. I was number one hundred and one. One SS officer grabbed me and was getting ready to throw me onto another car when Zsofi jumped off the train. She snatched me out of his arms and threw me up to my family on the car. Nobody breathed. I don't know why they didn't shoot her or me or both of us; perhaps this particular officer was one percent more humane than the others. All I know is that Zsofi saved me, and it was after this incident that I started to think of Zsofi as my surrogate mother. The Nazis closed the doors and the train started up. We continued on.

Some days, the train just stood without moving, the doors shut tight, the July heat beating down on us as we trembled, not from cold or even so much from fear of death but from the feeling of helplessness in the face of these people who were ready to kill us if we moved or stepped the wrong way – or even just for fun. We could still not believe such things could happen, that such behaviour was possible. I don't remember feeling terrified myself, I was too numb, but all my suppressed terror came to me much, much later in the form of nightmares that started after the war.

After we crossed what had been the Hungarian border, there were many stops. Although I didn't understand then, now I realize that the Germans literally didn't know what to do with the 12,000 to 18,000 Hungarian Jews whom the Hungarians had willingly thrust at them since March: Auschwitz could not handle that many people any longer, nor could Bergen Belsen. All I do remember was being tossed about like an unwanted carcass at a slaughterhouse. In the end, the Germans uncoupled parts of the train from the rest of the cars, and each section was sent on its way separately.

It was a horrible, long journey that finally ended when we arrived at Strasshof concentration camp. We didn't know the name of our destination at the time, let alone what they were going to do with us here. All we knew was that this was going to be life from then on. As soon as we arrived, the guards immediately began the selection process. Men were to go one way and women the other. We had to be listed and catalogued. We were not tattooed, but each of us was given a number and made to walk through a very narrow entrance that led to a huge gymnasium. There were already many people in that large room, lined up in two rows opposite each other: one line for men and one for women. We stripped, our clothes were put into a pile to be sanitized, and we were given soap and some kind of towel. In shock, we just did as we were told. What else could we have done?

I don't remember seeing any other children there, nor do I remember being separated from my mother, my father, or Tibi. There was no talking, and I could hear every breath I took. What I do remember is seeing all the naked men and the humiliation on their faces. Their penises and testicles hanging down looked to me so extraordinary, so bizarre. I was innocent and uneducated about sex, and the sight totally sickened me. All these naked people seemed not to be human any more, and I tried desperately to look away. It was such a huge shock to me that it took me a long time, even as an adult woman, to get over the revulsion of looking at a naked man. Perhaps, I now think, I concentrated on the ugliness and the strangeness so that I wouldn't have to think about what was going to happen to us next.

After a while, we were told that we were being taken to the showers where we would all be cleaned and sterilized, and then we would be able to put on some of the clothes that each of us had been given. We filed through into a shower room. I must have found my mother because I remember going into the shower with her. I remember her holding me very close and embracing me, and then something opening up above us. We had heard stories and thought that gas would come out of the nozzles. I really don't think that we believed for five seconds that we would survive. We were just standing there all ready to die, and I think we were more surprised than anything else when the water started to pour down.

We had heard about the gas and the ovens from people who had fled to Hungary in 1942, and although we believed them, we couldn't visualize what that meant. "Jews are being gassed," they would tell us. We just couldn't imagine it. It still turns my stomach upside down when I think that Polish Jews were the first ones taken in 1942, and the death camps were all in place already then. But now it was 1944 and we were in the same situation. Barely human, we just trembled. And starved. Strangely, I don't remember the feeling of hunger, even though I was scarcely more than bones at this point. I think it was here that we were first introduced to turnip soup that the Germans used make out of the big white turnips that were normally used for animal feed. I am sure we got some kind of bread ration, but I don't remember eating bread, only that watery tasteless turnip soup.

And once again, there were the open latrines I had first experienced in the Szolnok ghetto, and their stench, the sight of children drowning in filth, the sight of people performing private functions in public, became to me one of the most blatant examples of how we were being reduced to less than animals. I count myself lucky that I cannot remember all the disturbing things I saw in Strasshof, but what I do remember, I remember very vividly. The very dignity of our humanity was being stripped away day by day, and we began to see ourselves as the filthy pigs the SS told us we were, leaving us only the prospect of dying like dogs in the dirt.

In Strasshof, our family was still together, at least occasionally, and we sometimes saw each other during the day. I recall that people were taken away to work in the morning and came back at night, but because my parents never talked to me about it, either at the time or afterwards, it is difficult for me to validate my memories. I remember distinctly, however, that a friend of my father's who had arrived at Strasshof before us came to my father at one point, and very discreetly in case he was being watched, gave him some well-guarded advice. He told my father that sometimes the townspeople from the nearby occupied towns came to ask for workers. He suggested that if we wanted to have even a slight chance of staying alive my father should quickly come forward and volunteer for any work opportunities that came along.

Sure enough, when we had been in Strasshof for a while, the Germans announced that they needed some people to work at the brick factory in Auspitz, unloading crates of cooling systems that came in on the trains. By this time, everyone, including me, had all heard of the hellhole called Auschwitz, and we must have been terrified that we were heading there. But my father, who knew the difference between Auschwitz and Auspitz, immediately volunteered. My mother, who spoke very good High German, told the German officers making the selection that my father had had a grain business before the war and that she was a certified cook and pastry chef. She told them also that my grandfather had worked hard all his life in his bakery, so although he looked somewhat worn by now, we were lucky that he was taken as well.

Our family and some other lucky people were bundled into a farmer's large horse and buggy and sent to the factory, with my brother Tibi and me, both afraid of being left behind and being disposed of like all the other children, hiding in the hay of the cart. It was then that we were separated from Zsofi, and there were no goodbyes, no words, as we were just shipped off, leaving her behind. Even though we were reunited with Zsofi after the war, I never did find out what she had to do to survive in Strasshof. Her story and the stories of both the survivors and the butchered in my family are all missing pieces in my life that I will never be able to recover.

Auspitz, in the protectorate of Bohemia and Moravia in Czechoslovakia, wasn't too far from Strasshof. When we got to the brick factory, we were put into the northeast corner of the warehouse area of the actual factory, a very large building where we slept in bunk beds, three to a tier. No one said anything about Tibi and me. Our eating room and kitchen was in a separate, long building that had probably been used for the factory workers before the war. I remember that by this time there was very little food, and what there was consisted of turnip soup, potato peelings, and bread. The piece of bread that we were given – an inch thick and perhaps the diameter of a slice from today's large rye bread – had to last for the week. In our barrack, there was a man who taught us how to slice our bread so it would last for seven days. He had a very sharp knife with him, and I don't know where he got it or how he managed to hide it, but every week he would carve up his bread into seven pieces.

My father went to work unloading the heavy crates that came in on the trains. My mother was put in charge of the officers' kitchen, which was in a separate small building that housed the officers. My mother would often try to bring us food from the officers' kitchen, sometimes breaking off a piece of something she had baked for the Germans. It was a very risky enterprise, and if she had been caught, she would have been severely beaten. Maybe because of that, my brother, Tibi, always refused to eat his portion, always giving it to the others to share. I do not remember much else about Tibi at this time, and to this very day, he will not talk to me about his experiences or memories of the Holocaust. Each time I ask him to tell me something or to validate my memory, he becomes nervous and agitated and yells at me, "Do you want to kill me? Don't you understand that I buried it very deeply and I don't want to remember anything?" My most vivid memory of him at that time was that he would give his food away.

Even I worked in Auspitz. The town had a railway depot where trains came in every day, carrying large crates that we had to unload quickly. We had been told that the crates contained some kind of cooling system, but we soon discovered that they really held ammunitions and explosives. Winter was setting in, and I remember not having any shoes. I would tear the wrappings off the crates, using the packing and the cardboard from the crates to wrap around my feet to keep them warm. This packing from the crates also kept my feet from freezing when I was sent out into the fields in the snow to dig ditches. I remember standing in the snow half-frozen, digging ditches with the guards standing over us, telling us these were going to be our graves when we were shot. Other times, I was sent to simply sweep out the train cars after they had been unloaded. I was happy to do this work because, if nothing else, many times I would find some edible crumbs of food or seeds of grain in the cracks of the empty cars. I think of Auspitz always as a place of eternal hunger and equally eternal winter, and during that very hard winter, I looked forward to the times I would be sent to work in the kitchen with my mother, to sweep or do whatever I could to stay indoors.

Sometimes someone from the outside would throw some food over the barbed wire fence as they rode their bicycles to work. If they did it early enough in the day, before the dogs or officers were up yet, we had a chance to find it. Once I happened to be walking by the fence when someone threw a little bag over. In it was a small piece of a poppy seed roll. This had been one of my favourite foods at home, and I loved it so much I can still taste it. When I saw what was in the bag, I took it out and ate it right then and there. I didn't save it till I got back to the factory to share with my family, and I didn't tell anyone about it. I just stood there at the fence and ate every crumb, feeling both guilty and selfish but with that utter enjoyment of a cat licking its whiskers after drinking a bowl of milk.

My grandfather's death certificate from the Auspitz work camp,
December 24, 1944.

We spent the remainder of the war in Auspitz, and it was this place that changed our family forever in several ways. My grandfather died there. He was seventy-six years old in 1944, and the war took whatever little life he had left out of him. I do recall that when we got there, there was another old man with whom he used to talk all the time. Both of them were quite deaf, and they used to shout to each other all day long. It was the only thing that made everyone laugh in spite of our misery. But not for long. My grandfather, number 141, died on December 24 of hunger, cold, and his lack of desire to continue living. While my grandfather was alive, he always lit the fourth Hannukah candle in memory of his late wife, who had died on the fourth day of the holiday, and after he died, my brother Peter carried on that tradition.

We were afraid to tell anyone that my grandfather had died, and not knowing what to do with his body, Tibi slept next to him for a while so nobody would know he was dead. Once the others in the barrack became aware of my grandfather's death, however, they became agitated at having a dead body to add to the dirty, odious conditions we lived in, so we finally had to tell the Germans. The officer in charge of the camp was surprisingly humane and allowed us to have my grandfather buried in a corner next to the fence of a gentile cemetery, a place that could be easily identified as his final resting place. Only my father was permitted to go along for the burial. For the rest of her life, my mother wanted to visit this cemetery and have her father's body transferred, but circumstance made this impossible.

My mother was still relatively young at that time, not yet forty, and she was a handsome and very distinguished-looking woman. She was also open game for the Germans. Cooking for the officers, serving them dinner in the evening in their quarters when the officers would often get very drunk, left her vulnerable. One particular night, either at the end of January or beginning of February 1945, a high-ranking officer raped her. When she came back to our barrack that night, she was bleeding and her body was bruised from the force he had used. I heard her crying and talking in whispers with my father. I didn't know exactly what had happened, but I knew the Germans had done something very bad. I had turned eight the previous July, but I had no idea what sex and rape meant. All I knew was that my mother had been badly hurt. My father went looking for the officer, but before he had a chance to get to him, the Germans caught him. They decided to make an example of my father and shoot him, and they assembled the rest of us before the sun came up the next morning and ordered all of us to watch.

By this time, the officer who had raped my mother had sobered up and ordered a stop to the shooting, instructing that my father be beaten instead. Even as I write this today, more than sixty years later, the thought of my father's battered body makes me tremble. He was beaten and kicked so brutally that he could not move. Tibi, I think, tried to get closer and was thrown aside with one vicious blow. Not able to watch the beating, I just screamed for them to stop. I remember trying to memorize the officer's face, to imprint it in my mind so that when the time came, if it did, I could identify him. I looked at my father and couldn't believe that this lump of flesh soaked in blood was my gentle, pious, loving father. He couldn't have weighed much more than a hundred pounds by this time, and I could barely recognize the tender soul with the thick, black hair who was always so neat, so tidy, so kind. By the time we pulled and dragged him back to his bed, he was mercifully unconscious. Tibi and I and whoever else could help tried to keep him alive. It was our luck that by this time the ammunition shipments had slowed down and we had some time to be with him. He had a fever and no food or water, and my mother kept stealing torn sheets, cleaning liquid, and some kind of painkillers so we could attempt to nurse him back to health. Nobody thought he would survive, but he did. It took a long time for my father's body to heal, but between his own determination and all of our help, he did. As far as his spirit was concerned, those maniacs could not touch it. For me he continued to act as he always had before the war and would continue to do so for all of his life afterwards.

The Auspitz labour camp with its twelve-foot-high fence was on the outskirts of a small farming community, and the townspeople would often walk or cycle by the fence of the camp on their way to work. One day, a townsperson saw me standing inside the fence and threw something over to me. It was a little doll made of cardboard and wearing a dress made of cloth. I picked it up and held it as if it were a gift from heaven. I hid it under my dress, tucked into my panties, and kept it with me at all times. No one but my parents could know about it. God had given me back my Pani, my doll. How can I explain what that felt like for me. My heart is racing even now as I recall the feeling of touching it. It may have been the only moment during the war when I didn't think I was that filthy, hated, bad girl who was waiting to die and the sooner the better. Maybe as I felt the doll hugging me under my clothes, rubbing against the hollow remains of my stomach, I remembered Pani and my home. For a moment, I could feel like a child again, and a flicker of strength to survive surfaced in me. At night, I would kiss the doll and hide her under my "mattress" for fear that someone would take her from me when I was asleep or she would disappear just like the first Pani did. After all, whom could I trust anymore?

How Auspitz changed us! My mother had always been so proud of her spotless home, of how we were all dressed and groomed. Now we were covered in lice. Everything was infested with it – our hair, our clothes, our beds – everything. We had become creatures rather than civilized people. And my mother stopped smiling. I don't think I ever saw her smile again until her first grandchild was born. My father, who had always been so straight and strong, became very, very skinny, slightly bent, and very tired looking. Even his good nature and his optimism couldn't protect him from the brutality of the life we were living. My brother, Tibi, once a good-looking boy with blond hair and a heart of gold, now at twelve years old wanted only to sacrifice himself for our family. He was very devoted to my parents and wanted to help them. He wouldn't eat anything and always said he had already eaten and that his portion should be given either to my parents or to me. He would save his portions of bread and margarine, if we got any, so that we could divide it up for everyone else. Tibi was very badly affected by the war in ways that only manifested themselves later on, after we returned to Szarvas.

It is hard to imagine how we survived and where we found the strength to hold on and go on living, but spring finally arrived. The snow melted, and I was being sent into the fields to plant crops. As I turned the softening earth, it gave me some hope that maybe the hardest part of our suffering would be coming to an end. Maybe spring would bring a new beginning. For the Germans, the spring of 1945 meant that their dream of world domination was also melting. My mother was virtually invisible to the German officers, who talked openly in front of her, and she understood full well what they were talking about. They were losing the war, and word was out that the Russians were coming fast. It was sometime in March 1945 when the Nazis decided to abandon Auspitz and take us to one of the death camps, but it was too late for that and there was no transportation. And why should they bother with "another handful of filth"? We were often told by the officers who passed us by as we were working, "Watch out, you filthy pigs. Your heads are very loose on your necks." Why they simply didn't shoot us all since, as I recall, there were only eighteen of us left by then, who can say? Void of feeling and numb, we did not realize at the time how significant the number eighteen was in the Jewish tradition – eighteen being the numerical value of the Hebrew word for life – but I have thought of it many times since then.

When they marched us out of Auspitz, there were only two SS officers with us. I don't know why we didn't overpower them and kill them, but by then we were nothing more than helpless, beaten dogs. We were moving very slowly, even though the yelling and hitting never stopped, and we might have lost more people on the way since I remember only nine of us remaining at the end. We had been marching for about a day when we came to a small river with a little bridge over it. On the bank was a fence running along the embankment. If we looked up, we could see the surrounding mountains, and we could hear, and physically feel, the Russian tanks, the bombing and shooting everywhere.

We knew that the war would soon be over, and the Germans knew their end was near, too. The Nazis, who had shown great inhumanity where our lives were concerned, were still able to be afraid for their own skins, and they were getting impatient. They told us to stop, that we were not going any further, and ordered us to line up, faces towards the fence and hands above our heads so they could shoot us in the back. And then a miracle happened. We were all turned to the fence when my father stepped out of line and declared in Hungarian, "No, we are not going to be shot in the back like dogs." Telling everyone to turn back around, he started to pray, leading us in the recitation of *Shema Yisrael*, the affirmation of our faith in the Oneness of God that is the most sacred of all Jewish prayers. By the time we had finished praying, one officer had already run away and the other was just standing there. When he saw us turn around, he, too, just took off, afraid for his own skin. I can still see myself standing there beside the river, clutching my cardboard doll as if my life depended on it. We were alive.

But what were we to do now? We didn't know where we were, which way to go, where we would be safe away from the line of fire of the advancing front. I don't know how we decided, but we just started walking. After a day and a half, we wandered into the Czech city of Brno at night, our way lighted by *Sztalin gyertyak* (Stalin candles), flares like "firecrackers" thrown from airplanes. Brno looked like a very big city to me, and there was a lot of heavy door-to-door combat going on all around us. There was surprisingly little Allied bombing because, as we later discovered, Brno had been declared an open city.

We didn't know who was fighting the Germans there – the Russians or the Americans – but there was devastation all around.

Amid the rubble on the outskirts of the city, we stumbled on an apartment complex that had an inner courtyard, and there we found an underground bunker. Hoping for safety, we climbed in. The bunker was dark and damp, and inside, hiding among the civilians from the surrounding apartment buildings, were close to twenty young German soldiers, who looked terrified. When we entered, it was clear to everyone who and what we were because we must have looked like hell on earth. One of the Nazis, probably the highest ranking officer, came up to us and said, "We want to make a deal with you. When the Russians come, you tell them we saved your lives and we won't hurt you." We looked at him in wonder and didn't even bother to answer. We weren't afraid, and the civilians were on our side.

We remained in the bunker for a couple of weeks as the fighting and heavy shelling raged around us. The civilians in the bunker were kind enough to let us stay, and I think they must have shared their food and even their clothing and bedding with us. They knew we were Jews, but they must have been so afraid for their own lives at that point that it probably didn't make any difference to them *who* we were. Because we were cooped up there for so long, whenever the shelling subsided and it seemed a little less dangerous, someone would stick their head out of the bunker for a breath of fresh air. I was getting very bored and restless in the bunker myself. When I had had enough, I decided to go out and see what was happening outside, even though I had been strictly forbidden to do so.

I climbed out and began to run around the courtyard. On the ground, I found different coloured little "toy" airplanes, about an inch or so in length, with messages written in a language that I couldn't read rolled up around them; these, I later found out, were propaganda messages that the Russians were dropping from their bombers. As I was collecting these lovely coloured airplanes, a shell fell quite close by, and the detonation threw me to the ground, stunning me. I don't know how long I lay there before my parents came running out and found me and took me back to the bunker. I seemed to be fine, just a bit shaken, and it wasn't until much later, when I already had a daughter of my own, that I discovered I had sustained permanent damage to my hearing in both ears.

I was scolded for my disobedience, but I suppose I was just craving to be a child, to act like any normal child would. When the soldiers took my doll away from me the day they marched us out of our home, I had stopped being a child, stopped being myself. I had stopped wanting to live. I could never understand why I had to go through all that suffering. If we were just going to get killed anyway, why did we have to wait? I didn't care from one minute to the next if I would live or die. I didn't know when the end would come, but as far as I was concerned, the sooner the better. But now the child in me wanted to come out and play. I didn't feel any fear. Fear had become a part of me, and it didn't faze me to be out among the rubble, hearing the shooting.

Fighting from house to house, the Russians eventually took over the city and found us on April 13, 1945, my brother Tibi's birthday. The first thing they did was take the Germans away. They asked everyone for their papers, and we had papers, too – the numbers they had given us at Strasshof. Although we couldn't communicate with the Russians, when they realized who we were, they gave us food and were very nice to us. I even remember once sitting on top of one of their tanks, watching the soldiers guzzling vodka. For the Russians, one bottle of vodka was nothing, and I remember thinking, "What can they accomplish when they are this drunk?"

By now, people were emerging from bunkers everywhere, relieved and celebrating their liberation. But what about us? We were nowhere; Brno wasn't our home. What were we to do? We were in a strange city. Whom could we trust?

As far as we were concerned, all we wanted was to go home to Szarvas. My parents were desperate to find out what had happened to my older brothers and the rest of our family, and we haunted the railway station almost daily, trying to explain to the Russian soldiers that we just wanted to go home. But how? The trains were not running, and everywhere there was chaos. If a train did manage to come through, there were so many people on it, they were hanging out of the windows and climbing all over the cars.

One day, a train pulled into the station with a group of some twenty to thirty young women inmates from Auschwitz, still wearing their concentration camp rags. None of them had seen a Jewish child for years, and when they saw me, they formed a line and just picked me up and handed me around, hand over hand, so everyone could touch me and look at me. All of them were crying; they had all had daughters or sisters who had been murdered, and they were overwhelmed that a Jewish child had survived. For me, the experience was terrible. I think this was the first instance when I consciously felt very guilty about surviving. Why *did* I survive? I would have given them my life to bring their relatives back. That guilt has stayed with me; it is with me still. Why was I chosen to live? Why did I survive when so many died? So many had wanted to live and had died – why was I saved when all I wanted was to die?

As often as we begged the Russians, they told us there was no way to get us home yet. With no way to leave, we began to think of what to do in the meantime. A Russian commandant, it so happened, was looking for a cook, and my mother agreed to take the position. "I used to cook for Nazi officers," she said cautiously, "and I can cook for you." If there was no way of leaving, the Russian headquarters was a good place to stay and wait until we could. My parents were too beaten down and heartsick to start walking home, and Tibi and I were too young. So we made a bargain with the Russians and decided to trust them. They promised that when it was possible, they would make sure we could go home safely. In the meantime, we would come with them and my mother would be their cook.

They took us to a castle just outside of Brno where they were headquartered. I think Field Marshall Hermann Goering had used it as a summer palace, and now the Russians had made it their headquarters for the area. On the way, we passed by the factory at Auspitz and saw that the building where we had once been housed had been bombed and that the very corner where we had slept was now simply a pile of rubble.

Although we were the only non-Russians there and Tibi and I were the only children, we soon settled into life at the Russian headquarters. My mother cooked, and my father was out talking to people every day, asking if anyone had heard anything about Peter and Pali and looking for a way to get transportation home. As for me, the Russians were using only part of the castle for offices, and I was allowed to move freely around the rest of the building. I was still shell-shocked from the war, and I think I mostly roamed aimlessly. The castle was very beautiful, made of red clay with marble steps, and its courtyard was huge and well taken care of. I remember seeing a very large reception area and wandering through the rooms, examining them and the things in them. In one room, I found a gorgeous French doll. She was about three feet tall and made of porcelain. Every little part of her moved separately. She was so big, I could hardly hold her. I was in a dream. I was in a castle, I had food, and I had a doll. There was nothing I needed to be afraid of there, but to say that I felt safe, that I was comfortable, would be a lie. The war had taken a permanent toll on me.

One day as I was sitting alone in one of the rooms, a Russian officer spotted me. He came in, sat down, and gestured for me to come sit on his knee, which I did. Although he spoke to me in Russian, I somehow understood that he was telling me about his daughter who was my age. He began to cry as he talked about her, and before I knew it, he was patting me, his hands sliding further and further up and down my body. He was touching me in places that made me very uncomfortable. Suddenly, as if by magic, my mother appeared. She took my arm and led me away from him. Her voice trembled as she explained to me that I had to watch out for men. I must never again sit on a man's lap.

I don't know exactly when my nightmares started, but I think it was around this time. I could always tell, even during the day, that I was going to be sick at night and have a nightmare because I would start to smell cigar-like smoke. I don't know if the Nazis smoked cigars or not, but even now, if I am having a very bad day, I can smell cigar smoke, although a very different smell than the smell from cigars they smoke in North America. My nightmares started recurring almost every night. It got to the point where I was afraid to go to sleep. They were always the same: Nazi officers in high black boots running with their big dogs and shooting at me. There were dead bodies. And always I was running, running, running, forever ending up in a maze, a maze made out of wagons, and I was suffocating. In the nightmare, I was small and couldn't find my way out of that maze. It was pressing in on me, and it was very grey, like the colour you would see on mouldy bread. In the end, there was always a grey-coloured, sponge-like thing bearing down on me, and I couldn't breathe. That was when I would scream or just wake up.

I remember having this nightmare in the castle and later for as long as we lived in Szarvas after the war. Once we moved to Budapest, the dreams subsided a bit. Strangely, when we came to Canada, the nightmares came back and continue today. The only difference is that now in the dream, there is always someone close to me who has died. And still I am running and still I'm being pursued.

The Russians kept us at the castle for three months. One week turned into two, two turned into a month, a month turned into three. It wasn't until the end of June 1945 that we arrived back in Szarvas. We were the last to return, and everyone had given us up for dead.

CHAPTER 4

Return to Szarvas

Mourn not: weep not at a time like this/Nor bow your head... –
"Mourn Not," *Sabbath and Festival Prayer Book*

My family had lived in the town of Szarvas since before my grandfather's time, and on our street, Jokai Mor Utca, we knew everybody and everyone knew us. There were pleasant people across the road who had always been our very good friends. On the corner, one-armed Mr. Kukovitz, owned the cigar store where my father would send my two older brothers to buy him cigarettes. I think my brothers were quite young when they would sneak the occasional cigarette, and every time they came to the store, Mr. Kukovitz would make the same remark so that it soon became a family joke. In English, it would translate as something like: "If I ever catch you smoking one of your father's cigarettes, I will hit your hand so hard that it will be full of shit, and I will make you eat it." He was a nice man, but he had no manners. But he did have great respect for my parents. One Shabbat, my brothers, not being particularly observant, went for cigarettes, and Mr. Kukovitz, realizing that smoking is forbidden on the Sabbath, threw them out of his store.

There were also two Catholic maiden sisters living in a house near us, and I knew them very well. They had a gorgeous garden and an artesian well. There was a well in the middle of town, too, but almost every day, I would go to the sisters' house, accompanied by our maid, to fetch water in my little child-sized metal water jug. They would tell me stories about themselves and proudly show me their beautiful flower garden. These two sisters were the nicest people.

But that was before the war. Now when we came back from the camps, everything and everyone had changed. There was greater anti-Semitism now than had ever existed before, and our best neighbours and former friends would not even talk to us. The Christians in our town had never really exhibited strong anti-Semitism before the war, but they were fast learners. The Nazis had taught them that Jews were to be hated, and this had brought out the latent anti-Semitism in everyone. It was something that I had never felt before the war, and it shocked me. They were not at all pleased that we had come back, and I couldn't understand the change in them. All these people who had smiled at me and been friends with my family for years, these people who had rung the church bells to herald my birth, now just turned their heads away. They said that more Jews had come back from the war than had left. Our synagogue had been burned down, and older children like Tibi got into fights. The two Catholic sisters crossed themselves and shrieked as if they had seen an unbelievably frightening sight. "These are not real people. They are ghosts," they cried. And probably we did look like ghosts – but we were real.

Because we didn't come back till late June of 1945 – so much later than some other families – we found our house occupied by a Jewish family who had come back before us and whom we had known before the war. Surprisingly, though, the house was in good shape. Peter and Pali had been taken away to forced labour camps shortly after the Nazi occupation of Hungary in March 1944, but Peter had managed to escape and returned to Szarvas that fall. I don't really understand how he did it, but he managed to rent out my grandfather's bakery at that time. He also rented our house to a Jewish couple from Budapest with whom Pali had been staying and studying his trade before he was taken away to the labour camp; this family needed a place to live until it was safe for them to go back to Budapest. Because there were people living in the house during the war, it had not been completely ransacked as many others had been. Of course, many things were missing, but all our furniture was still in the dining room, including my mother's silver candelabrum and our chairs with seats made of the finest *petit point*. My parents told me later that they had buried some of the silver, including our candelabrum, in the back of the house where the *succah* usually stood. It didn't take long to convince the Jewish family to give us back our house, and we began to settle in.

In September, I started back at school. Of course, I couldn't go to a Jewish school because it no longer existed, and our synagogue had been burned to the ground the previous October. So I was sent to the Szarvas Evangelist School. The pain and humiliation I had felt during the war was not to be over for me just yet. I can still hear the school bell ringing three times on that first day, the shuffling, the last-minute rush of the latecomers, and then the quiet as the teacher arrived. We stood, said the morning prayers, and sat down in unison. "Olga Berger!" the teacher shouted out as she began the roll call. "Here," I answered shyly, looking up at her as she peered in my direction over her glasses. As the new girl in school, I felt timid and uneasy. It didn't help that my name sounded German, not Hungarian, and everyone knew that it was primarily Jews who had German names.

I don't remember if the children made fun of me, but I do know that all I wanted to do was disappear, hide from their curiosity and their endless questions, and be left alone. I couldn't stand being different and didn't want anyone to hurt me anymore. I tried to make myself invisible, and for the first time since the horrors of the war, I was glad that I was small and skinny. It made it easier for me to go unnoticed most of the time. But the more I didn't want to be different, the more I stood out. At that time, religious classes were still mandatory several times a week, and being the only Jewish child in that particular school – neither Tibi nor Kati attended the same school as I did – I had to leave the class during these lessons and during all the Christian celebrations. One more degradation to make me feel labelled and outcast.

I worked hard, trying to complete all of grades three and four in one year so I could catch up with what I had missed during the war. By the spring of 1946, my school work was coming along fine, but I still felt alienated and alone. It was Easter time, and the local stores were filled with chocolate bunnies and other delicious Easter treats. The other children at school were painting Easter eggs, something that looked like fun. There were preparations going on at our house, too, for Passover, but the endless scrubbing and bleaching brought back painful memories of the smell of disinfectant in Strasshof, reminding me of how uncomfortable I was being Jewish. To make matters worse, I could vividly remember the spring before when we had barely been alive.

I did make one new friend at school. My classmate Ilona lived on a farm just outside of town, almost an hour's walk from our house. She was Christian but just as lonely and shy as I was. Her family was poor, too, and I shared my lunch and clothes with her. She often came to my house after school so we could do our homework together. She frequently stayed for dinner, and sometimes my parents would let me walk her part way home. As our house began to take on a festive look and smell of Passover, with the sweet aroma of my mother's cooking and baking filling every corner, Ilona, who as a Christian had never experienced Passover, asked if she could come and join us for our celebration. My parents agreed, and they invited Ilona to spend the *seder* night with us. I was thrilled, and our excited giggles filled the house. That night, Ilona ran all the way home to ask her parents.

On the night of the *seder*, my happiness and anticipation were boundless as I waited anxiously for Ilona to arrive. But she never came. Seeing my anguish, my parents invited my old friend Kati to our *seder*. Kati's family had also been deported, but they, too, had returned to Szarvas after the war. Her presence soothed me somewhat, and soon we were both enthralled by the celebration, the prayers, the songs, and the delicious meal, especially my favourite chicken soup with matzo balls and tiny yellow unhatched eggs floating in it.

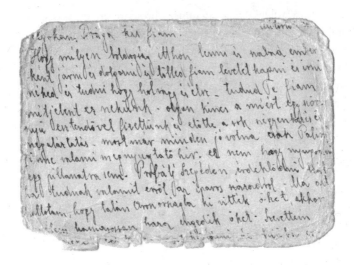

My mother's reply to Peter's first letter after we returned to Szarvas, June 1945. In it, she tells Peter that everything would be fine if the family would only hear that Pali was still alive.

Ilona did not come to school for several days after our *seder* celebration. It was only later that I learned that missing school had been her punishment for having made a Jewish friend. Ilona was now a little scared to be friends with me, but our friendship slowly returned to the warmth it had had before the "ill-advised" Passover invitation.

As soon as we arrived home in late June of 1945, my mother had gotten in touch with the Red Cross and began looking for my two older brothers. Peter sent us a message from Szeged that he had enrolled in medical school there after it was finally safe for him to leave Szarvas. It took another three months, however, before we heard from Pali. He had been in Dachau and Mauthausen and had survived, although just barely. Liberated near a sugar factory, the starving survivors had been drawn to the big sugar blocks, which they licked until they got sick. Pali was lucky that my father's brother, Miklos, was with him, and when Pali lost consciousness, Miklos made sure that his nephew was taken to a hospital. Pali was sick with typhus and had been given up for dead at first. Slowly he did recuperate, and my mother went to see him in September. When she came home, she was clearly broken-hearted at the state he was in.

I was ecstatic that we had found Pali. He had always been my favourite brother and I could hardly wait to see him, but we had to wait until the end of September for him to be well enough to come home from the hospital. When he finally did arrive, I ran to greet him and tried to hug him. Weak and overcome at his homecoming, he just fainted and fell to the floor. Of all of us, he had had the worst time of it, and to this day, he suffers from heart problems and other related health issues.

When our family was finally reunited, I wanted to talk to my brothers about what we had all gone through. They, however, did not want to speak about what they had faced even though I was aching to discuss it. I wanted to tell them my story and to talk about what I was feeling. It made me sick and miserable when friends told us how lucky we were to be alive. I felt only guilt and sadness. "Why?" I asked myself. "Why am I so lucky?" And my friends who were taken away, where were they? It would have helped me to talk to my brothers, to hear what they had experienced and what they felt. But to this day, I know very little about their Holocaust experiences, and they know very little about mine.

My parents wouldn't discuss the war either. Whenever I approached them with questions about our survival, they brushed me off. But I knew that they had been permanently changed by our ordeal. My mother hardly ever smiled any more, and my father's face had taken on a new, strained look. Memories of lost sisters, brothers, nieces, nephews, and other relatives hung in the air, making it difficult to breathe. I think there are two types of families that came back from the Holocaust: one that could not stop talking about the war whenever they got together with friends or family, and the other, like ours, that totally ignored what had happened, suppressed it, and wanted only to get on with life.

Exactly one year after our liberation, on April 13, 1946, my brother Tibi celebrated his *bar mitzvah*. Although things had stabilized somewhat for the Jews by this time, there was still no synagogue in Szarvas. A Jewish school had been converted into a conservative synagogue that still had separate seating for men and women, and it was here that the holidays were observed and where Tibi's *bar mitzvah* took place. The *bar mitzvah* party, though, was held at our home and became not just a celebration of Tibi's special day but a celebration of survival for all of us. I don't think I have ever again experienced such a joyful party since that occasion. Because his birthday is in April, there were already flowers. My mother also ordered violets that grew in abundance in Hungary, and their heavenly aroma filled the house. The dining room table was pulled out, covered with a damask tablecloth, and sprinkled with violets. The table was then covered with bridal veil netting to hold the flowers in place and set with beautiful china and heavy silverware with a bunch of violets laid next to every plate. It was breathtaking.

To get to the dining room, guests came in through the front gate and stepped up onto a long, open veranda leading to the sunroom, which looked out over our garden. From there, they entered the dining room through my father's office and library. The entire congregation must have been invited because tables had also been set up in the sunroom with yet another table in the big kitchen for us children. My mother baked and cooked her specialties: *challah*, Hungarian carp in aspic, and other delicacies. There wasn't a dry eye in the house. Everyone was celebrating their lives, hugging and kissing each other and whispering, "Dear God, we are alive!"

By 1946, Peter and Pali wanted to get on with their lives. They did not spend much time at home in Szarvas any more and were usually away at school – Peter at medical school in Szeged, Pali at a tool-and-die-making trade school in Budapest. But they would come home for the summer, and even though we tried to spend as much time together as we could, I was constantly aware of the changes in us and in our lives. It became clear to me that nothing ever remains the same. I remember once standing on the banks of the Koros River, just looking at the scene, watching the river change minute by minute. I was fascinated by bridges and rivers and loved watching the sun reflect off the water slowly flowing by. I knew that every minute, everything in the world changes, just like the river.

When my brothers came home for the summer, however, we did not do too much thinking. We concentrated on having fun and were thrilled just being together. Peter would often have friends over to play cards, and I just wanted to hang around all evening and admire them all. I suppose I was too chatty or rambunctious and kept them from concentrating on their game, so they all said that they would marry me someday if I would just keep quiet and let them play cards. Cheaters!

My brothers had taught me how to swim before the war, and the lessons continued that summer of 1946, now that I was a "big" girl and all of ten years old. They were tough and would throw me in the middle of the Koros River from our boat and make me swim back to shore. I struggled, but I would always make it back. They watched to make sure that I made it to shore, just as I knew they would. They loved me and were good teachers. Once I could swim, we would play other games in the water and see who could swim the furthest and for the longest time. Once when we were fishing from our little boat, Tibi tossed the fishing line out, and the hook landed in my left palm. He told me that it had happened because I had not been sitting quietly and carefully enough, but still he ran all the way to the doctor with me.

Some people owned cottages or small parcels of land on the Koros River, and we shared one of those parcels with Pali's girlfriend's family. There was a small shack to change in, and someone had built a dock on the shore out of a small, downed airplane. The wing was very hot to step on with bare feet, but it made a perfect place to stretch out on a towel to read and suntan. It was also our jumping-off spot when we raced each other across the river. On the other side of the river was Peppi Kert, an orchard where the owners were experimenting with very special fruit, and we often swam across the river and sneaked into the orchard. We would fill our bathing suits with delicious fruit and swim back to feast on our stolen treasures.

Our laughter during these special times together carried through the air and across the water, and we tried very hard to enjoy each moment. Even though the airplane wing reminded us of the war, it also reminded us of how lucky we were to be together, reunited after the horrific event that had swept through Europe and through our own lives. But we also knew that we had changed. We might still have looked the same, but we had each experienced tremendous changes both in our bodies and in our minds. As we laughed and swam through those long summer days, we knew that we would never be the same as we had been before. The Holocaust had been a turning point in our lives, yet nobody else wanted to talk about it. I desperately needed to share those experiences with someone, but I couldn't find anyone who would listen, not even my beloved parents or brothers, the only people I knew I could trust completely.

That autumn when Peter and Pali went back to school, Tibi and I spent a lot of time together. We would walk in our famous park, Erzsebet Liget, where the magnificent colours of autumn were on display. I always found the sight breathtakingly beautiful and am still, every autumn, filled with awe at the ability of nature to surpass the talents of the greatest human artists in creating the splendour of the changing leaves. We strolled over ground that was littered with many shades of fallen leaves, and to this day, the crunch of autumn leaves under my feet transports me back to the sensation of pleasure and companionship this time of year gave me when I was young.

All the crazy things my brothers and I did together come flooding back into my mind. Once, seeing my big brothers smoking, I was curious and wanted to try it. After some hesitation, they rolled me a cigarette made of a tree leaf. Once I had taken a big puff of that and began throwing up violently, I was instantly cured of ever wanting to taste a cigarette again. Sometimes when they wanted me out of their hair for a while or wanted to bribe me not to tell on them for something they had done, they would leave me at the Frecska movie theatre to watch a movie or buy me ice cream as a bribe at Brachna Bacsi's beautiful pastry shop. With treats like those, they knew my mouth would be truly sealed.

Although it was a rough start at first, we did begin to live once more. By 1946, my father had begun to work, and slowly but surely, he re-started and built up his grain business again, buying grain from the small independent farmers in our area. There was a lot of competition now that many Jews were back in business, but my father always paid a little bit more than everyone else so the farmers wanted to sell to him. My mother, a very intelligent businesswoman, worked alongside him, and they began to make money.

I resumed my friendship with Kati. We were so lucky to have both survived the war, and we continued where we had left off, but now that we were older, we also got into our share of trouble. One night when I was sleeping over at her house, we decided to crawl out through the window after everyone else had gone to bed. This escapade, one has to keep in mind, took place at a time when two girls aged nine or ten, could imagine going out in the middle of the night in their nightgowns or pyjamas, just for a laugh. It was just lucky for us that nobody noticed or we would have gotten a good licking for our trouble. I also remember that Kati's grandmother was hard of hearing, and it was very difficult to communicate with her. We would sit and giggle as Kati's mother tried to talk to the old woman, not realizing how frustrating it must have been for everyone concerned. At the age of twenty-three when I discovered that I myself was hard of hearing, I certainly thought back sympathetically to what that must have been like for her grandmother. Sadly for me, when Kati was about thirteen, her family moved to Israel.

By 1947, my father's business was doing well enough that we could afford a live-in maid. We also had a woman who came in to help with different chores like ironing, making all kinds of pasta including *levesteszta* (noodles for soup), and putting up jars of jams and fruit preserves. We also hired Lujza, a woman who came once a week to sew for us. Our servants were all gentiles but were happy to work for us. I would call Lujza "*Lujza neni*," or Mrs. Louisa, because that was the polite form of address that I had been taught as a child to use. I used to watch *Lujza neni* make curtains and bedding, items that in those days you couldn't just go to the store and buy. She was gifted in embroidery, and of course, everything we owned, from serviettes and towels to bedding, had to bear our initials. In Europe, mothers began when their daughters were very young to collect a trousseau for them. These beautiful items were kept in a large wooden chest, and by the time the girls were brides, they had enough linen to start their own homes. I had a wardrobe again, and I could watch for hours as *Lujza neni* sewed my initials, "BO" (Berger Olga), in pink ribbon on my things and then embroidered the ribbons with white polka dots. I loved the polka dots.

I remember so many things from those first years after the war, things that were brand new for me but helped me move forward from the total chaos of the Holocaust to focus on the here-and-now. Sometime in the summer of 1947, after I finished grade five, we went to Budapest to visit Peter and Pali, who were already living there, and my father's brother, Miklos, who was now married to my beloved Zsofi. Miklos and Zsofi were working again for the elderly Jewish couple who owned the large restaurant on the corner of Mester Utca. At the entrance, there was a pub where people could go and drink, and behind that was a very elegant restaurant. I remember the thrill of being allowed to sit on Miklos and Zsofi's laps and play with the cash register. They had no children of their own, and they loved me and spoiled me rotten.

The most significant thing that happened to me in the first few years after the war, though, occurred in 1948 when I was twelve years old and the *Mizrachi* organization came to Szarvas. *Mizrachi* was a Zionist organization that came from Israel to Europe after the Holocaust to look for surviving children, especially orphaned ones, to take back to Israel. The leaders who came to Szarvas were all in their twenties, and they had already been gathering some children from the small cities and towns around us. They settled into a building at the end of our street close to our house, and it was there in this *maon* (Hebrew for residence) with these people that I found something to live for. There were already children staying there, children who had been traumatized and orphaned by the Holocaust. I had finally found some kindred souls; that was how good I felt with the *Mizrachi* group. Finally, here were people I could talk with, people who would listen to me and who understood me, people I understood, people who had gone through the same traumatizing experiences as I had.

I became very active in the organization, and life finally became something with meaning. I felt I could be truly Jewish there. They cooked kosher meals and talked about Israel. I made friends with the children who lived there, orphans whom I had never known before. They had been hurt more deeply than I had by the war, and when I held their hands, they trembled in mine. I wanted to be with them so badly and decided to go to Israel with them. Of course, my mother and father categorically refused to let me go. They asked one of the *Mizrachi* leaders to come to our house and told him that our family needed to stay together. They said that we were planning to go to Israel one day and that I would come with them. They begged him not to take me.

Within a year or so, the organization was ready to move on. I remember the last evening I spent with them. We lit fireworks before Shabbat on their last Friday evening in Szarvas. It was the first time in my life I had seen fireworks. They used cotton wool soaked in gasoline and wrote in Hebrew letters in the sky: SHALOM.

L'HITRAOT. (Goodbye. Peace. We'll see each other again.) When they left, it was very, very hard for me to get over their departure. It was only with them that I felt truly alive as a young Jewish girl, and it was my dream to go to Israel, the homeland of my soul. But I did not blame my parents. I understood them. And I really believed that soon they would take me to Israel. We were making plans, but political events in Hungary would again prove to be more powerful than our private desires and dreams. Communism was about to become a fact of our lives.

Indeed, as far back as September of 1945, our family had begun to talk about leaving Hungary and going to Israel as soon as Pali came back from the hospital. But we all needed a little time to recover, to get some money together, to see what was going to happen in Hungary. By early 1948, however, Hungary was starting to fall into chaos, and money was becoming so worthless that you couldn't buy anything. Barter became the only method of trade, and rape, murder, and looting had become everyday occurrences. My father had two stepbrothers, and when they left for Argentina, they begged us to come with them. But Argentina was equally unstable at that time, and we decided we wouldn't trade one set of troubles for another. By the time Israel became a state in May 1948, a Communist government had been "elected" in Hungary, and we were stuck.

We decided we would try to escape to Israel, our spiritual homeland, and start a new life. Tibi had been studying at a rabbinical seminary in Budapest since the year after his *bar mitzvah*, but the Communists closed it down in 1948. We decided as a family that Tibi should try and cross the border and escape to Israel. There were people who promised that for money they could get him safely out of the country. We hoped that he would lead the way and we could follow, but he was caught at the border and sent to jail. Although he was released after a few days, we didn't dare try and leave then.

The year 1948 was one of turmoil for Hungary and for our family. It seems fitting that after that year of unrest, I got my first period during Shavuot in 1949. Because we didn't have indoor plumbing, we used to go to the bathhouse in Szarvas twice a week to take a bath. I loved swimming, and in the summertime, I would sometimes swim in the large, open pool connected to the bathhouse as a break from swimming in the river. On that particular day, I had gone to the pool with my girlfriends. When I undressed, I saw that there was blood on my bathing suit. At first, I was afraid to tell even my friends, but finally I found the courage to say, "I don't know what's wrong with me, but I think I'm pregnant. Maybe floating things in the pool made me pregnant. Or do you think I have an incurable disease?" Of course, they didn't know either.

Frightened, I went home where I knew my mother would be preparing for Shavuot. Even in my distress, as I walked up to the front of our house, I was overcome by the beauty and fragrance with which summer had graced our home. The two large acacia trees were in bloom, and I smelled the glorious aroma of their blossoms. There were huge wild chestnut trees, two or three different types of lilac bushes, and several splendid peach tress, all in full bloom.

As I entered the house, my mother was making her final inspection of our elegant home. Every holiday at home was prepared so beautifully, like preparations for the coming of the Messiah. The whole atmosphere in the house was special, and flowers were everywhere. Her face beamed with approval to see around her all that she admired and held dear. When she saw me, she asked, "What is the matter, *kislanyom* (my little girl)?"

"Nothing." I replied.

"Something's wrong with you," she insisted.

"Nothing," I repeated and went to my room. But I was feeling really, really sick and came back. "I'm really not pregnant. And don't blame me."

"What are you talking about?" she said, exasperated but worried.

"I have blood on my bathing suit."

I had to stay in bed for two days because I was so sick. In the meantime, the whole family was called in to hear the news that I had become a woman. It became a celebration. I hated my mother for telling. How could she tell my brothers that I was bleeding? How dare she tell everyone a thing like that? But while I was naive enough about the facts of life to be embarrassed about my brothers knowing, still I did feel very proud of myself. Now I really *was* a big girl. In those days, we were so backward, so naive, but this memory is so ingrained in my mind. How silly and ignorant I was, how strangely innocent, even after all I had seen and experienced.

By late fall of 1949, things had reached the breaking point. The Communists declared us *kispolgari csokeveny* (an upper-middle-class family not favoured by the Communists) because we had been well off before the war. Because religion was now against the law, my school was nationalized and its name changed to the Szarvas State School. Once again, we could no longer be openly Jewish and celebrate Jewish holidays. If we wanted to acknowledge the holidays, we had to do it in a very subdued and quiet way. My parents continued to go to synagogue secretly, but I didn't want to. I was afraid of being caught and punished by the Communists. If that wasn't enough, the Communists confiscated my father's business, and no one would give him a job because he had not been accepted by the Communist Party.

Worst of all, our home was being taken away from us and we were forced to sell most of our belongings. There was great mistrust and intrigue everywhere around us. We didn't know who was a friend and who was an enemy, who was telling the truth and who was lying. Everyone had to weigh very carefully every word they said. Faced with a new, constantly changing world that was being ruled and transformed by ruthless, brutal people, I was finding it hard to keep my sanity. First, I had been ostracized for being Jewish, and now I was being punished for being born into a middle-class family. On top of all that had happened to us in the war, these new traumas were almost too much for me to bear. They compounded the physical and psychological toll I had suffered in my formative years and ended up leaving permanent scars on my body and soul. My hearing was getting worse, my nerves were bad, and every month I was laid low for a couple of days during my period. By the time we moved to Budapest, I was suffering bouts of dizziness, nausea, and migraines.

It was in 1949 that we decided to move to Budapest with the understanding that it would only be for a short time, just until we could get out of the country. Peter, Pali, and Tibi were already there. I was in the middle of grade eight at the Szarvas gymnasium (middle school), and we were to leave in December so that I would be able to begin the second semester of grade eight in Budapest. Szarvas before the war had been my home. It was the place where I learned all the important things in life: love, kindness, sharing, giving, and much, much more. Now Szarvas would no longer be my home.

I do have two beautiful memories of the last days before we left Szarvas. The first is of Pali and Zsuzsi's engagement party. Pali had always been my special angel. He could never stand to see me hurt or neglected, and I loved him unconditionally. When he saw that I was bored or had nothing to do, he often took me out with him, even when he was dating Zsuzsi, the girl he would marry. Zsuzsi was five years older than I was, and her school was adjacent to the school I went to. We became very good friends, and I found I could confide in her. Still, there was a part of me that was unhappy about their marriage. I was so attached to Pali and loved him so much that I worried I might lose him now that he was getting married. But I needn't have worried; we have all remained very close friends, and Pali and Zsuzsi are still married after all these years. Their engagement party took place in our beautiful dining room and was the last happy occasion we celebrated in Szarvas.

My father went to Budapest ahead of us to try and find a place to live, which was very difficult because, being considered second-class citizens, we were not allowed to have our own apartment. My mother and I remained behind in Szarvas to oversee the transportation of the few pieces of furniture and belongings we still had left after selling off most of our possessions. We had almost nothing, not even carpets, but I remember that last night alone with my mother as a very special night. As my mother and I lay on the floor trying to fall asleep during the last hours we would spend in the house where all her children had been born and raised, where she herself had grown up, she began to tell me the story of her life. I lay beside her, painfully aware that this was the first time that my mother was speaking to me so openly and intimately about herself. She talked about her childhood, her mother whom she adored, her first period, and her marriage. She told me how she came to marry my father, that she had never really loved him as deeply as he loved her. And she told me she was unhappy in her marriage. I lay in the dark, afraid to breathe, afraid to break the spell of this incredible event, of this love and honesty between mother and daughter that I had never experienced before. And I have never forgotten it. I see my mother still, in her navy blue dress with the beige polka dots, her ageless aristocratic face and posture shadowed by this new uprooting, this new occasion for good-byes and sorrows.

CHAPTER 5

Budapest: My Teenage Years

Life is either a daring adventure or nothing. – Helen Keller

The next morning, my mother and I set out for the train station and boarded the train to Budapest, leaving behind Szarvas and a way of life that would be a bittersweet memory for all of us for the rest of our lives. We spent the few hours of the trip totally immersed in our own thoughts, neither one of us any real comfort to the other. I am sure that my mother's feelings were much deeper and sadder than my own, but I myself had a great deal to think about. I had just recently turned thirteen, the age of birthright in Jewish tradition. Ironically, it was at this time, too, that I was coming to realize that as Jews, we could not truly live and have roots in a country where our countrymen despised us. Even though I had my blessed parents and brothers, all I could really expect from life was a few pleasant memories that I would try to carry with me as buffers against the hostile outside world. I was becoming aware, too, that from here on in, I could not afford idle self-pity or backward glances; I would need to focus on the present and think ahead as little as possible to the uncertain future.

When we arrived in Budapest, the large, echoing train station with its busy comings and goings seemed dark and dirty to me. Although I felt very small and out-of-place in this legendary city, its people looked so shabbily dressed to me and its buildings so drab and damaged by the war. "Is this Budapest? Hungary's capital city?" I asked myself. Is this the city whose natural beauty was once so admired as a landmark of Europe and whose setting, surrounded as it is by the Duna River, inspired the architecturally famous bridges that link the hills of Buda to the plains of Pest? I had learned all my life about our art and culture, which had been influenced by the Romans, the Ottomans, and the Habsburgs. Here at the crossroads of Europe, this site of several historic sieges was now also a city that bore the scars of the more recent Nazi and Soviet conquests. These scars were more relevant to me than all the stories of the distant past because I myself had witnessed the war that caused them. Everything about Budapest seemed an unpleasant dream to me, a dream that I would suppress for years to come. Who would have thought that it would take another generation before I would be able to let myself feel proud of my heritage again?

The apartment that my father had found for us on the fourth floor of the building at 53 Nepszinhaz Utca was a far cry from our house in Szarvas. The neighbourhood, which was not far from the Teleki Ter flea market, had a bad reputation, and we had to contend with the noise of the traffic and streetcars that clanged by our building from early morning until late at night. Still, we consoled ourselves that all the windows faced west, which made it sunny and bright most afternoons ... *and* there was indoor plumbing. On the other hand, the Communists had in place the policy of *tarsberlet*, or co-tenancy, and we had to share our apartment with another Jewish couple, the Ulmans. Luckily for us, they were a middle-aged couple who kept mostly to themselves. I never saw children, relatives, or other people visit them, and they rarely spoke to us either. They left for work in the morning and returned at night, seldom using the kitchen, one of the rooms the two families shared.

Ours was the first apartment next to the staircase and elevator on the fourth floor. Just to the right of the entrance to our unit was the kitchen. The laundry had to be done in the attic of the building, something that was very hard for my mother, who had to carry the dirty laundry up the stairs and the wet wash back down to the kitchen. In the kitchen were clotheslines called *fregoli* that could be lowered from the ceiling to hang the wet laundry and pulled back up to let it dry. From the kitchen, a door opened onto a *U*-shaped, outdoor walkway that overlooked the inner courtyard and led to other apartments to the left of our apartment's entrance.

To the left of the entrance was a long dark hallway, which led to three rooms: the first a cold room, the second the toilet, and the third the bathroom from which there was a door into one of the bedrooms, the one belonging to the Ulmans. There were double French doors in their bedroom, which had at one time opened up into the combination living-dining room, but those doors were permanently closed as the living-dining room belonged to our family. Straight past all the doors, at the end of the long corridor, was the entrance to our living quarters. Through the doors, we stepped into a living room, and from there, another set of double French doors led to the second bedroom, which was my parents' room. From their bedroom, a door opened onto a very small, crescent-shaped balcony that overlooked Nepszinhaz Utca with its busy traffic and noisy streetcars.

At first, I found very little pleasure in this big, noisy city. It took me six to eight months to settle in, to fit in and get to know the sites once named after famous Hungarians like Liszt, Bartok, and Petofi but whose new names reflected political propaganda and the Communist regime. I started school after the winter holidays and was determined to finish my gymnasium years with good grades. Although there were two schools available in my district, my parents and I felt that I would be more comfortable in the all-girls' school on Koztarsosag Ter, located three or four blocks from our house, where I could complete the last half of grade eight, all I needed to graduate. I worked hard at school, leaving myself little time to develop a social life.

I was thirteen, lonely and miserable – a teenager whose emotions were bouncing in all directions. Also, I was a *falusiliba*, a simple girl from a small town, and I found it difficult to communicate and make new friends with the girls at school who seemed much more sophisticated than I with my much slower-paced and very strict upbringing in the country. Where my hair was still in braids and my clothing childish, their hair was stylish and they dressed in grown-up clothes. I had never been to a professional theatre or dance. I had never ridden a tram or been to a hairdresser. In short, I was the proverbial "country mouse" suddenly thrust into the heart of the "big city."

I did become friendly with Emma, a Jewish girl who lived in my building with her aunt and uncle because the rest of her family had been killed in the Holocaust. Under her tutelage, I quickly acquired a new vocabulary, what I thought was an extensive sex education, and many other behaviours that were fascinating to me but that my parents were not as enthusiastic about, and they effectively put a stop to our budding friendship. Although Emma and I did manage an occasional clandestine meeting, our relationship was ultimately doomed. It took me a while to realize how many orphans were being brought up by relatives and how that left a mark on children like Emma.

Seeing how unhappy I was, my aunt Zsofi began to make inquiries with people she knew and soon introduced me to a girl whose mother had died. Juli Sarlos, an only child, lived in Budapest with her grandmother and widowed father who had remarried. His new wife was having a hard time relating to her newly acquired daughter. Still, her family had Jewish values and her upbringing had been similar to mine, so we took to each other instantly and forged a very loving friendship. We became inseparable, and even today, more than a half century later and an ocean apart, with Juli still in Hungary and me in Canada, we still correspond and speak on the phone, and she and her husband have come to visit me.

Although I now had a friend, I still had many other obstacles to overcome.

The situation at home had become unbearable. I was a teenager who had no privacy. Because the Ulmans had to walk through the bathroom to get to their rooms, I would often be taking a bath when there would be knock at the door and Mr. Ulman would barge in heading to his bedroom even though I had told him that I would be using the bathroom for a while. A year earlier when I had gotten my first period, my mother had given me flannel rags that I was to use during the bleeding, change often, and then soak in a covered pail of soapy water. At the end of each day, I had to wash them to get them ready for the next day. The lack of privacy made these small tasks shameful for me.

On top of that, I did not have a room of my own. When we first moved into the apartment, I slept in the living room on a daybed, but that changed when Pali and Zsuzsi got married. They had a very quiet family ceremony on May 26, 1950, at a neighbourhood synagogue on Nagyfuvaror Utca, followed by a small celebration dinner. Then they moved in with us and took the daybed in the living room. From then on, I had to sleep in my parents' room on a narrow, single folding bed.

As difficult as I thought things had become for me, I wasn't the only one having a hard time adjusting to this new way of life. My parents had been through so much already in their lives, and now things were becoming more and more difficult. We were living in the midst of a Communist hell where nothing was private anymore and everything belonged to the Hungarian state. This ideology might have worked in theory, but in practice, the Russians believed that everything belonged to them. Consequently, many goods and commodities like wheat, potatoes, and meat were being shipped out of the country, and that meant we were left to line up for even the most basic food supplies. To make matters worse, my parents, no longer young, were ostracized from society by the Communists because of the social status they had enjoyed before the war. For a short time, my father worked at an office and my mother found a job in a supermarket, but mostly my parents were not able to find employment. My brothers helped out a little, but we were struggling.

Anti-Semitism was also rampant at this time. The Communists strongly discouraged any practice of the Jewish religion, but my mother and father went secretly to the closest synagogue, the one where Pali and Zsuzsi were married, for High Holiday services, and I went along when I could. But when my brother Peter married Manyi later that year on November 14, it was in a civil ceremony in a public hall set up by the Communists. I first came to know his new wife, Manyi, after the war back in Szarvas, where she lived with her parents and brother in a small house in back of my friend Kati's house, and both families used the same garden and entrance to the property. I instantly bonded with Manyi, as did everyone who met her – she was an unforgettable and beautiful person both inside and out – and I was thrilled when Peter started dating her.

As my graduation from gymnasium approached, I had to face the serious issue of my future education. When we were still in Szarvas, I had hoped to study medicine in university and become a pediatrician. I even began taking private Latin lessons from the elderly gentleman who had taught my mother as a young girl. I loved taking those lessons both because my teacher was a sweetheart and because I wanted to prepare myself for university. But the Communists had put an end to my dream of a career in medicine. I had had too many privileges before the war, it seems, and now I was declared a "class alien," who would not be allowed to attend university. My best option, therefore, was to learn a trade. I decided to go to a technical school to prepare myself for employment and chose a fashion college, the Dress Industry and Related Technical College, located on Raboczy Ter. I was delighted to discover that my friends Juli, Agi, and Marika would also be going there, and from 1950 to 1954, we learned how to design patterns, cut fabric, make clothing, finish garments, and knit and weave on machines at the school we sarcastically called *Cerna Egystem* or Thread University.

The Central Dress Designing and Planning Industry (the Hungarian "ministry of fashion") was located on the other side of the square from the college, and among other things, they designed clothing that would then be copied at various factories across the country and sold to the public. During the time I was at the fashion college, when I was about sixteen, the ministry sent officials to look for girls who could model the clothes the ministry was designing for teenagers. Because my figure was closest to that of the pattern size for my age, I was a perfect candidate and was chosen as one of the models; no one knew that I was Jewish or, if they did, they ignored the fact. Being picked for this job was a great privilege and a wonderful opportunity for me. I loved being a model and was proud of the day-clothes, sleepwear, and bathing suits I got to wear. I especially liked the perks that went with my job, particularly the winter vacations when we were taken to resorts to build up our tans and work on our diets and figures. By this time, I had grown from a shy ugly duckling into a confident budding rose. Suddenly, I was thin and tall and had sex appeal. For the first time in my life, I cut my long, dark blond hair to shoulder-length and was often told that my large hazel eyes, which had a certain sadness in them, were very appealing.

Although we had to be careful about practising our religion, during Shavuot in the year I turned fifteen, all Jewish girls were invited to the world's largest *neolog* (Conservative) synagogue, the Dohany Temple, to celebrate our coming of age. There must have been over a hundred girls taking part in the joyous confirmation ceremony. Since we could not have *bat mitzvah* celebrations, I felt delighted to be acknowledged as a Jew and receive a blessing and certificate from the rabbi. Our names are inscribed in a book that is still available at the synagogue today.

Because my family and I were very discreet about being practising Jews, the Communists did not come down hard on us. So even though I hated the Communists, I still joined the Communist Youth Organization when I started at the fashion college to help me begin to get used to my new circumstances and to boost my social life as well. It was considered a great "honour" to belong to this organization and to wear our uniforms of navy skirts or pants, white shirts, and red triangle kerchiefs around our necks. I belonged to one of the youth dance groups and remember clearly our participation in the May 1 celebrations every year throughout my time at the school. As we danced through streets that were closed to traffic and lined with people watching us go by for five kilometres or more, high-ranking officers and Communist party delegates sat on high stages and watched the parades below them. All day long, singing and dancing groups performed in the streets, and bands and workers marched by the stages, paying their respects to the government bigwigs whom we hated and secretly ridiculed.

In the evenings, street dances were organized in suburban districts of Budapest with the specific purpose of making the unhappy youth more content. My friends and I would go in groups to these dances to try and secretly meet some other Jewish kids – especially boys. I remember in particular one dance in May 1952 when Juli and I decided it was time for some adventure, especially as we were both approaching our sixteenth birthdays. The music was tempting, but we still hung back until we noticed a group of teenage boys eying us. Two of the boys came over to us, and one, Jancsi, asked me to dance while his cousin asked Juli. Jancsi and his cousin, who had both been orphaned by the war, walked us home that night. Jancsi and Juli eventually started going out together, which made me very happy because I loved them both. They were married on July 26, 1956, Juli wearing a wedding gown we made from old drapes, just before my family left Hungary, and Juli and I have kept in touch throughout the years.

By 1953, Hungary was slowly emerging from its darkest period, which my family had been able to survive only because we had trained ourselves to pay very little attention to the outside world. As the country began to relax, I, too, began slowly to emerge. To begin with, I had made some lifelong friendships. Along with Juli, I was also very good friends with Agi, who now lives near me in Toronto and has been my closest friend since we were fourteen years old, and Marika, a great friend of mine who eventually became my sister-in-law when she married Tibi. And I had acquired some sophistication as well. As I grew and my tastes expanded, I found that the little girl in me continued to love the zoo and amusement parks, but I had also acquired a love for the theatre, museums, and music. There were many theatres in Budapest, and tickets were very affordable, so my family had season tickets to two or three theatres in the area. I became an avid reader and went to museums and art galleries.

More and more, I was beginning to again notice the natural world around me. Budapest is made of two parts, Buda and Pest, which are connected by many bridges. Pest is flat and mainly residential, while hilly Buda is the more elegant and beautiful part with its old forts and very expensive homes, night clubs, and churches dotting the hills. Between Buda and Pest is the famous Margit Sziget, the Margit Isle, with its hotels and an outdoor swimming pool that has artificial waves that go on every hour or so. I loved swimming, and in the summer, I would go with friends to this great pool. In the winter, I chose an indoor pool close to our apartment and would leave home early in the morning at least four times a week to have a swim before school. The lovely hills surrounding Budapest on the Buda side were perfect for picnicking, and I found that the natural beauty of the landscape helped me attain serenity in the insane world around me where contradictions were the norm and fervent ideologies rose and were toppled without warning.

Along with learning to speak Russian, I was finding out all about Communism. I remember that when Stalin died in March 1953, we had to stand beside his large bronze statute on the school grounds to show our respect. Agi and I were together in the fashion college lobby holding our flags when I laughed at some remark she made. Someone reported me to the principal, who proceeded to kick me out of school for laughing during such a solemn occasion. As luck would have it, certain rumours soon began to circulate that tarnished Stalin's reputation, and, miraculously, I was allowed to return to school.

I hated politics and the Communist slogan "Labour Glorifies" and decided to concentrate instead on surviving ... and boys. I was very popular and had an active social life, and soon I was in love. For my "sweet sixteen" birthday party, I invited both boys and girls. It was the first co-ed party I ever had ... and my first kiss from a boy. The party was in July in the early evening in our apartment, and we had sandwiches, cake, and lemonade. But what I really remember was the game we played where a boy and girl would go outside onto the *U*-shaped walk to "see if there were stars out." If you liked the boy you were with and he was quick enough, the "sighting" ended in a kiss. On the day of my birthday, a friend of mine introduced me to Janos, an extremely good-looking young man who was studying to be a doctor at an out-of-town medical university, and he was my star-gazing partner. When his lips slightly brushed mine in the kiss, I thought I would die of embarrassment.

But I liked him very much, and he became my first real boyfriend. My mother finally took notice when I came home with a small bunch of violets after a date with Janos. To her great surprise and worry, she realized I was growing up. "*A kislanyom szerelmes!*" ("My little girl is in love!"), she shouted, and from then on I had to have a chaperone, either my mother or my brother Tibi, whenever I went to a dance or on a date. Of course, Janos and I could only get together when he came home for the holidays, but the rest of the time we corresponded through passionate love letters. This kind of relationship suited me just fine, actually, since I myself wasn't ready to get serious with anyone at this point. In 1953, I was seventeen, entering my last year of fashion college and having a great time.

December 6 is St. Nicholas Day, a very big holiday in Hungary and in other parts of Europe. Janos was away at school, so Jeno, another boy I knew, asked me to come dancing with him in Buda to celebrate the holiday. At that time, it was very popular to hold dances at five o'clock in the afternoon, which was perfect timing for me. I wasn't allowed to stay out later than ten o'clock at night because that was when our apartment house entrance was locked. You could ring for the superintendent who would let you in after ten o'clock, but my parents didn't want their daughter to be thought of as a "loose" girl and talked about by the neighbours.

Jeno and I went to the dance and had a wonderful time. We danced, had some dessert and coffee, and were ready to come home at what couldn't have been later than eight or nine o'clock. As we were standing at the bus stop waiting for the special bus that would take us back over the Duna River to Budapest, a jeep full of drunken Russian soldiers came careening around the corner and hit us. We were both hurt and rushed by ambulance to the hospital. Jeno sustained only some minor injuries – a torn earlobe and cuts and bruises on his face – but I was badly hurt with a broken knee and shin bone. Of course, there was no such thing as suing for accidents or even reporting them to the police. At first, the hospital was going to operate on me, but one of the young doctors was against it, arguing that an operation would mean I would have a scarred leg for life. I can still hear him saying, "We are not going to cut Olga's leg. I want to put it back together so there will never be a scar on it because one day, I would like to dance with her." They put me in a cast up to my hip and kept me in the hospital for a only couple of weeks, although I would remain in the cast until the following June.

Unfortunately, this was my graduating year and the worst possible time for me to be laid up with a broken leg. I was lucky to have good friends who came over in those difficult months to bring me homework and help me study. Marika, with whom I had been good friends for four years, came the most often and would stay with me until late into the dark, winter evenings. It would not have been very nice or proper to let a young lady walk home alone in the dark, so when she was ready to go, my brother Tibi would be enlisted to walk with her and make sure she got home safely.

Marika was an extraordinarily good-looking girl, the prettiest of all my group, with gorgeous blue eyes, which even today are very expressive. At first, I think Tibi was reluctant to walk her home all the time, but eventually he became much more willing. As for Marika, even after she no longer had to bring me my homework, she still kept coming over. It was no great surprise to anyone, then, when we discovered that she and Tibi had started seeing each other and later on when they announced that they were getting married.

Jeno also visited me on a regular basis. He was feeling very sorry for me and guilty because I had been out with him when I was hurt. As he came around more and more, we became very close, or so I thought. Around Christmas time, he bought me a beautiful red dressing gown and surprised me by proposing marriage. I didn't know what to think and put him off, telling him I needed time to think.

But when Janos came in for New Year's from medical school, I had no hesitation going out with *him* on New Year's Eve. Because I was still in a cast and couldn't dance, he took me to a house party at the home of an older woman he knew.

We had a great time at the party bringing in 1954, and I was happy. After all, I was in love with Janos and wanted to be with him. What I didn't know about him, though, was that he had a secret. My parents had given me permission to stay overnight with the lady whose home we had gone to for the party, and as she and I sat talking when everyone left, she told me some very disturbing things about Janos. She said that Janos was a gigolo and disclosed that she herself had been living with him and keeping him. What's more, she said she knew she wasn't the only one who was romantically involved with him. I was shocked and devastated by the news. I confronted him several times about what I had learned, and we had a real showdown.

I had come to the realization that he was just not for me. It was a realization that would change the course of my future.

Although it would take almost a full year of physiotherapy before I could walk again without crutches, my cast came off in June, just in time for final exams. The exam process was very stressful, especially since we had to sit for both our oral and written exams, one student at a time, in a large room in front of a select group of teachers and Communist dignitaries. At the end of this difficult process, I was relieved to discover I had done very well.

By the time exams were over, I was ready for what I thought was a well-deserved graduation party. My mother bought me a beautiful white dress that was made of cotton pique with a full skirt on which Zsofi appliquéd pink butterflies. It was Zsofi's graduation present to me. Our class went out with our teachers and had a lovely celebration of dancing and dining at a beautiful restaurant set in a lovely park-like setting in Buda.

But once school was over, I had to begin to think about my prospects. I was very concerned about what life would be like after school and worried about all the responsibilities that were waiting for me. I saw myself on the threshold of life and wondered where I would be going from here. My brother Pali and his wife, Zsuzsi, who had just had a baby daughter, Kati, took me out to celebrate my graduation. As we ate ice cream, we talked seriously about what lay ahead for me, and as they advised me about what I might do, I remember thinking, "But where? And how?" Looking back now, I can see how full of teenage angst I was and how unrealistically and dramatically I saw my life then.

By a stroke of good luck and because of my years as a model, I was offered a job at the Central Dress Designing and Planning Industry. My job involved laying out coat and dress patterns on fabric and calculating the least amount of material required to make the item. My calculations determined the amount of fabric the factories would be allowed to use to manufacture these ladies' fashions. I was also required to travel to different cities in Hungary to check if the manufacturers were complying with the material allotments. I would fly or go by train to these cities and stay at stylish hotels. I was thrilled and very proud to be given such a high position. A government job like that came with a lot of privileges, not the least of which was the opportunity to travel anywhere within the borders of the country, something that was not affordable for most people. I felt pretty important to have such a prestigious job at the age of eighteen. I even continued to do a little modelling for the ministry from time to time, but by then, I was becoming too old for the teenage clothing while not old enough for the more sophisticated fashions.

Just as my career began to take off, though, my personal life fell into turmoil. After I broke up with Janos, Jeno still wanted to get married and was pushing me. Even though I had a wonderful job, I was still disappointed that I would never be able to go to university and have the profession I had dreamed of. In addition, Janos had let me down very badly, and I knew my dreams of a life with him were over. Looking back, I think I just wanted to get on with things and try to accomplish something. Picking a partner, getting married, and settling down was what girls my age did at that time, and it seemed the easiest way to get on with my life. I had heard rumours that Jeno drank too much, but decided to marry him despite all the misgivings I felt.

My parents were also very much against the marriage. Jeno was a nice boy, but they felt I could do better. They were sure I was making a terrible mistake. In the end, they gave in because they wanted me to settle down. Imagine, they wanted me to settle down at eighteen! On my nineteenth birthday – Sunday, July 10, 1955 – and a year after my graduation, Jeno and I went to City Hall and got married. Afterwards, we had a luncheon party attended by my whole family, and that was that. We set off for our honeymoon on Lake Balaton, one of my favourite places in Hungary, the day after my beloved Manyi gave birth to her first child, Eva.

Of course, I had never had sex with anyone before, and I can honestly say that I was very innocent about it all. On the first evening of our honeymoon, Jeno got drunk. He forced himself upon me and all but raped me. I was traumatized, and all I remember of the experience is that he smelled of liquor and vomit. When he was finished, I couldn't look at him and couldn't stop crying. I simply got my things together and went home to my parents. Jeno and I had planned to move in with my parents because, of course, no one could get living quarters right away, but I immediately ordered him to remove his things from our home. We quickly had the marriage annulled, and I have never seen him again since that time, have never contacted him, and don't even know if he is still alive.

This disastrous experience affected me greatly. I felt that as far as sexual contact was concerned, I did not want to have anything to do with men ever again. I vowed I would never trust a man again in my life or ever get married. Feeling great shame, I thought of myself as a piece of used merchandise and just pulled back, licking my wounds. Now I had to cope with the fiasco of this marriage. I could not tell anyone what really happened and just said that we weren't meant for each other and had gone our separate ways.

The marriage was a terrible, terrible mistake and one I have paid for very dearly throughout most of my life, carrying a great inferiority complex within me. From my more mature perspective many decades later, I see now that I had had very little opportunity to learn how to pick a life-partner. The horrors of the Holocaust and the upheaval of Communism cost me my formative and impressionable years when I could have looked for and benefited from role models in life. With only my own experiences as my teacher, I was forced to accept the hard realization that romance and love were not necessarily the best criteria for choosing a partner for life.

I know now that the Holocaust affected me emotionally more that I ever realized at the time. I sometimes feel that the adults who survived the Holocaust were better able to get on with their lives than the children. Perhaps adults had a stronger sense of the meaning of life, having come so close to losing it. But the younger ones, like me, came out confused and lost. We had been living in chaos and just couldn't put the pieces of our lives back together again. Many young girls came out of the war and got married very quickly. We just wanted to live before we died! But we didn't have the skills to chose our partners wisely.

My own emotional confusion manifested itself in bits and pieces as time went by and influenced every relationship that I had and everything I did. I never felt good in any of my relationships and finally started to question whether I even had the ability to love. I started to believe that I would just see everything through a kind of fog forever. I think I was very lucky that eventually I did find a partner for my life and that even though he was twenty years older than I was, it made all the difference that I could trust him. It was only with someone very gentle and caring that I could ever have achieved a successful relationship.

CHAPTER 6

Leaving Hungary

> *Then from our shackles we must first emancipate ourselves —/From fear, from self-contempt, /From ignorance and blinding hate, /And set our own souls free.* – "The Blessings of Freedom," *Sabbath and Festival Prayer Book*

October 23, 1956, started out like any other ordinary day. I had tried to put my failed marriage behind me to concentrate on my professional life. I was travelling on business, making money, and having fun, and I enjoyed my work very much. When I woke that morning, I looked out my window and saw a picture of a perfect autumn day. During the night, nature's exceptional painters had been at work, and as far as I could see from our small, fourth floor balcony, all the trees and bushes were dressed in their new, brightly coloured outfits. As I looked at the golden yellows, burning reds, and varying shades of rusty orange, I was reminded of the enchanted forests of my favourite fairy tales. Even today, I can still occasionally smell the tang of those musty leaves and the slightly frost-dampened earth that I inhaled on that eventful morning.

But, of course, my euphoria couldn't last. I was startled from my reverie by the ringing telephone. Pali, the most caring of my brothers, was phoning to warn us that a full-fledged uprising against the Communists was about to erupt in Budapest. He didn't say how he knew, but he told us to stay inside and listen to the radio. It was the last phone call we were to receive for a long time because, shortly after that, the phone lines went down. Suddenly, there was chaos everywhere. The young revolutionaries had taken over the radio station and began a barrage of announcements describing every small victory against the Communists. As we listened, we could hear gunfire in the distance. By early afternoon, thousands of unhappy people were marching in the streets, ripping down Communist flags and toppling statues of former Communist leaders and smashing them to pieces, including the famous larger-than-life statue of Stalin.

I was twenty years old when the revolution broke out, certainly old enough to understand that what I was seeing was nothing less than the outbreak of a civil war. But I felt utterly emotionless – no elation, no concern, not even any fear. This is the only way I can explain how on that very evening, I got dressed, packed my suitcase, and left on a planned business trip as if nothing were out of the ordinary. My parents were distraught. "Where are you going?" they asked me. "Are you crazy?" And I answered them, "What do you mean? I must go." What was happening didn't faze me in the slightest, and I went off to work as usual, not believing for a moment that this "uprising" would come to anything serious before the Russians would brutally suffocate it. I suppose I did not know what else to do and did not yet realize what people can accomplish when they are truly unhappy. But I had no one to talk to, our telephone lines were cut, and I did not know where my brothers were. I certainly did not trust a soul outside my family. Who was who? Nazis were masquerading as Communists, Communists as Nazis. What was real at this point? Best to hide in the shadow of normalcy and just carry on as usual, I thought, and the whole thing would blow over in no time. I could never have imagined that we had the capability to overthrow the Communist government. In the end, we didn't, but it was a time of many decisions when people took a deep breath of freedom, something they had been craving for a long time.

In the streets, I saw people marching and chanting for freedom, but I simply got on the night train to Debrecen. That this would probably be the last train coming or going for the next few weeks, if not longer, did not occur to me. By the time I got to my destination, however, the factories were all closed, and my trip was in vain. There was a large, popular university in Debrecen full of unhappy students who had taken to the streets. That made it extremely dangerous to leave my hotel. I had close family in Debrecen, but phone and telegraph lines were down there, too, and there was no way to get in touch with them. The ministry was paying for my stay at a beautiful hotel, the Arony Bika (Golden Steer), and there was nothing to do but to stay there and wait. It would be more than two weeks before I would be able to leave the hotel, get out of the city, and return to Budapest.

I knew my parents would be frantic, but I had no way to communicate with them. On top of that, they would be worried sick about my brothers. They as well as my brothers were in a lot of danger, too, even though none of us knew exactly how much danger there was until after we had already been in Canada for a few years. It was only then that we realized that this uprising had allowed the Hungarian anti-Semites to again openly declare their hatred of the Jews. And that was when we realized, astounding as it may sound, that Jews were better off under the Russians, who simply prohibited the practice of our religion but didn't advocate annihilating us physically as a people. Even now, I know very little about what my parents or brothers did and how they lived through those turbulent weeks in the late fall of 1956. We were the "silent family," never discussing our feelings or fears with each other.

The hotel I was staying at was full, and I soon learned that a famous entertainment group from Budapest, whom I had seen on stage many times, was also stranded there. The troupe was made up of ten to fifteen well-known singers, dancers, and comedians, who were touring together and had been caught in Debrecen when the revolution broke out. I did not know any of them personally, but sitting around the hotel lobby day after day, we got to know each other quite well. We commiserated, sang songs, joked, cried, and simply waited. They were all quite a bit older than I was, perhaps my father and mother's age. But we bonded strongly because of the similar circumstances we were in, and I was soon "adopted" by them, especially by the famous comedian and actor, Arpad Latabar. They would be heading to Budapest when they were permitted to leave, he told me, and he swore to me that they would take me with them. Being actors and actresses, they would be among the first people allowed to leave when the fighting died down because they were considered apolitical and not affiliated with any political party or group.

After more than two weeks of waiting, our lucky day finally arrived when we were given a travel permit and allowed to leave. The troupe had their own luxurious bus, and our trip back to Budapest was uneventful. But, by now, the whole country was in chaos. The Russians had come in with all their power to quash the rebellion. There was constant fighting in Budapest, and Russian tanks were everywhere. Since my street was fairly close to the theatre district, the bus dropped me off at the park just a few blocks from my apartment building near the all-girls' school I had first attended in Budapest. Just walking through the park and those few blocks to the apartment was dangerous, and I was terrified. My determination and ordinary looks were my only allies, and I ran home, stepping over dead bodies – something I had gotten used to during the Holocaust – and trying to ignore the ugly sight of people hanging from trees, some by their necks but most by one leg.

I found my parents hiding in our apartment cellar with many other people. Most people felt safer huddling together while they waited for the worst to be over, despite the appalling conditions of the cellar, which was dark, dusty, and stale-smelling, with a mud floor and no water or toilet facilities. For those necessities, we had to make an early-morning run back to our apartments. Food, too, was in short supply, and we had to make do with what we had brought with us, something we had learned to do in the ghettos and labour camps.

The situation outside our little cellar microcosm continued to be chaotic. The Russians, who had promised to pull back, simply withdrew from Budapest and surrounded the city but would not leave. I remember feeling brave enough to return to my office a few days after the Russian "withdrawal" and finding that meeting after meeting was taking place every day. Everyone's biography was printed up and handed around. We had no access to correct what was being said about us nor any input into what our superiors wrote. I remember reading my biography, which stated that I was unreliable and could never be a Communist Party member because I had come from a family who could not be trusted, part of what they called the *kispolgari csokeveny* (the bourgeoisie).

The Russians soon began shelling the city and re-entered a few days later, giving rise to several days of heavy street-fighting. Suddenly, too, we were all back to those terrible post-war, pre-Communist days with people dressing in SS uniforms and openly declaring themselves Nazis while anti-Semites and old Nazi party members everywhere were making speeches about "the filthy rich Jews amongst us who should just get up and leave." Even the fashion ministry photographer who had always let me into the darkroom to watch him develop the models' photos was parading around in a Nazi uniform and talking about getting rid of all the Jews. He obviously didn't realize I was Jewish, but I don't know if it would have made any difference if he had. Anti-Semitism was quickly reaching its highest level in Hungary since the war had ended. We were very, very scared. How could we go on living in this country?

My children have often asked me what it was like for us to leave our home, to simply shut the door on our lives, possessions, family, and friends. Can I honestly answer that question from a distance of fifty years? When my family returned from among the dead after the war, we had developed a detachment in regard to possessions, deciding that henceforth only the family's health and welfare mattered. I think we all wished at times that we had been among those who had perished rather than having to continue living with the memory of the nightmare we had lived through. We had emotionally shut down.

I did not, could not, allow myself to become attached to material possessions. The hurt of any loss took too much energy, energy I no longer had.

Under the Communist regime, our lives consisted of simply going through the motions. Losing so much time and again, having to conform to an ideology that was both foreign and hostile to us made us numb and left us little time to grieve. Most of the time we did not even know what to think. Were we under surveillance? Were our phones tapped? When would the police come, fabricate an excuse, and take one of us away for no reason? And if they took away my father or one of my brothers, would we ever see them again? When it began to dawn on us that there was a chance to get out of the country, it was all that we could think about, the only thing that mattered. Maybe we were all dreamers and romantics, believing in a sentiment that Kalman Imre expressed in a charming duet in his operetta *Csardas Kiralyno* (*The Gypsy Princess*): "*Tull az operencian boldogok leszun.*" ("Over the ocean, we shall be joyful.") All we knew was that we needed to get out at any cost from the hellhole Budapest had become. Even dying in the process would be better than slowly suffocating under the intolerable circumstances we now called living. "Freedom at any price," declared the great Hungarian poet and freedom fighter, Petofi Sandor, in 1847. We agreed with him. Maybe, we hoped, we could still find a place where a new, peaceful life would be possible. It still surprises me to think that we could have mustered that much faith and desire.

I cannot remember exactly when a sort of normalcy returned to Budapest, but by late November, we had returned to our apartment and started to hear rumours that the borders were not being watched all that closely and that it might be possible to get out. We started to hear of people leaving Hungary, and we began to talk more and more in secret within our immediate family about taking a chance and trying our·luck escaping. Large numbers of young people set out to cross the border to Austria, which was the easiest to approach as well as the least guarded. No one spoke openly about escaping for fear their names would be given to the authorities, but everyone "knew" what was happening.

The fever grew day by day. Some made it; others just disappeared. Reports circulated via an active underground grapevine and even in banned radio broadcasts that we had to decipher. Some people were killed or thrown in jail, but for many that was a better alternative than being hung on a lamp post as a "decoration" without even trying to get to freedom. Some of the escapees were important Communist Party members who were afraid for their lives. At the other extreme, there were many young people, especially young Jews, who had been dreaming all their lives of getting out of Hungary and now had their chance. I was one of those young people, and so was my girlfriend Jutka, who wasn't Jewish but who had decided to come with me.

So my whole family got together very discreetly to make some very serious decisions. The difficulty was that my mother's main focus was to keep the family together. My two older brothers were already married at this time, each with an eighteen-month-old baby whose welfare had to be taken into consideration when contemplating such a treacherous journey. My mother was adamant that she would not leave if she knew that my brothers and their families would be left behind and had no way of getting out. As for me, I was determined to get out but knew that she most definitely would not let me go alone.

In the end, it was decided that Tibi, who was still single at this time, would be the first to try to escape and reach Austria. We devised a code so that if he got out, he could let us know. He did manage to get to the border but was caught there. He was arrested, brought back, and put in jail. I'd like to think it was fate that led to his release after only two days in jail, but it could have been a guard, many of whom were sympathetic to the would-be fugitives, who let him go. Although Tibi's capture was a huge disappointment to us, this time we could not and would not be deterred. At the end of November, Tibi tried again and this time managed to get through. When he arrived in Vienna, he sent us a telegram in coded language, advising us that the coast was clear and we should follow. I begged my parents to let me go next on my own. I told them that I would send for them as soon as I was settled, but they refused to even listen to me. I was so scared for them, so worried for their safety, but now I can say how very proud I am of them, of their courage and strength to decide to escape with me. They simply would not let their family be torn apart, no matter what danger and hardship they had to face.

We also wanted Zsofi and Miklos to come with us, but they refused to leave. Saturday afternoon visits at our apartment had become a family ritual when we moved to Budapest, and Miklos loved my mother's cheese buns so much that he and Zsofi continued to visit even during the revolution when it had become dangerous to do so. By now, however, the streetcars had begun to run again, and it was at one of these Saturday afternoon visits that we saw them for the last time. Miklos had never totally gotten over Ilonka's death. Moreover, the couple they lived with and were working for in the restaurant and who were virtually adopted parents to him and Zsofi were getting old and he couldn't just abandon them.

I would have to say that I loved Zsofi almost as much as my own mother. I thought of our time together when I was a small child as a golden time and remembered how she would sit, with such patience and love, and curl my long hair with a mixture of water and sugar so that I would look like a doll out of a box with my long curls. I've always hated saying goodbye, and it was especially painful for me to have to say goodbye to her. In fact, we never did say a final goodbye because Zsofi and Miklos could never know precisely when we planned to leave. The entire enterprise was extremely dangerous and had to be carried out in secret. You couldn't tell anyone, not even extended family or close friends, about your arrangements. You simply did not know whom you could trust. There could be no goodbyes to anyone, not even your closest relatives or friends, even though you knew you might never see them again. But truly, we never thought for a

My calendar/diary from 1956 to 1957. It is open to my last entry that reads in part: "Your perception changes every minute according to what happens in that minute in life."

moment that this "temporary" goodbye to Miklos and Zsofi would be forever. We were sure that once we were settled in our new home, we could send for them. They had no children of their own, and we would just bring them out. Unfortunately, they never did immigrate to Canada.

Once we heard from Tibi, my parents and I began to make plans. We had learned that there were farmers living near the border who were helping people get across. They knew the area and the terrain very well and would gladly provide information as long as you paid them handsomely. My father and brothers looked around for contacts and tried to approach trusted friends. They finally got some leads, and the rest was trial and error. We made arrangements. By now, our co-tenants, the Ulmans, had disappeared, and this made things a lot easier. Still, we knew we were taking great chances, but desperation is a great incentive.

In the cold pre-dawn of December 6, 1956, I looked around the apartment and silently said my goodbyes. I had no desire at this point to ever see Hungary again and took only a small, leather-bound calendar with me to write in on the way. We did not take a change of clothes or anything else that would give us away. We didn't know what the situation would be at the border, and we needed to travel light. If we were captured, we could all be shot.

At four in the morning, my parents, Jutka, and I left our apartment and walked into the night, shaking but determined, toward one of the two large train stations. My brothers and their families were to follow later. Once we were on the train, we were asked several times for our papers. Thanks to my government job, I had a letter saying I was required to go to different Hungarian cities for work, and this proved a perfect alibi. I said that the girl with me was a co-worker and we were taking my parents to the city of Sopron to a rest resort. We added that my parents were sick and required fresh air and good food. Incredibly, the guards let us stay on the train.

I don't remember where exactly we got off the train, but it was at one of the small farm stops long before we reached Sopron. We were met at the train station by a farmer who took us to his farm and put us up in his barn with horses, cows, and several other people waiting for their try at freedom. The farmer allowed only four to six people go at one time, so we had to wait our turn. The farmers had scouts combing the area for army and police, and they warned us that there were Russian mines in the fields around the border that they were not sure had been dismantled. At this point, who knew what was truth or hearsay, and anyway, we had no choice but to trust them. It was very dangerous, but we wanted so desperately to escape. I don't remember how long we were there, perhaps a few days, but there was no turning back now.

Then one night, *our* turn finally came.

The open fields between the borders were ploughed every day so that footprints could be easily detected. Luckily, the morning we left, it had rained all the previous day so the earth was soaked, making footprints hard to see. We started out just before dawn on that dark, freezing morning after paying off the farmer with money we had kept hidden. He headed us in the direction of Austria, pointed out the watchtowers, and told us how often the Russian searchlights swept the fields. With the full moon giving us some light and with each other's support, we hiked into the deep mud of the ploughed fields of no man's land and took our first steps towards freedom. Without hesitation or a single backward look and hoping we were headed in the right direction, we left our country of birth behind and just started walking.

Even though the soggy earth in the border area between Hungary and Austria made footprints hard to see on that particular morning, the flat open areas meant there were hardly any trees to hide behind or hills against which we could take refuge on our flight to freedom. When we were about half-way across, a searchlight passed over us, and we threw ourselves to the ground, holding our breath and lying very still to blend into the mud so we wouldn't be detected. The searchlight moved on, but when my father got up, he felt a sharp pain in his right foot. He had twisted his ankle and couldn't walk. He was too heavy for Jutka or me to even lift, and my mother certainly couldn't carry him. Without much time to think, I half-dragged, half-carried him for the rest of the seemingly endless journey.

Finally, we detected a faint light in the distance. Was it Austria or had we lost our way and ended up back where we came from? Then we saw some people walking around who appeared to be shouting to us. Exhausted but excited, we realized we had walked to freedom. We had made it! Tired, confused, and covered in mud from head to foot, we fell into welcoming arms. The Austrians were well prepared by this time for the influx of Hungarians who were fleeing every day, and they had set up camps for the refugees. In no time, they had taken us to a nearby school where we were given blankets and warm drinks and settled into makeshift beds. Kissing each other, we fell into a deep, relaxed sleep.

But we had no time to waste, nor could we afford to rest for long. We had a little money with us, enough for train fare to Vienna, and the next morning, the Austrians helped us clean up, gave us some clothes and food, and provided us with papers. We said goodbye to my friend, Jutka, who was going on to Belgium to stay there since her whole family had been left behind in Hungary. I know that she eventually got married, had a little son, and moved to the Belgian Congo, but then I lost track of her and never heard from her again. I often think about her and wish I knew where she is and if she is well.

My parents and I boarded a train for Vienna where we located Tibi, who had been staying there while he waited for the rest of the family to get through. In Vienna, he figured, he would be close to all the important information sources regarding our future. Now we started the next phase of our lives, waiting in long registration line-ups to get some help. It was in a Jewish International Rescue Committee line-up, where we were given food vouchers and small packages of sanitary supplies, that we learned about a camp in the mountains outside Vienna, where there were more Jewish refugees. This camp, run mainly by Norwegian volunteers, was called Bad Krajcen and was less than an hour's train ride from Vienna so Tibi could easily get in touch with us by telephone or even come to see us. We decided to go there and wait for Peter and Pali.

As soon as we arrived in Bad Krajcen, we immediately sent messages to Peter and Pali, finally getting word back from them that they were a week to ten days behind us. They had had to take a different route than we had and go by boat. We later learned that they were forced to sedate the two babies so they wouldn't cry and give everyone away. But they, too, did get out, accompanied by my friend Marika.

Finally, we were all together again and spent three weeks at Bad Krajcen where we were looked after and had time to rest. A spa in the mountains, it was a beautiful place, and we were housed in the luxurious main building where well-to-do Europeans, there for therapeutic bath treatments, had stayed before the war. Although volunteers served excellent meals at communal tables in the dining room, we had access to the kitchens, and I remember how my mother and Zsuzsi baked *tortakat* (layer cakes with a cream filling and decorations on top) to celebrate both New Year 1957 and the upcoming marriage of Tibi and Marika. These festive cakes, ironically, almost caused a tragedy. Zsuzsi had put them out on the snow-covered balcony of our room to keep them cool, not noticing that the balcony had been weakened by the heavy snow. When she went out to bring the cakes back inside, she dropped up to her thighs through a hole in the balcony floor. Making a human chain, we managed to grab her and drag her back inside, not losing even one cake in the process.

During our stay at Bad Krajcen, I tried to restore my mental balance by taking long walks in the mountains and writing in my journal. But now that we were all together again, we had to make some difficult decisions. The most problematic was where would we go to start our lives again. Our most important goal was to stay together so everyone had to compromise, although all my parents cared about was keeping our family together.

I wanted to go to Israel and so did my father, but Peter and Manyi were not comfortable going to live in Israel. My father had two step-brothers who had left Hungary in 1948 and were well established in Argentina. We met my father's full brother, Ferenc, in Vienna, and he, too, was moving to Argentina. His wife, Boriska, and their son, Andris, who had been my age, had perished in Auschwitz, and Ferenc had remarried. His new wife, Joli, had a sister living in Argentina, and Ferenc and Joli wanted to go to her. He would have liked my parents to join them, but they weren't interested. America's borders were closed to refugees so it was decided that we would all go to

Canada. Everyone had such wonderful things to say about Canada, but we knew almost nothing about the country. Interestingly enough, Ferenc and Joli ended up not liking Argentina, and they moved to Winnipeg a couple of years after we did to be closer to us. After Ferenc died of a heart attack, Joli moved to Toronto.

Even though our family was scattered, all my uncles were very special to me, and they all spoiled me rotten. Before the war, Ferenc and his son, Andris, used to visit us in Szarvas; Ferenc loved motor bikes, and it was my mother's constant fear that he would give me a ride. After the war when his entire family was killed, even though he was happily remarried, I never saw my uncle until the day he died without tears in his eyes. But my children became his children, and we celebrated all the holidays together at my home.

For Miklos, who stayed in Budapest, I was the child he had never had, and he, too, along with Zsofi, treated me like a treasured daughter. Even Sanyi, who remained in Argentina, wanted me to move there to be with him and his wife and children. The great tragedy in his life came when his two children were run over by a milk truck before they even reached their teens, and his wife, a psychiatrist, succeeded in committing suicide after several attempts.

Our family stayed in Bad Krajcen until the beginning of January 1957, celebrating our first free New Year's with a great festivity. Then on January 4, Marika and Tibi and I travelled to Vienna where they took their marriage vows. It was too expensive for everyone to travel to Vienna so I represented our family at the wedding because Marika had been my girlfriend and it had been through me that she and Tibi had met. But we vowed that once we were settled in Canada, they would get re-married in a synagogue with the entire family present. We spent their wedding night with some relatives of ours in another Jewish refugee camp in Vienna where we somehow found a spot to sleep with what we felt were hundreds of curious eyes looking on. The three of us snuggled up together for the night, me sleeping with the shy bride. We had been friends for almost six years, so it was just another sleep-over party for Marika and me. The next day, the newlyweds set out for a short honeymoon in a small town near Vienna where Marika had relatives. Before they left, the three of us went to the movies together to see a film we had heard so much about. Even though we did not understand everything, we had all read the Hungarian translation of the book by that time, and it was thrilling to see *Gone with the Wind*.

Refugees were coming to Bad Krajcen daily and leaving regularly to many different destinations. Soon it would be our turn to leave, and we were certainly anxious to get going. For our part, Tibi and I stood in line every day at the Canadian embassy in Vienna to get our papers for Canada. We were going to someplace called Winnipeg. Finally, everyone had their papers, and that's when we discovered that, because I was over eighteen, I needed my own visa. We hadn't realized that I couldn't go on my parents' papers and needed documents of my own. Frantic at this point, Tibi and I returned to Vienna, once more lining up day after day at the Canadian embassy. We asked everywhere for help but without any luck. Then one day, I saw a poster in Hungarian on a wall somewhere, saying that on a particular day at a particular hotel suite, a gentleman from Toronto, Canada, would be interviewing girls wishing to go there. It seemed like a stroke of luck.

When we got to the hotel suite, there were other girls waiting in a room. One by one, they were called into another room to be interviewed. When they were finished, the girls were led out through another exit, and we never saw them again. When my turn came, I was ushered into a room furnished with a large bed, a cabinet, a small desk, and several armchairs. The man I met there was dressed in a loud chequered jacket and tie, and he looked Jewish and had a Jewish-sounding name. He was quick to assure me that I was very beautiful and clever and that I would have no trouble obtaining what I needed to get to Canada, and fairly quickly, at that. There was something about him, though, that set off my inner alarm about men.

Once burned (with Jeno, of course), twice shy! I was needy, but not desperate.

Soon enough, he asked me to remove my coat and make myself comfortable. He pointed to the bed. As soon as I sat down on the bed, he sat beside me and started explaining to me how rich he was and that one of the girls, the cleverest one of us, would benefit from him personally. He told me that I was everything he could want in his otherwise empty life, all the while roughly pushing me back onto the bed. He clamped one hand onto my chin and lunged for my lips, while with the other hand he stroked my breasts. I managed to kick him between the legs and ran, leaving behind my coat and purse. Luckily, the door was unlocked, and Tibi was waiting outside just in case I had needed him for reassurance. I was so shook up that I don't remember where we went after that or how. I do know that this experience confirmed once again one of my greatest resolutions – to never trust a man. In fact, some of the first words I would learn in English would be "Men no good!"

Shortly after this incident, Tibi did manage to buy a visa for me, and sometime at the end of January, we were taken to a transit camp in Austria to wait for our journey to Canada. When it was time to leave, we travelled by train through the breathtaking mountainous scenery and crossed a river on our way to Trieste, Italy. There we boarded our ship, the *Saturnia*. The ship would be making several stops in southern Europe, and when we stopped in Milan, we all went into the city. My father's step-brothers in Argentina, Gabi and Sanyi Ban, had sent each of us $100 in American money for our journey. We had very little time or patience to really tour Milan or any other city on our way and just idly strolled and bought ice cream. I splurged and bought a pretty pair of shoes, an act that felt very good.

Our ship was an Italian vessel, built in 1927, that had returned to transatlantic sailings in 1946 and was to continue sailing until 1965. There were many refugees on our voyage, around 1,400 in second and third class accommodations. We travelled along the coasts of Italy and Spain, and as the ship passed Gibraltar with its statue bearing the inscription, "This is the end of Europe," we all stood and cried and sang "*Arrivederci, Roma*" ("Farewell to Rome"), a popular song of the time. I don't know exactly why I was crying; perhaps I was overwhelmed at seeing a little of Europe, and all that beauty was not easy to leave behind. Or perhaps I was just overcome by my memories, both bad and good – who knows?

It is likely that I was just frightened of the unknown that lay ahead. What was waiting for us on the other side of the world where I would be an immigrant in another people's land? How would they know who I was, what I had inside me, where I was coming from and why? Would they believe us or understand the ways in which we had been damaged and how we survived? Would they be kind and embrace us? Could I bury all that I knew and learn to be a new me? Could I forget and find enough trust to start again?

What I did know was that, whatever awaited us on the other side of the ocean, it would never be as natural to us, as beautiful or as innocent, as the life we had once known in Szarvas. Never again would I run into my beautiful house, surrounded by acacia trees in blossom and the sweet smell of the flowers blooming in the yard. Never again would I hold my Pani in my arms and offer her tea at my little table. Never again would my parents have that sweet, happy look on their faces that they used to have around our beautiful dining room table during the Passover *seder* or on the High Holidays. And never again would I look at the world with the innocence and joy I knew in those first six years of my life before hell broke loose upon us. I was a different person now, and so were all those whom I loved and cherished. I stood in the cold ocean air with tears running down my face saying my last farewell to Europe, to the horrors of the Holocaust and Communism, to my home and to my childhood.

Little did I know then that for the next forty years, I would suppress all my memories of the great physical beauty of my birthplace and bury inside me the language, all the melodies, the poetry, the books, and the art that had been such an integral part of my life. I would not even allow my children a glimpse into my heritage. But at the same time, I also learned that I should "never say never" (especially about getting married) and that even though my spoiled upbringing did not prepare me for it, I would soon adapt to my new life and do anything required of me with a smile. I would do it all to immerse myself into my new environment and to embrace my new life without a single glance back, not even talking to my loved ones about all the missing pieces from my old life that I cherished and was still keeping closely guarded in my heart.

CHAPTER 7

Coming to Canada

We perceive a community great in numbers, mighty in numbers, mighty in power/Enjoying life, liberty, and the pursuit of happiness...
– "A Vision of the Future," *Sabbath and Festival Prayer Book*

I first laid eyes on Canada from the deck of the *Saturnia*, the ship that brought my parents, my three brothers and their families, and me into Halifax harbour on February 12, 1957, after a very rough, ten-day voyage across the Atlantic Ocean. We had survived the horrors of the Holocaust as well as the upheavals, cruel restrictions, and rampant anti-Semitism of Communism in Hungary, and now the eleven of us found ourselves standing on the verge of a new life in a strange country, foreign to us in every sense of the word. For me, coming to Canada seemed a mixed blessing. Even after all the suffering during the war and all the hardships and pain afterwards, it had been a very monumental and wrenching thing for me to leave my country of birth, the only home I had ever known. Although I knew we had no choice but to leave, I also knew I was leaving my childhood and youth as well as other missing pieces of my life behind in Europe.

As the ship ploughed through the stormy waves of the Atlantic, there were many things I had to think about and come to terms with about my life up till now and about the future I was sailing towards. But I decided not to think about that during the ten days on board ship. I was young and had had enough of thinking and worrying. I just wanted to enjoy myself, to feel free. The Atlantic is turbulent during the winter, and it took a little while for me to develop my sea legs, so during the first few days I simply stood and watched the dolphins as they playfully followed behind the ship. Then I discovered there were European students on board returning to university in Canada and there was dancing every evening. Everyone was always telling me I was an attractive girl with a good figure and that I could have as many boys around me as I wanted. I loved dancing and I liked being popular. I wanted a little pleasure in my life, in this upside-down world in which I had been living for the past twelve years. I knew that building a new life would be hard for me when we got to Canada, and I just wanted to be happy. I decided from the beginning of the journey that if it was going to be a choice between standing miserably at the ship's rail and vomiting over the side or having fun, I was going to have fun.

So I danced my way to Canada. Most of my partners were students from Norway, and, although they were travelling first class and we weren't, on most nights they'd smuggle us upstairs where the dance band was playing. Even though we couldn't communicate in words, we made up for it with friendly smiles and a mutual love of dancing. On the last night of the voyage, my new friends and I stayed up and "talked" away the night until we could see the first traces of land silhouetted against the rosy dawn sky.

As our ship finally sailed into Halifax harbour, we could just make out the contours of a building that seemed to be beckoning to us through the thick, early morning fog. It had a large sign on it with big letters that read "PIER 21." As my family and I staggered off the boat in a daze of bewilderment and curiosity, I could almost hear someone saying, "Welcome to our land, your future home." I don't know if those were the actual words that were spoken or if I just heard them in my imagination, and it hardly matters any more now anyway. But at that time, after so many years of yearning, we could hardly believe that we had arrived. We took our first deep breaths of the fresh, clean air of freedom and walked towards the Immigration Hall.

Before we entered the building, my father gathered us together for a moment. We had no belongings except the clothing we had on our backs, clothes we had been given in Vienna that were hardly suitable for the cold, damp February weather of Halifax. We stood together shivering on the pier, holding on to one another. It was so hard to let go of the fear and the anxiety, to know where to put the excitement and the curiosity. So we thanked the Almighty and recited the *Shecheyanu*, a blessing thanking God for bringing us to this new country. Now, my father felt, we could be on our way.

As we waited around for all the medical tests to be completed, we were shuttled back and forth, confused, not able to communicate verbally with anyone but somehow going through the necessary paperwork, waiting to be accepted into Canada, and getting our landing papers stamped "Landed Immigrant." Each of us had our own anxieties about standing on this strange new soil, about this new culture that was totally alien to us, and we were all acutely aware of the vast ocean that separated Europe and our former lives from our lives-to-be in Canada. Would I be able to go to school? How would I master the language? And what about my parents? We owed them so much for coming with us to this new land, but how would they fit in at their age, a time in their lives when they deserved to take it easy?

The next day, we were put on a train heading west. It seemed so strange, yet so exciting, that we were here and on our way across the North American continent. It was also very frightening. By the time we left Hungary, a country mired in the isolation of Communism, everyone had already heard a little about Canada, particularly about Montreal and Toronto. But we were going to Winnipeg. What kind of place was this Winnipeg? I felt as if I had come to the end of the world.

Our first stop was Montreal, and when we arrived at the train station there, I could hardly believe my eyes. The whole station was decorated with hearts. The entrance was hung with two halves of a great big red heart and inside the station, everything, including the chocolates and candies at the concession stands, was heart-shaped. I had seen some American movies, and I knew from those movies that in America you could have things like heart-shaped swimming pools, heart-shaped beds, and even heart-shaped bathtubs. At twenty, I was just the right age to look at all the hearts in the train station and think, "So those Hollywood movies were true. Look at where we are. Everything in this country is made out of hearts." But I knew nothing about Valentine's Day and had no idea that I had arrived in Montreal on the one day in the year when the entire country was thinking about love.

It didn't take me long, though, to find out that in Montreal, under all those shiny red decorations, people's hearts were not made of gold. I had been so excited about my surroundings that I hadn't been paying attention to what was happening beside me. My brother Peter's daughter, twenty-month-old Eva, was very sick and running a high fever. Even though we had no money, Peter, himself a doctor, ran around with someone from the Red Cross looking for a doctor near the train station who would look at Eva. He had very little money and couldn't find a single physician who would talk to him, even just to advise him on what medication to give the child. And so I learned my first lesson about Canada. This country was not so different from most other places where money makes the world go round. It would take some time before I could laugh about my "land of hearts," whose big heart seemed only to be visible on Valentine's Day.

After the two-hour stopover in Montreal, we were back on the train bound for Winnipeg. The train ride from Montreal to Winnipeg seemed to take forever, and it was a revelation. Our porter must have been seven feet tall, and he was the first black person I had ever seen in my life. Although I was curious about him, my parents had taught me never to differentiate people by colour or race. My father always used to say, "There are two kinds of people, a *mensch* (a good person) and an *unmensch* (a bad person). Admire the first and pray for the other." After the first few minutes, what really impressed me about this man was the fact that as he went about doing his work, he made us feel totally comfortable. He lowered the beds for us at night, showed us where the washroom was, delivered our food, and made sure with gestures that we understood the announcements.

On that first night on the train, the unfamiliar rocking and clicking noises of the train kept me awake at first, but I finally fell into a peaceful sleep and woke early in the morning just as the light started coming in through the window. I watched the changing landscape, taking in the huge differences between this land and the overpopulated, crowded European countries I was used to. I marvelled at the vegetation, even the difference in the soil and rocks. When our breakfast came – tiny boxes full of cereal in colourful shapes and different tastes – my father was delighted. "Look," he cried out. "We got coloured candy and popcorn that looks just like the candy at home." We soon learned what it actually was and how to eat it with milk, and then we asked for more to save as treats. My father was very happy. I think he was the biggest and happiest child in our family at that moment.

For the rest of the journey to Winnipeg, I entertained myself by looking out at the vast distances we were covering. As far as the eye could see, everything was blanketed with the splendour of sparkling, untouched snow. As the train chugged along, leaving behind one sparse little town after another, we looked at the houses with TV antennas stuck to their roofs and reassured ourselves. "Yes," we told each other, "there is civilization here after all." Coming from Budapest, from Europe, we were used to an urban environment and the culture that goes with it. After all the losses we had endured – our religion and all our other freedoms – culture was all we had left.

When we arrived in Winnipeg on February 17, there was so much snow we could hardly see the houses. We were welcomed by the Salvation Army and taken to a place we did recognize because it looked like a refugee camp. It was Winnipeg's Immigration Hall, which was overflowing with immigrants. On our first day there, we ventured out to have a look around our new city. The bitterly cold weather scared us, and most of us soon scurried back to the warmth of the building. Only Tibi and Marika were more adventurous and their curiosity – and appetites – soon led them to a restaurant. The only writing on the menu they recognized was "Chicken, 99¢," they told us later, so that is what they ordered. At the end of the meal, when the Chinese waiter brought them little bowls filled with clear liquid with a slice of lemon, they quickly drank it down, thinking it was some kind of weak tea. It was only when the waiter gave them each a towel that they realized that the liquid was for washing their hands. But the chicken they ate was delicious.

We would all have many stories like this to tell each other over the next while, stories that kept us in stitches for years to come. Extremely anxious to get started with our new lives, we threw ourselves head-first into every experience. We soon got used to people pushing us and stepping on our feet or burping in our faces and simply saying "sorry." By the time I knew what the word "sorry" meant, I had learned to push and shove like everyone else.

Once the Salvation Army deposited us at the Immigration Hall, we saw no one else for a while. No one from the Winnipeg Jewish community came, not even to say hello. Finally, when someone from either HIAS (the Hebrew Immigrant Aid Society) or the Canadian Jewish Congress, I can't remember which, did come to talk to us, they found eleven anxious members of an observant Jewish family who wanted to stay together and were impatient to get started in their new lives.

HIAS provided us with a three-bedroom house on Inkster Boulevard for six months rent-free, and we moved in at the beginning of March, about three weeks after arriving in Winnipeg. Peter, Manyi, and their daughter, Eva, took one bedroom. Pali, Zsuzsi, and their daughter, Kati, took the second bedroom, and my parents took the third. Tibi and his new wife, Marika, simply converted the living room into their bedroom each night. I had the walk-in closet where my parents put a bed that just fit. I loved the privacy and peace this tiny room gave me. There I could read and sleep and be all by myself.

By the time we moved into the house, some of us had already started to work: Marika and I at a coat factory, Tibi and Pali at Lux Electrics. It was decided from the start that my mother would stay at home and that Pali's wife, Zsuzsi, would stay home with her to help with the household chores and looking after the children: her own daughter, Kati, and Peter's daughter, Eva, both of whom were almost two years old by this time and handfuls. My mother did all the shopping and cooking. With her German and Latin along with a lot of hand gestures, she could usually make herself understood, especially with the Jewish butcher, but elsewhere, she often ended up with something completely different than what she had asked for. It was trial and error. For a long time, our meals consisted of soups she fashioned out of bones and whatever else she could find that was inexpensive enough to feed so many hungry mouths. She truly was a "kitchen witch," and no matter what she put into her soup, we wiped the bowls clean and licked the bones.

Our first contact with other Hungarians in Winnipeg was with some people my father had known in Hungary who came to Immigration Hall to look for any friends newly arrived from the old country. They invited us to their home one Sunday afternoon, and it was there that I first saw a television set. Much about that visit was odd for me, but particularly curious and rude was the fact that they were all gathered around this television set, engrossed in some kind of sporting event, and no one even bothered to talk to us. Finally when the game ended, we did have a chance to chat. To my dismay and shock, they told us that they were in Canada under Christian papers and were bringing their children up as Christians. They informed us that we were not to tell anyone that we knew them. As a matter of fact, my father's friend said that when his sister and her husband came to visit from Israel, they lied to the children and told them their uncle and aunt lived in Nairobi. It would only be in 1967, during the Six

Day Arab-Israeli War, that their Jewish roots were ever mentioned at all, and they finally told their children that they were Jewish. I later discovered that this family was not unique in their denial of their Jewish ancestry, that many other people had been so affected by the Holocaust that they no longer wanted to live a Jewish life.

Many things were strange and new to me in Winnipeg. For one thing, it was very, very cold in the winter or very, very hot in the summer with very little in between. Also, in the fifties, there was nothing to do there. Winnipeg was a barren city with very little entertainment and no cultural activities. It did not help that I couldn't speak the language. I was eager to begin speaking and writing English and was learning by reading about Dick and Jane and Spot and Puff, who featured in the grade 1 level school books I was using. Still, it took me a few years to learn English well enough to have a meaningful conversation with someone outside the house.

And then there was the work. I wanted to help make our new life in Canada a success and took many menial jobs so we could get started. I had to work very hard physically, something I wasn't used to doing, and I often walked ten blocks or more to work so I could save the 10¢ bus fare. My first job was sewing coats at a coat factory where I worked with my sister-in-law Marika. There were many Polish Jews working there, which initially seemed like a great advantage to me but to my amazement turned into a huge disappointment. They did not receive us with enthusiasm and even seemed contemptuous of us. They called me a *shiksa* (gentile woman) because I did not speak Yiddish, and they were constantly comparing Holocaust experiences, debating who had suffered more. This "I suffered more than you did" talk was a trivialization of the horror we had all shared, and it made me very sad. What I did not know at the time but was to learn later was that Polish Jews tended to hold their Hungarian cousins in thinly veiled contempt. The coat factory was the first place – but certainly not the last nor the only time – where I was confronted by this prejudice from Polish Jews.

As it happened, this job did not last very long, and I was more than ready to leave when it was over. Before I left, I bought myself a spring coat, but to my great surprise and disappointment, the Jewish owner of the factory took all the money I had earned in exchange for the coat. How, I wondered, could such a rich man take advantage of a poor fellow-Jew? It took me a long time to break my habit of automatically expecting kindness from other Jews.

My next job involved painting ceramics in a ceramics factory, the most pleasant of my jobs because my father worked there with me. We had been amazed and crushed when my father, a grain specialist, could not find work in his field. Instead, he came to work with me where he had to carry heavy trays of painted ceramics to the ovens all day long. Although he worked very hard and was disappointed not be able to work at a more meaningful job, I have some loving memories of the time we worked together. By the time we were working there, it was summer and very hot. My father loved cold drinks, so much so that he would even chew on ice. So even though we couldn't really afford it, every day as a treat I would buy him a Coke, which he loved, and he would drink it straight from the bottle with great enjoyment. "You see, sweetheart, this is big America," he would say. "For this alone it was worth coming to Canada. Where else could we have a drink like this?" We didn't know at the time that he had a heart condition and that he would not be with us long enough to enjoy his life in Canada and get the *naches* (great joy) from us that he so deserved. My eyes grow moist even now when I think of him working so hard, and I still find it difficult to accept that with his expertise in the grain business, no one in the heart of Canada's wheatland would give him a job or help him find work.

When the job at the ceramics factory came to an end, Manyi and I worked together at a candy factory during the later and hottest months of our first Winnipeg summer, filling five-quart bottles with hot mustard or peanut butter, then lifting them onto a counter and sealing them. Meanwhile, Peter, who had been a doctor in Hungary, had to start all over again in Canada and was working as a male nurse in a hospital until he learned English well enough that he could pass his medical exams again. As a nurse at the hospital, however, he was paid only a very small salary.

Although we had no help from outside, everyone in our family seized every opportunity to get ahead. We had all been trained in useful professions, and as our grasp of the English language improved, we tried to find less manual, stressful jobs and concentrated on getting better paying work. Around the middle of July, while we were still living on Inkster Boulevard, my father met three younger Hungarian refugees who offered him an opportunity to go into business with them, selling carpets, sewing machines, or other household items that became available. They had a broken-down truck, which served them well enough to drive into a different district of the city each day, park, and go door to door with their wares, selling them at give-away prices.

I am often amazed at how well they were able to communicate, but with a strong will you can, I suppose, accomplish anything. One hot day, my father left home in the morning as usual, and when he returned for the family meal in the evening, he recounted this delightful story of what had happened to them during the day.

The four partners were doing business as usual. They had parked their truck and were carrying a large and very heavy rug two blocks to a potential customer's home when a police car pulled up to the curb beside them. When the policeman got out of his car, they realized to their surprise that he wanted to question them. He wanted to know where they were taking the rug. Their English was still rather spotty, but my father answered the policeman, using whatever German he knew and, I am sure, some Hungarian. It was soon obvious to the partners that the officer wanted to see their vendor's permit, which they did not have. Not only did my father manage to talk the policeman out of giving them a fine, he also got an extension to obtain a valid permit. And if that wasn't enough, he managed to convince the "gentleman" officer to give him a lift back to the truck because he was hot and tired. I don't know how he did it, but I don't underestimate his great charm. Even when I am in pain or depressed, thinking of one of the many wonderful anecdotes about my father always puts a smile on my face. God bless him and grant him eternal rest.

My father did well in this business for a while because he was a very good salesperson and because people were drawn to him. He looked the way he lived – honest and trustworthy. What we didn't know at the time was that his partners were taking advantage of him because of those very attributes. Once we discovered what they were up to, my father had to find some other way to make a living.

My brother Pali started his business soon after this, with my father standing beside him at every step. Pali had heard through the Hungarian grapevine of a man who wanted to sell his business of sharpening knives and scissors. Pali had been trained in fine tool-and-dye manufacturing and sharpening in Budapest, and he saw this as a good business opportunity. Marika and Tibi had saved some money so they bought the business, which consisted of a motorized tricycle, a sharpening wheel, and other sharpening tools, for $400 so that Pali could start out on his own. While Pali stayed at his day job at Lux Electrics, our father would go from house to house asking homeowners if they needed anything sharpened. He would collect their knives and scissors, carefully writing down where each implement had come from, and Pali would do the actual work on them after work and on weekends. After supper, he and my father would go out together to deliver the sharpened items and collect more things that needed sharpening. They continued in this way for a while, my father running up and down apartment building stairs and coming home in time for supper with a great smile on his face, gleaming because he had been able to collect more and more work.

When Pali could finally give up his job, he established his company, PGI Gemini and Paul's Grinding Industries Ltd. He still has that company forty-five years later, and as it proudly says in his yearly expanded customer list, he now owns a company that serves Canada from coast to coast in addition to some parts of the United States. He has even expanded into Europe. Zsuzsi along with their two daughters, Kati and Yvette, have been instrumental in making the business the success it is. Pali inherited all my father's qualities that both helped him build his company and earned him the admiration of our entire family. Now with everyone in his family except one son-in-law working in the business, perhaps Pali and Zsuzsi will be able to take it easier, to have time to play with their four lovely grandchildren and look after their failing health.

The last menial job I worked at was at a large laundry where Manyi and I again worked together. By this time, the summer heat had become unbearable. Manyi and I would head out at five in the morning and work at the steam machines all day in the sweltering heat. It was not surprising that one day I simply fainted and slipped under one of the machines. I was rushed to the hospital, and to my shock, the company deducted the time of the hospital visit from my pay. This experience became the excuse I needed to decide to stay at home for a while and make a final decision about going to university. I also started to feel it was time to meet more young people. I had already gone out with a few Hungarian boys, war orphans who had arrived in Winnipeg before us, but I was now ready to socialize more widely.

Looking back now, it was a blessing that we were sent to Winnipeg first and not to a big city like Toronto. It was easier in a smaller community to get to know people, most of whom I found to be very warm and friendly, and to become known to them. The slower pace of life in Winnipeg also gave me the time I needed to get used to being openly Jewish again. Coming from a Communist country where we weren't allowed to practise our religion openly, it was wonderful to be able to go to synagogue and to celebrate the holidays without fear. And I did love the traditions of Jewish life.

Orland (Avraham Yitchak) at Rosh Pina Synagogue, 1957,
as my father first met him.

As soon as we moved to Inkster Boulevard, my father had begun looking around for a synagogue to attend. One of the two largest conservative synagogues in Winnipeg, Rosh Pina, just happened to be around the corner from our house. On the first Shabbat after he had found Rosh Pina, my father got dressed up in his best clothes, went to synagogue, and came home a happy man. As we all sat down to our noon Shabbat meal, a delicious *cholent*, my father told us about the outstanding welcome he had received. When the congregation heard him pray, they knew instantly that here was a *mensch*, even in his shabby suit. They tried to converse with him but soon realized that he did not speak English while none of them spoke Hungarian. Suddenly, someone remembered that their new cantor spoke some Hungarian. I cannot express in words what that meant to my father. He had always cherished cantorial music and had been very impressed by this cantor whom he had just heard singing. "His name is Avraham Yitzhak," my father told us as we listened intently around the table. "He has a melodious voice and a way of praying that must go straight to heaven. I have invited him to come to our home this afternoon to meet our family."

After our Shabbat meal, I was glad to finally be able to go to my little closet-room and think about my plans to attend university in the fall. Whenever I stepped into my tiny sanctuary, I was struck by how different this closet of mine was from the beautiful childhood home I had in Hungary before the war, a home now gone forever. But I loved my closet and never complained about it, and I never wanted to look back at what had been, even though sometimes I wanted to tell people I had come from a good family and a beautiful home, that I was civilized and had manners, and that I hadn't left Hungary because I was a criminal but because I was in jeopardy as a Jew. Still, I was learning to be happy again and beginning to see a future here in Canada, one I could be excited about. As I lay there dreaming about university and new friends, there was a loud knock on my door, and my mother stepped into the open doorway. "Put some decent clothes on," she announced, "and come to meet our highly respected visitor, the cantor." Whatever I had been planning before that moment would be utterly changed in the next few minutes, and I would learn another valuable lesson on my life's journey that would make me a great believer in fate and destiny. For every plan or decision one takes in life, a higher power is always there, ultimately taking that decision out of our hands.

CHAPTER 8

The Cantor's Wife

Even the Smallest Event is Orchestrated from Above. – The Baal Shem Tov

I dragged myself down the stairs in my long, green, hand-me-down housecoat. This was the best I could manage after a hard week at work, and it would have to do. Besides, I was not interested in meeting this man, or any man for that matter. I had but one ambition – to go to university – and had already been accepted at the University of Manitoba for the fall semester. Tired and resentful of being summoned, I found our esteemed guest in the living room sitting on a chair surrounded by my whole family, including the two toddlers running around in diapers. He looked embarrassed, almost childish, sitting there and was looking down at the floor, twisting and turning his hat nervously in his hands. What kind of person is this, I thought to myself, who cannot even look someone in the eye when they walk into a room? Still, I had to admit he was good-looking, with a round face capped by prematurely greying hair and young, almost girlishly attractive features. I also couldn't help admiring his European way of dressing, so clean and elegant compared to most of the people I was meeting those days.

"Olga," I said, introducing myself, shaking his hand and murmuring, "*Shabbat shalom.*"

"Please call me Orland," came his soft reply in a beautifully modulated voice.

"Oh, gee," I whispered to my parents in Hungarian, "may I leave now?" But the murderous looks they both gave me stopped me in my tracks. I sat down.

Will I ever forget those first few moments with Orland? I think they will remain with me throughout my life. One could ask whether we were fated to meet, both so far from our birthplaces, both strangers in a strange new land. In 1956, when the Hungarian Revolution began, I had never heard of Winnipeg. And when Orland came from London, England, to visit his brother in Vancouver that same year and heard that Rosh Pina Synagogue in Winnipeg was looking for a cantor, I'm sure he could never have imagined the outcome of his little trip east to audition for the position. Orland later told me that he fell in love with me the moment I entered the room. He said he had never met anyone like me before, and he just couldn't control his feelings. As for myself, I still hated men. I didn't want them in my life, and I'm quite sure I felt nothing for Orland that day I was introduced to him. But fate took a hand in our affairs, and I am a great believer in fate. Life is a huge maze, and as I have walked around in it, I have often taken wrong turns, ending up at seemingly dead ends, stuck searching for a way out. Luckily, I have always found the way meant for me.

Orland spoke some Hungarian so we managed to converse for a few moments on that first day, but mostly he spoke with my father. Then after tea and some of the delicacies my mother always made for Shabbat, he wished us well in our new country and left. It took him a few days to call me, but when he did, he asked me out on a date. On our first date – my first real date in Canada – he picked me up in a pink Lincoln Continental and took me for a drive. I couldn't get over the car's elegant leather seats and its radio. We drove around for a while, but March in Winnipeg, with its lingering winter, isn't terribly pretty, and there wasn't much to see except piles of dirty snow everywhere. But Orland kept me enthralled as he talked about his life and serenaded me with Italian songs.

When he delivered me home, he asked me out for the following weekend. This time, we were going out to dinner at a fancy hotel with his good friends, the Glesbys. How excited I was, although at the same time very anxious about the prospect of going to a nice place when I didn't have anything to wear and couldn't afford much. I went to Eaton's bargain basement and found a pink taffeta dress with small flowers on it that fit me perfectly. I could wear the spring coat I had bought for myself at the factory where I was working at the time. And now I finally had a place to wear the shoes I had bought in Milan just before our long voyage to Canada.

The following Saturday night, Orland picked me up again in the pink Lincoln, which I later discovered he had borrowed from the Glesbys, who had told him they wanted to meet me. We went to pick them up at their home, and when we arrived, Orland introduced me to the couple: a good-looking man and his wife, a beauty with burning black eyes. I also met their daughters: four sweet, lively, and exceptionally pretty girls who also seemed anxious to meet me. I was only slightly older than the eldest daughter and was very taken with all of them and with their elegant home, but with my limited English, I couldn't speak with them very much. In any case, I figured no one wanted to hear about my experiences in the war and under Communism even though I was finding it difficult and frustrating to put my previous life in Hungary behind me so soon. I was also disheartened to learn again and again that most immigrants just wanted to forget their wartime and post-war experiences and not be reminded of their past.

When we arrived at the beautiful hotel where we were to have dinner, Mrs. Glesby and I headed up the long staircase to the cloakroom while the men waited for us at the bottom of the stairs. I took off my coat and boots, changed into my shoes, and checked my hair, which I had pulled back and clasped with pink, plastic flower clips. I felt like a fairy-tale princess as I walked down the Scarlett O'Hara staircase, and I was very aware of Orland and Mr. Glesby standing at the bottom of the stairs watching me and exchanging glances. Maybe, it suddenly struck me, they were comparing me to beautiful Mrs. Glesby and had noticed how my Eaton's basement outfit looked rather shabby compared to her elegant clothes and black mink coat. But I have never felt threatened by beauty or wealth; only the ability of others to analyze and discuss complex ideas clearly and simply used to and still does intimidate me sometimes.

As it turned out, we had a wonderful evening. The Glesbys were charming, and by the end of the evening, I was a little dizzy from the wine and from all the new experiences. All the way home, Orland sang songs to me in Italian and told me that when they had watched me come down the staircase, Mr. Glesby said I was so beautiful that I took his breath away. Like Eliza Doolittle, I could have danced all night. It had all ended too soon.

From that night on, Orland called me frequently, and we began to see a lot of one other. At first, he came around under the pretext of helping me learn English. He soon hired a Jewish girl and later a qualified private English tutor to teach me English. Overwhelmed and very grateful for his encouragement, I worked hard to prove myself worthy of his blind faith in me. In the meantime, we were becoming closer all the time, although sometimes I felt our relationship was moving ahead too quickly for me. Nonetheless, I was learning to trust and rely on him. Perhaps it was because he was twenty years older than I was and had a very proper and respectful demeanour, something that was enhanced by the fact that he spoke good English with a charming British accent. Or perhaps it was because I was beginning to see that underneath the immaculately dressed gentleman was an extraordinary, cultured person with whom I was very impressed. Aside from the fact that he also spoke fluent Italian, French, German, and Yiddish, he was a talented and beautiful vocalist whose glorious singing went straight to my heart.

As we got to know each other, I began to learn something of his past as well. Orland, or as he was known at birth, Avraham Yitzchak

Zicherman, was born in 1916 to a large Chassidic family in Cerna, Czechoslovakia. Along with his parents and twelve brothers and sisters, many of whom were already married with children by the time World War II broke out, he also had many aunts, uncles, and cousins. From very early on, it was apparent to both his parents and his teachers that he had a true calling to be a cantor. He dreamed of becoming an opera singer, but his parents wanted him to be a great *chazzan* (cantor), so he attended the Galanta *Yeshivah* (religious school) and later studied music and voice production at Presburg.

In 1938, when he was twenty-two, he was called up to join the Czech army, but his family decided to try and get him out of the country so he could continue his studies and fulfill their dream for him of becoming a *chazzan*. It was decided that his younger brother, Jankel (who changed his name to Jack when he moved to Canada), who looked very childlike and frail, would take his place and pose as Avraham. Jankel presented himself at the army office and was declared unfit for military service. In the meantime, the family managed to obtain false papers for Avraham, who fled to Amsterdam. There he began to study voice production under the well-known choir leader S. H. Englander, with whom he developed a strong and lasting friendship, the two of them corresponding for years after.

When Holland was invaded by Germany, Avraham Yitzchak moved on to London, England, where he was appointed first reader at the Southport Hebrew Congregation in 1940, at the same time enrolling in the Royal Academy of Music to further his voice studies. But the continuing attraction opera held for him, along with his ambition to study secular music, drew him to seek the advice of Beniamino Gigli, one of the greatest opera singers of his time. Gigli recommended that Avraham settle in Italy and change his name to Orland Verrall, a name switch that along with his blond Aryan looks would help him stay out of the hands of the Nazis. With a letter of recommendation from the opera director of the British Broadcasting Corporation, who had heard Orland performing charity concerts for the Red Cross, Orland travelled to Rome for the first time at the end of 1940. Although he did not move to Italy as Gigli had suggested, he was to make many trips there on his vacations during the war.

Orland loved Italy and opera. He was a quick study in languages, soon speaking Italian perfectly. He knew most Italian operas by heart and studied with great fervour under the tutelage of Manlio Marcantoni, singing mainly from the Italian opera repertoire. He would have made a wonderful opera singer, but his love of cantorial music, combined with the promise he had made to his parents, won out in the end. In addition, he was totally cut off from his family during the war and had no idea what had happened to them. He felt terribly guilty (and would continue to do so for the rest of his life) that he had been safe in Holland and England while his family had all probably died.

When the war ended, he immediately began searching for any family members. It was through the Red Cross that he found his sister, Hencsi, and two brothers, Jankel and Zalman, in Budapest. The four of them were the youngest children in his immediate family, and except for a couple of cousins, the only survivors of the entire extended family. The rest had all perished at the hands of the Nazis.

Orland went to Budapest to meet with his remaining siblings. At first, all four wanted to return to Cerna to see for themselves if anyone else had survived, but some of their friends had gone back and been beaten or killed by the locals so they decided not to chance it. It was time for them to get on with their lives and build their own futures. Hencsi, who had married a cousin right after the war, and Zalman both decided to emigrate to Israel, but the youngest brother, Jankel, chose to settle in Vancouver, Canada, with his new wife, a Romanian Jew and herself a survivor of a large religious family. Orland returned to London in 1947 where he served as cantor at the Palmer Green United Synagogue, a position he would hold until 1956. During those years, he frequently received invitations to return to Italy, where singing in operas with other great artists was something that always gave him great joy.

In 1956, Orland decided to take a year's sabbatical from his cantorial duties in London and went to visit his brother, Jack, in Vancouver. While he was there, he started thinking of staying on in Canada, and he began to inquire about any cantorial positions opening up in Vancouver, working as a real estate agent while he looked. Then he heard that the congregation of Rosh Pina Synagogue in Winnipeg was looking for a cantor. He applied, auditioned, and was hired. By the end of the summer of 1956, he had settled in Winnipeg and was preparing to take on his duties at the High Holiday services that autumn. The following spring, he met my father.

By June of 1957, Orland and I were seeing each other more or less steadily. By that time, too, word had spread in the Jewish community in Winnipeg that there were new Jewish immigrants in town with an unmarried daughter. There were many single young Jewish men in Winnipeg, mostly orphans of the Holocaust, who had been brought to Canada from displaced persons camps after the war. I myself had gone out with some of them, but very few Canadian Jewish parents wanted their daughters to go out with orphans who had nothing to offer and weren't established in any way. But these boys were really looking for wives with similar backgrounds to their own, and I suddenly found myself very popular. Even though I did not have any special feelings for any of them, I wasn't sure how I felt about Orland either. I knew that I felt secure with him and trusted him, but I certainly wasn't ready to commit myself so soon to a one-on-one relationship. So I started going out on dates with some of these young men. We might go out to a bar or a movie or to the lake on a Sunday. While I enjoyed my dates with these boys who were very pleasant and ambitious, they were just not meant for me. They simply could not compete with "O Sole Mio" and the gentle charm of Orland.

In July, Orland received a letter from his brother in Vancouver saying he had suffered a herniated disc in his back and was in tremendous pain and stuck in bed. Orland decided to visit him, and I saw him off at the train station, still unsure of where our relationship was going. As I stood at the bus stop after we said good-bye, thinking about what I felt for this man, I discovered that I did not have any money with me for the bus. I was beside myself. How would I get home? It was such a long walk. When the bus pulled up and the doors opened, I tried in my broken English to communicate to the driver that I did not have the fare. As I lowered my eyes in embarrassment, I noticed to my astonishment that there was 10¢ lying on the ground, the exact fare I needed for the bus. With tears in my eyes, I bent down quickly to pick it up. Was this a coincidence? Or was it a sign? I recognized at that moment that my life had held so many extraordinary coincidences, signs that came to me to show me the way. Call it fate or destiny, but I have come to be a true believer that at whatever point we are in our lives, whatever we accomplish, whatever happens to us, we are predestined to it. Looking back, I realize that at that moment, despite all my hesitation and doubt, I knew for a fact that Orland was my destiny.

During the month he was away, Orland called me from Vancouver every second day. Often I was out with one of the boys who had started coming around, and my mother would tell Orland the truth, that I was out on a date. On one occasion when my mother told him I was out, he told her that he would call again at a particular time and that he wanted me to be home. He needed to talk to me. When he called, Orland told me that he loved me and wanted to marry me. He said that he would like to announce our engagement when he came home so we could get married after the High Holidays. He told me that he had already bought a one-carat diamond for me to have an engagement ring designed to my taste.

"You bought a what?" I asked him. "How could you buy a diamond when I haven't said yes yet?" Although I trusted Orland, I still had serious misgivings about marriage, especially because my heart was set on going to back to school.

When Orland got back, we had many a talk about my apprehensions. Even though he promised to let me go to university, we had many other disagreements and some serious fights and even broke up a couple of times. But he wouldn't give up, and in the end, I agreed to marry him, discovering to my surprise that the more I contemplated getting married, the happier the idea made me. I was in love, and my love and happiness were starting to wash away all my fears and all the bad memories of my previous marriage and prior experiences with men. All I could think of was how much I cared for Orland, what an honour it would be to marry him, and how happy my parents would be. At the same time, however, I felt that many people in Orland's congregation were not happy with his choice for a wife. All the well-to-do parents at Rosh Pina wanted him to marry one of their pretty daughters, but he wouldn't hear of it, and the congregation didn't take too kindly to the news of our engagement. Who was I, after all – just an immigrant, a girl from nowhere – and here I had landed a man whom many in the Winnipeg Jewish community considered the biggest catch in town.

My parents were delighted, to say the least, and once I said yes, I looked forward to the festivities of getting married. Orland and I picked out a ring design together and had the diamond he bought in Vancouver set into it. We had a traditional Jewish family engagement party in our home, with a festive meal and all the time-honoured prayers and blessings. We even broke a fine bone-china plate and gave each of my unmarried girlfriends a fragment of it; tradition in Hungary has it that once a girl collects seven shards, she'll be the next to get married. Later on, a wonderful family in the Rosh Pina Congregation, the Summers, threw us a most beautiful and elegant engagement party in the garden at their home. Most of the congregation was invited, and many people told me afterwards that I was aglow with love and happiness. We remained good friends with the Summers until we moved from Winnipeg in 1969. Unfortunately, we lost track of each other, but I shall always feel a great sense of indebtedness to them for the generosity and friendship they showed me then and at many other times during our time in Winnipeg.

Autumn 1957 was a busy time for me. At the beginning of September, two months before our wedding, I registered at the University of Manitoba, planning to start school the following year. I was taking extra English courses and felt that I needed the winter and spring to prepare myself for my studies. November soon arrived, and on the Shabbat before our wedding, Orland had his *oifruf* (calling up to read from the Torah). Then on November 17, 1957, we got married at the Rosh Pina Synagogue, with three rabbis and two cantors officiating as we exchanged our vows. There were four hundred guests: all the members of the congregation; Orland's brother, Jack, with his wife, Estelle, and their son, Harold; and of course, my whole family. Orland paid for most of the wedding, from my wedding gown to his brother's train tickets, and my mother baked all the cakes for the sweet table, cakes that were, God bless her hands, glorious confections the likes of which people had seen only in pictures and had tasted only rarely.

Right after the High Holidays, most of my family had moved to an apartment building on Salter Boulevard: Pali, Zsuzsi, and little Kati in one apartment; Tibi and Marika in another; and my parents and I in our own small unit. Only Peter, Manyi, and little Eva had moved away to be closer to St. Boniface Hospital, just over the Red River on the French side of town, where Peter was training. Before the wedding, though, we all congregated in my parents' small apartment to get dressed. Some congregants had given Zsuzsi, Marika, and Manyi used dresses to wear at the wedding, but these dresses were all too small for them. I still remember how much we all laughed as my sisters-in-law held onto the fridge and my brothers pulled in their girdles and tugged on the zippers to try and make the dresses fit.

Our wedding was the most beautiful I had ever seen. Of course, it was different from the weddings we had gone to in Hungary, and as I walked down the aisle of the synagogue filled with fresh flowers and candlelight, I felt like a Hollywood movie star from some of the old films I had seen. I chose as my matron of honour the wife of a Hungarian survivor friend of ours, and I asked the daughters of four of the synagogue leaders to be my bridesmaids. I had the prettiest wedding attendants from the wealthiest families marching down the aisle for me. Best of all, though, my whole family was there. My parents were absolutely elated that I was marrying a *chazzan* and proudly escorted me down the aisle, giving me away to the handsome groom, the respected cantor of the synagogue. If I ever gave anything back to them for all they did for me, this was it. Here I was, Cinderella with her handsome prince, about to live happily ever after and giving some well-deserved *naches* (overwhelming joy) to my parents after all the years of turbulence in their lives.

After the ceremony, we all stood in a formal receiving line, but since I knew very few of the congregants yet or spoke much English, it felt like an endless line of kissing until my lips were swollen and I had no more strength to speak. Then began the whirlwind of dinner courses and dancing. I felt I was living a fairy tale. At midnight, we said good-bye to our guests and set out for our honeymoon in Niagara Falls. Not only was I overwhelmed by the magnificence of the falls, with the coloured lights playing over them at night, but I was with a man I adored.

How different this honeymoon was from my first honeymoon and "marriage" to Jeno! Orland and I were a perfect match in many of our interests, and we both had dreams about having a family. With his gentle, patient approach to love-making, he awakened in me a physical longing that lent our union a strong physical satisfaction. It was a magnificent honeymoon and a perfect start for what would be our many wonderful years together.

It seemed unbelievable that in less than a year since I had come to Canada, I had become a married woman and was embarking on a new and exciting chapter in my life. Yet it still would take some time for all the events of my spectacular wedding day and honeymoon to sink in and quell the residual fear in my heart that I didn't deserve this joy and would wake up and find that it had all been just a dream.

When we came back from our honeymoon, we settled into a two-bedroom apartment that was close enough to the synagogue for Orland to walk there. The new phase of my life began in earnest as I returned to face my newly demanding social life serving a large congregation run by wealthy, powerful people. I don't think I fully realized when I got married what a tremendous adjustment this would be for me, coming from a Communist country where we weren't even allowed to practise our religion and had to do everything in secret. Now I found myself the cantor's wife in the second largest congregation in Winnipeg.

Even though I loved the Jewish life and all that came with it, I was twenty-one years old with no appreciation – or training – for the role that a cantor's wife was expected to play, with its almost full-time commitment to the congregation's wants and needs. In my parents' house, I had always been watched over, and I really thought that once I was married, I would be able to do whatever I pleased. Instead, I suddenly found I had a lot of responsibilities to take on. I was expected to join Sisterhood and was asked to perform all the honorary duties of a cantor's wife: attend all the meetings, participate in fundraising functions, and be present at all *bar* and *bat mitzvahs* and weddings, even if there were two or three on a given weekend. I had to come to grips with the reality that my husband's success depended on my being able to hold up my end of this partnership. It was this aspect – looking at our life as a business – that was hardest for me. I had been through so much that I found it hard to trust anyone, and on top of that, I was not the kind of person who found it easy to kowtow to people. But these people were my husband's employers. It took me quite a while to learn how to try and please them and to be accommodating even when I didn't feel like it. Eventually, I did learn to be what they wanted – a nice decoration in the synagogue

– but that didn't satisfy me: I would have preferred to contribute something intellectual, not decorative, to the synagogue.

On the other hand, there was a great deal about my new life that I cherished and that has stayed with me in the form of pleasant memories. Perhaps I was not good friends with all the leaders of the congregation, but I did form close bonds with the people who mattered to me, people with similar backgrounds and values as mine, people I could feel comfortable with and not inferior to because we lacked a house full of material goods. In the thirteen years we lived in Winnipeg, the many strong friendships we made there gave me immense pleasure. Most people in the congregation were very warm and hospitable. As I got to know them, we became very close, and even after we moved to Toronto, many of them would come to visit us.

In September 1958, I had barely started my studies at the University of Manitoba when I became pregnant. This was my second pregnancy; a few months after my wedding the year before, I had missed my period, and it turned out that I was pregnant. The doctor I saw at that time told me that my uterus was turned the wrong way and I was very weak inside. He said that he was surprised I had even been able to conceive, and if I wanted to have this child, I would have to stay in bed. However, to Orland's and my sorrow, I lost that baby in my first trimester.

But now here it was a year later, and I was pregnant again. I said nothing to anyone, fearing that I might lose this baby, too. But I was at my parents' apartment one day when I was in my third month. My mother had some of her friends over for lunch, and when I told her I'd like some cheese blintzes, one of the ladies said, "Mariska, I think your daughter is pregnant." Soon after, I learned that Tibi's wife, Marika, was also expecting their first child. We were thrilled that our children would be so close in age. Both of our due dates were on the same day, and together we awaited the great day, comparing the symptoms of our pregnancies step by step.

This time, I paid heed to what the doctor had said and spent most of my time resting in bed. But I didn't care if I had to stay in bed for the whole nine months, I was just so happy to be pregnant. I have always loved children more than anything else and had long craved a child of my own. Orland was also delighted. If I was crazy about having a child, Orland was even more elated. For him, having children was a miracle after having lost so many people in his family to the Holocaust. There was a bittersweet aspect to my happiness, however. Even though we were thrilled at the prospect of having a child, my personal dreams of a university education were effectively over.

As soon as I was able to get out of bed during my seventh month of pregnancy, I began taking prenatal classes with a doctor who offered painless, natural childbirth through self-hypnosis. Although I had only a little time left to master the technique, I jumped at the opportunity to experience the birth of my first child totally awake, without the need for drugs or gas. And it proved to be a great and fulfilling experience.

I delivered my baby girl, Judy, on May 27, 1959, half an hour after Marika had her daughter. My brother Peter was allowed in the delivery room where he told me about Marika. Then he added that the family would have liked me to have a boy. At the time, in my pain, I told him not very politely to just go and get lost, but we laugh about it now. I called my mother right away and broke down on the phone. I told her that I knew everyone had been hoping for a boy but that, more than anything, I had wanted a girl. My mother was, of course, ecstatic, as was my father when he heard. As I held my baby girl in my arms, my happiness was beyond measure. While I was in the hospital, Zsofi sent me a beautiful bunting she had embroidered for the baby. It was so pretty that the nurses at St. Boniface Hospital took Judy around to show everyone before we left for home. I was aware, though, as I looked at that tiny baby in my arms, at that child I adored so much, that there is no instant bond you forge with your child. The bond is created and strengthened, and your love grows as you go through many experiences together. You can only hope that as you both grow and learn, a healthy, respectful love will bloom in both directions, a love that will last a lifetime.

Once Judy was born, we decided it was time to move. We found a bright, three-bedroom apartment on the second floor of a duplex in a predominantly Jewish neighbourhood that was even closer to the synagogue than our old apartment had been. A lovely elderly couple, Nellie and Morris Yarmos, owned the duplex and lived on the main floor. They were in the restaurant business and would leave early every morning, returning about supper time, so we had the house practically to ourselves for the whole day. I settled into motherhood and caring for my baby. At last, life was taking on a pattern in which I could feel safe and secure. Orland and I were happy, our family was growing, my family was around me, and we were becoming more at ease in our new country.

It was only after Judy was born, all those years after the war and the explosion near the bunker in Brno that left me unconscious, that I noticed I was having problems with my hearing. Judy started having a lot of ear infections when she was about six months old. When I took her to the ear specialist, I told him that I, too, suffered from earaches and was extremely sensitive to noise. Running water, the floor polisher, in fact any noisy situation was too loud for me, and I would have to shut off the source because it was so irritating. He told me I must have very sensitive hearing and to put cotton batting in my ears. I let it go at that, and it was only after we moved to Toronto that I started to notice I could not hear well. If I turned my head in a certain direction when I was watching television, I couldn't hear and when I talked on the phone, I had trouble hearing what was being said. In 1972, I went to see an ear, nose, and throat specialist who told me I certainly did have a problem. He told me about a new procedure from England that could help me, and I underwent a seven-hour experimental procedure at Mount Sinai Hospital. They only did one ear because they did not know how successful it would be. My hearing was never completely restored, only to about sixty-five percent, and I have been wearing a hearing aid since I was thirty-five years old.

On Mother's Day in 1960, when Judy was about a year old, my world suffered a great blow. We had gone for a drive in the country with my parents, and my father, who was particularly crazy about his newest grandchild, was holding Judy in his arms as we strolled together beside a lake. At one point, he said a strange thing to me, "Don't ever let her forget me." Then he kissed her little nose and said to her, "That's from your grandfather. Remember!"

After we ate lunch, he began to feel unwell and even jokingly complained that perhaps we had fed him something that wasn't fresh. We just laid him down on the back seat of the car, thinking it was indigestion, and rushed back to Winnipeg because he was in such pain. We took him to the hospital, where he was immediately admitted. It wasn't till the following day that tests indicated that my father had had a mild heart attack. We were a bit shocked at the diagnosis, but because my father was only sixty-seven years old at the time, we didn't really expect that the problem would be that serious. He would be in the hospital for a while, we reasoned, then he would come home and take better care of himself.

We were so wrong with our prognosis. On the second day of Shavuot, June 2, 1960, I got the call from the hospital that my father had died. My mother had gone to visit him in the hospital earlier in the day, but my husband and I did not travel on holy days. Not realizing how serious his condition was because even the doctors had made light of it, Orland hadn't wanted me to go with my mother. Now she was on her way home and did not even know that my father had passed away just after she left his side. When she arrived home, Orland had to break the news to her because my own pain was so great that I could not face her. It would take me a long time to get over the anger I felt at Orland for not letting me travel on that occasion to visit my father before his death. I had acceded to his wishes because I had not yet come to a point in my life where I felt old enough to do what I wanted to do without asking my husband's permission. My father's death was a tremendous blow to me, and I felt very guilty that I hadn't seen him before he passed away. Had I told him, I thought to myself, how much I loved him? I would have loved to hug him just one last time, but now I could only say good-bye to my wonderful father in spirit.

I was also devastated that my father had to leave us and go to his eternal rest now when he was finally so happy. He loved living in Canada and enjoyed so many things about his life here. I remember how overjoyed he was when we bought him a little car for $350. It still makes me laugh to remember how my mother would starch and iron his shirts, and then he would go outside and shine his little car with his sleeve. After all the years of horror and deprivation, he had just begun to live again and see the fruits of his labours, watching his children settle down and have children of their own. He could finally relax and bask in the warm glow of his beloved family around him. Most importantly, though, my father was able once again to live the Jewish life he so loved. It meant so much for him to be able to go openly to synagogue to pray and to listen to his son-in-law, the cantor, sing. He would sit there with a look of such contentment on his face, one would think he was in *Gan Eden* (paradise). He was a warm, loving person and a wonderful father, and the blessed memories I have of him have always been a comfort to me.

Immediately after the crushing loss of my father, my thoughts turned to my mother and the impact that his death would have on her. I did not want her to be alone. Having a granddaughter, a loving son-in-law, and her daughter beside her would, I hoped, make things easier for her. We closed up my parents' small apartment, and my mother moved in with us permanently. I took care of her for the rest of her life.

During the year or so following my father's death, I was so engrossed in dealing with the impact it had on my mother and with my own feelings of loss that I didn't realize that I was pregnant again.

I almost lost this baby, too, before I knew what was happening. Once I knew, though, it was a wonderful thing to look forward to a new life coming. My second daughter was born on April 29, 1962, and she was so eager to come into the world that she was almost born in the car on the way to the hospital. As we were driving, I could feel her head coming through, and we had to stop a police car at four in the morning on that Sunday to escort us to the hospital where she was born very quickly. She had a particularly round head, a beautiful complexion, and lots of lovely dark hair. We named her Lesley, after my father (Laszlo), and Pearl, just because she looked like a real shining pearl. When I brought Lesley home from the hospital, Judy wasn't jealous of her at all. She loved playing little mother to Lesley, constantly watching her and reporting to me, "She took her thumb in her mouth" or "She's laughing," and even helping to bathe her and change her diapers. I'm sure, though, that as the older sister, Judy could hardly wait till the two of them were old enough that Judy could boss Lesley around. Nevertheless, anyone could see the love growing between the two sisters even in those early days.

The duplex where we lived was on a large lot and had a big yard for the children to play in. Our home became a nursery with me as one of the children. We lived a mere ten-minute walk from the synagogue, and I often bundled my babies up on Shabbat and took them to show them off to the congregation. Now I had two living dolls to play with, and the three of us remained playmates well into their teen years.

Nellie and Morris's only child, a baby boy, had passed away many years earlier at the age of five months. Now they fell in love with my children, and my children took to them as if they were second grandparents. Morris was a tall, lean, grey-haired man of few words, but he was kind and obliging. My children were that much richer for having him as a grandfather figure after my father passed away. Nellie was small but had a great big heart. She loved children, especially my girls, and they loved her back. She became like a second grandmother to them and they even called her Nanny. She loved to talk and would often come upstairs and play with the children while I baked a cake for her and her husband.

When Lesley was about six months old, she developed a near-fatal intestinal disorder called intussusceptions, in which part of the intestine telescopes into another part of the intestine. It was during the High Holidays that Lesley started screaming in pain. I called her pediatrician and tried to describe the symptoms she was experiencing, but he must have thought I was exaggerating and said I was just being a hysterical Jewish mother. By the first day of Succoth – the eighth day of her being in agony – she was so sick I simply rushed her to the Children's Hospital in a taxi. Within thirty minutes of our arrival, the doctors operated on her, telling me to say goodbye to her because they had so little hope for her chances of survival. But Lesley is from a long line of survivors and came through the operation well. I remained at her bedside for ten days, staying awake at night by helping the nurses. She recovered completely, but the experience left me drained. When you are young and happy, though, you rebound quickly.

With two growing children, we soon started looking around for a house of our own. We wanted to stay in the same neighbourhood so Orland could continue to walk to synagogue, and we found a ranch-style bungalow that suited all our needs. It was a lovely house, and I was very proud of it, our first real home in Canada. The backyard faced a large historical park, and I enjoyed the old trees and serene beauty of the landscaping. We also had some delightful neighbours, particularly Ida and Nat Roy, who lived on the other side of the park; our houses were situated so that our kitchen windows looked out at each other across the park. Ida was a short woman of medium build with a attractive face framed by grey hair that she wore swept up in a bun. Nat, who was in the fur business, was a bit husky and a real joker, always full of fun. The two of them soon learned that I always baked late on Thursday afternoons for the coming Shabbat, a habit I had picked up from my mother. Whatever else I was baking – *kuglof*

The Verrall family in Winnipeg lighting the menorah for Hannukah,
1963. L to R: Orland, Judy, me, Lesley.

or yeast buns filled with either cinnamon or chocolate – I also had to
bake cheese buns for Orland. He always used to say, "If there are no
cheese buns on Friday morning, then it isn't Friday, and I'll have to
go back to sleep until it is Friday again." Ida loved to bake, too, and
in the years we lived in that house, it was not unusual to find us both
baking together and sharing tea or coffee on Thursday evening.

I don't think I fully realized or appreciated it at the time, but those
years in Winnipeg were good, rich years when I grew up as a person.
Winnipeg is famous for both its very cold winters, with snowstorms
so bad the police sometimes had to come and clear our doorways so
we could get out of the house, and its sweltering, mosquito-infested

summers. But it was a wonderful place to raise a family, and the children flourished, grew, and began school along with ballet and swimming lessons. We celebrated birthday parties and threw "just-because" parties in our backyard in the summer for our children's friends and their parents. We started renting a cottage every summer not too far from the city on Clear Lake or at Gimli, both of which were close enough to Winnipeg that Orland could join us during the week whenever he had time. We had friends in the congregation and outside the synagogue as well as good neighbours, and some of these friendships have endured even now that I'm in Toronto. I am grateful to all our friends whose warmth made Winnipeg an excellent place for me to acclimatize to my newly adopted home and country. We also had a wonderful family life, surrounded by my family, and we often exchanged visits with Orland's brother, Jack, and his family, sometimes going to Vancouver and taking my mother with us, sometimes being visited in Winnipeg.

As soon as we moved into our own house, we started entertaining, and I loved the way our home became a meeting place where people felt they could just drop in. Orland would bring people home from synagogue for dinner as well. We also hosted many out-of-town guest cantors, and my association with my husband's fellow-cantors and my role as hostess when they came to our home gave me great delight. My husband, as a member of the Cantors Assembly of America, a New York-headquartered but world-wide professional organization for cantors, was responsible for organizing many fundraising concerts, all of which were well attended and well received. We were also privileged to have some of the greatest cantors from all over the world, like Cantor Moshe Kossevitzky, Cantor Sholom Katz, Cantor Moshe Herstik and his two sons from Israel, and many others, stay at our home. With my mother's help, I learned to be a very good hostess and became quite adept at throwing some of the best and biggest parties for the Winnipeg Jewish community in my home.

It wasn't until years later at a large cantorial concert in Toronto that I discovered how Orland had been instrumental at that time in setting Naftali Herstik, the elder of the Herstik boys, on the road to being a cantor. It was at one of the cantorial gatherings at our house in Winnipeg that Orland listened to the sixteen-year-old Naftali sing, offering him advice and inviting him to sing at a particular concert. This concert was the boy's first public performance, and he was a sensation. When I met Naftali again a couple of years ago in Toronto, he told me that he was now the chief cantor at the Great Synagogue in Jerusalem.

During those years early in my marriage, I learned and experienced so much. Some of my most beloved memories are of the summers we went to the Catskills for the cantors' conventions. The first one we went to was held at Grossingers, and I cannot describe my excitement and joy the first time we arrived at that luxurious hotel where, to my amazement, everything was kosher. There must have been close to five hundred cantors there, many with their wives. Subsequent conventions were held at the Concord Hotel, and it was a wonderful thing, meeting there year after year, sitting around eating, singing, and exchanging stories. It felt like a big family gathering, and we made many very good friends. With so many cantors, the singing was more beautiful than any opera could be. Just their regular prayers were so meaningful and celestial, I still get shivers thinking about them. Each word of every prayer, each chanted by a different voice, was an incredible treat for the ears. There were all night singalongs, and when one cantor sat down at the piano, three others would join him to sing, each one wanting to outdo the other, all giving spontaneous and marvellous concerts.

My first visit to New York City in 1965 had a tremendous impact on me, too. I was overwhelmed by the skyscrapers, Broadway, and the Statue of Liberty. We saw Margot Fonteyn and Rudolf Nureyev dance for The Royal Ballet at the Metropolitan Opera House. It was a joy for me and a very special performance. I was thrilled to find myself sitting in that splendid theatre next to Robert and Ethel Kennedy and many other celebrities. At intermission, we saw them having coffee with Barbra Streisand and her husband, Elliott Gould, and I managed to work up the courage to get their autographs. It was the year of the World's Fair in New York, and we saw many marvellous things including Walt Disney's *It's a Small, Small World*, whose dancing and singing dolls in costumes from around the world fascinated me.

Best of all, though, we went to see *Fiddler on the Roof*, which was playing on Broadway. I don't know what I was expecting, but I just couldn't believe that in America there could be such a thing as a Jewish play like this on Broadway for all the world to see. The songs moved me so much, particularly "Sunrise, Sunset." Years later at Judy's wedding, Orland sang that song at my request. The play brought back many cherished memories for me of my childhood and of the special Jewish holidays and how we had celebrated them. We had not been allowed to practise our faith openly in Hungary since 1944, and now, here in America, our faith was openly celebrated on the stage. It was a new world for me, a free world, where anything and everything was possible.

In 1965, we began to plan our first trip to Israel. Orland wanted to visit his sister and brother and their families, whom he had not seen for almost twenty years, and I very much wanted to meet his family, too. So when our children were six and three years old, we left them with my mother and went to Israel. I found Orland's family to be outstandingly warm-hearted albeit very religious. They were so religious, in fact, that a man would not stay alone with me in a room, and if one of the men took me sightseeing, he would walk on the other side of the street from me. Orland's sister and some of her children live in Bnei Brak, one of Israel's most religious cities, and to see the young mothers with their children walking or playing on a holy day and to see the respect the children accord to their elders makes my heart glow with Jewish pride. The houses had no radio and no television, and the entire lifestyle seemed so much more meaningful to me than the North American one. We also visited Orland's brother Zalman and his family who were living in a *moshav* (communal settlement); although Zalman has since died, his wife and son are still living there.

I had always dreamed of going to Israel, and that first visit was a very moving experience for me. I loved our ancestral country and everything about it, and as soon as I got there, I fell in love with its people. During that entire trip, I thought constantly about my father. It was so sad that he had not lived to come to Israel. Everything I knew about Israel I had learned from him, and I cried whenever Orland and I saw anything wonderful that I knew he would have loved. My father had always said, "If I would go there, I would get down on my knees and kiss the earth. I would not be ashamed." So when I came to Israel, I did that for him. And when I stood for the first time in the midst of the ruins of the ancient Jewish fort on the high cliff of Masada, I thought about our forebears who had fought until their last breath to hold this fort and of their faith in the face of the Roman conquerors, and verse 5 of Psalm 137 sounded loud in my mind: "If I forget thee, O Jerusalem."

I have experienced many wonderful things in the years that followed, but nothing has been quite as meaningful for me as once again being able to be proud of being a Jew, celebrating our Jewish heritage in joy and freedom. I have become proud of my Jewish heritage and could not be more humble and grateful.

CHAPTER 9

From Winnipeg to Toronto

You shall not fear – "Fear Not, O Israel," *Sabbath and Festival Prayer Book*

Much during those years when I was a cantor's wife in Winnipeg was wonderful. It felt good to be a "somebody," a "cantorina" as some of the older and friendlier members of the congregation fondly called me. I loved the title and frequently compared myself to Margaret Trudeau (albeit only in terms of the age difference between us and our husbands). I adored my husband and worried in little wifely ways about him: Was he eating properly? Was he perhaps working too hard? Was he taking care of his voice? When I saw him on the *bimah* (the platform at the front of the synagogue sanctuary), he was my fairytale prince come to life and praying with such heavenly fervour, both by himself and with the choir, that my soul was sent soaring up to God. As for my children, I doted on them. As soon as they were old enough, I would dress them up in similar dresses and take them to synagogue to show them off.

But I still suffered from residual guilt and pain for having survived the Holocaust when so many others had perished, and I was at odds with some of the wealthier congregants who, I felt, never empathized with me. I was even criticized for not allowing my daughters to run around in pants and for being too protective of them. But they were my "gift from God," my real life little dolls, and through them I think I was making up for my lost doll, Pani, as well as appeasing my guilt for having survived the Holocaust when so many other children had been "discarded." It was, I think, my destiny to live and to have children. I would smile on the outside at my critics, but sometimes I was crying and screaming inside even though I could never speak of my feelings.

As time went on, one area of our life became a constant worry. I was concerned about the tension between Orland and the congregation. While we both had many good friends in the congregation, there were some members I was uneasy about. I had been brought up to have and to show great respect to our religious leaders and was troubled by the sheer disrespect shown for our faith by people who should have known better. Certainly, Rosh Pina had its share of devout congregants, but there were also congregants who would bring comic books to service, hiding them inside their prayer books and reading them instead of praying. Moreover, was it really necessary to announce the score of a football game from the pulpit? And how could people not be transported by the melodious and soulful prayers Orland sang, accompanied by a fully trained choir of men and women, and instead sit fidgeting and wanting the service to be over with? These same individuals paid Orland lavish compliments to his face while criticizing him behind his back. I just could not reconcile the fact that these people could be so wealthy and successful in business, yet lack the rudimentary respect and honour for their rabbi and *chazzan*, treating them instead like employees. Every time my husband would come home and tell me about the bickering, unkind remarks, and snide jealous comments, I would take it very much to heart.

Orland, however, was determined to make the best of it. I would often oppose him and ask him to quit and try another line of work, but he wouldn't hear of it. He continued to work hard and was a very active cantor, officiating at Shabbat and holiday services and celebrations, teaching the *bar mitzvah* boys and *bat mitzvah* girls, and visiting the sick. He tried in many ways to enrich the lives of the members of the congregation and the wider Winnipeg Jewish community by writing articles about Jewish liturgy and liturgical music in the Rosh Pina Bulletin and organizing annual fundraising concerts, which were outstanding cultural events with many guest participants. He also worked tirelessly with the synagogue choir director and the choir of twenty-five men and women.

He and I worked as a team, making our life within the congregation and the community a success. I became active in the synagogue and did some fundraising of my own. To my surprise, I was good at it. We also became very good friends with Rabbi Irwin E. Witty, head of the Winnipeg Hebrew School that our girls attended, and his wife, Shulamith, and together we accomplished a lot of good work, including organizing fundraising drives for the school.

By 1965 when Judy was six years old and Lesley was three, I was finding it increasingly more difficult to attend all the luncheon and dinner events I was invited to as *chazzante*. It was hard for me to be the "decoration," to be expected to put on a smiling face at the head table of every event – and on some weekends, there could be two or three celebrations – regardless of whether I could or wanted to do it. I wanted to spend more time with my children, to say nothing of the fact that it was very costly having to buy new clothes for these occasions and having to hire reliable babysitters, paying for all of these things from my husband's salary.

I tried hard to comply with all the demands on my time, but slowly I began to realize that no amount of co-operation and good will on my part could influence how successful Orland would be. It became obvious that a cantor was not appreciated in North America the same way as he was in Europe where he was looked upon as someone special and accorded a great deal of respect. I heard about some congregations in North America that even changed cantors every few years and tried someone new, as if cantorial singing was a form of entertainment. The rabbi–cantor relationship can also be a very delicate one. During our time at Rosh Pina, we had three or four rabbis come and go. Some were pleasant and easy to get along with; others could be quite difficult and overbearing.

And then there was the ever-present politics, something that now I realize is probably part of all organized religion but at that time truly bothered me. The misunderstandings, jealousy, pettiness, and rudeness became increasingly difficult to bear as time went by, and I often wished I were not Jewish so I wouldn't have to deal with the politics of the congregation. How naive I was then, but having survived so much anti-Semitism in Hungary, I really expected some kind of ideal perfect synagogue here in Canada, something that did not and obviously could not exist in real life.

In the summer of 1967, a month or so before the High Holidays, Orland began to experience severe back pain and could hardly walk. His pain was so bad he couldn't even go to the bathroom. We were at the cottage that we used to rent for two months every summer when the pain started, but I found a doctor who came and gave Orland an injection of Demerol, a powerful painkiller. As soon as he got the injection, though, Orland had a serious allergic reaction. His eyes rolled back in his head, and I thought he would die. As soon as he could be moved, I drove him, Judy, Lesley, and all our belongings back to the city, making three round-trips of more than four hours each, first leaving Orland at the cottage and taking home the children to my mother, then bringing home Orland as he lay in pain on the back seat of the car, and finally closing up the cottage and bringing home our belongings.

His pain became so severe that I insisted he go to the Mayo Clinic in Minnesota for a complete check-up. There they told us it was definitely a slipped disc in his back, and he was put in a full body cast from breast to hip. That was how he chanted the High Holiday services that year, leaning against the podium in extreme pain, yet singing his heart out. Orland's rendition of the *Musaf* services on Rosh Hashanah and Yom Kippur, his chanting of *Kol Nidre*, and his blowing of the *shofar* to conclude the Yom Kippur service were so heartfelt that it must have been hard for the congregation not to feel that his prayers were going straight to heaven. He put so much love and true talent into his prayers to God that I think we all believed he was singing on behalf of each one of us, and we could feel assured our prayers would be answered.

To add to the pain from the slipped disc, Orland caught a bad cold right after the High Holidays, and I tried to get him to stay home to take care of it. Nevertheless, when he was asked to come to a meeting at the synagogue, he decided to go in spite of being ill, and by Succoth, he was in bed with viral pneumonia. When the doctor came, he held me responsible for my husband's utter foolishness, but Orland was determined and officiated all through Succoth with pneumonia. His devotion to Rosh Pina was not reciprocated. The following summer when we went to Israel to visit his family, I had no doubt in my mind that when we returned, it would be high time for us to negotiate a long-term contract with the synagogue so we could plan for our family's future. When we got back from our trip, however, we learned to our shock and dismay that the congregation had been interviewing other cantors.

Orland received many recommendations from the Cantors Assembly of America for bigger and better positions, mainly in the United States, but some in Toronto as well. We travelled together to these interviews and auditions. I found these "trials," as they were called, very degrading. The protocol was that the Cantors Assembly of America would be notified of an available position, and they would contact any qualified cantors who would then get in touch with the congregation. Then the congregation would ask for an audio tape with samples of each cantor's singing. If they liked what they heard, they would follow up with an invitation to the cantor (with the more respectful synagogues asking the cantor's wife, too) to come for an interview. The interviews would be conducted at the synagogue by a handful of congregants who would ask the cantor to sing random prayers from the Shabbat and holiday services. Sometimes the contract would be negotiated there and then, but other times, the leaders of the congregation would notify the cantor in writing a week or two later. Occasionally, a synagogue would ask the cantor to come for Shabbat services and give the entire congregation the opportunity to hear him and to voice their opinion. To me, this approach gave the candidate cantor the proper professional respect he deserved. Most of the time, however, these "trials" felt to me like just another cold, business transaction, something not befitting men who had devoted their lives to learning a holy art requiring mind, body, and soul.

In the end, however, these interviews helped us make up our minds that this was not the life we were looking for. We also came to realize that we did not want to raise our children in the United States. We had both moved around quite a bit in our lives and decided it was time to settle down and make a home in a place where there was a good environment in which to bring up our girls. We did not want a life that depended on the whims of a handful of people. We trusted in a Higher Being, Who would lead us in the right direction.

Two of my brothers, Peter and Tibi, were already living in Toronto, so we decided to move there. Orland left for Toronto right after Passover, but I stayed on in Winnipeg with my mother and the girls to sell the house and ship our belongings, which took most of the summer. My mother, ten-year-old Judy, seven-year-old Lesley, and I arrived in Toronto on the overnight train from Winnipeg on October 31, 1969, just in time for Halloween. Orland had found us a three-bedroom basement apartment on Fraserwood Avenue, a street in a neighbourhood of six-plexes that seemed home in those days to almost every Jewish immigrant to Toronto, but we were all staying at Peter and Manyi's house until our furniture arrived and we got the apartment ready.

Moving to Toronto allowed us to open a new page in our lives, but it also meant some painful closures. Of course, it was difficult to leave Pali and his family, and it was heartbreaking to have to leave my father's remains as well. After we moved, my mother, Peter and

Manyi, and Orland and I often travelled back to Winnipeg to see my brother and his family and to visit my father's grave. As big a change as the move was, though, Orland and I never regretted our decision, and I have often felt that the next few years were the most productive and harmonious years of our lives, right there in our basement apartment with my mother, God bless her, living with us.

There were many things to attend to as soon as we arrived, the most important of which was to find a school for the girls. We enrolled the girls at the Associated Hebrew School where Orland was teaching music. Moving to Toronto and changing schools was a difficult adjustment for the girls. Coming from a relatively small city like Winnipeg where everyone knew them as "the cantor's children" to this big city of Toronto where no one knew them or thought they were anything special was a harsh new reality for them. Of all of us, they found it the most difficult to adjust to their new lives, and they missed their classmates at Winnipeg Hebrew School. But in time, they settled into their new school and lifestyle.

My mother and I spent a week cleaning the apartment and waiting for our furniture to arrive from Winnipeg, and then I began to check the daily newspaper ads for work. Our financial situation was a difficult one. We began our life in Toronto with only the one year's severance pay that Orland had received from Rosh Pina after thirteen years as their cantor. When someone told us about an investment that could double our money, we decided to take a chance, and, needless to say, we lost almost everything, managing to retain only about $4,000. Nor was it easy for me to find a job with no particularly marketable skills and my still-limited written English, but I was determined. I looked in the newspaper every day and finally saw an ad in the Thursday paper a week after we arrived in Toronto saying that a company that manufactured children's clothing was looking for a Girl Friday. I didn't know what a Girl Friday was, but I called them anyway. Before I had a chance to tell them all about the qualities I had that would make me perfect for the job, they told me that they had received so many applications that they weren't even going to take my name. They said they were going to begin interviewing at eight o'clock on Monday morning and that I should call back on Tuesday; perhaps they would look at some more people then. At seven-thirty Monday morning, I showed up at the company. Half an hour later, I was hired for what I was told was minimum wage at the time – 58¢ an hour – without ever having seen a single other applicant. This was my first experience working in sales – I had, in effect, "sold" myself – and I found I had a built-in aptitude for it. Perhaps I had inherited this ability from my parents.

A more significant change, though, occurred in Orland's work-life. As soon as he came to Toronto, Orland began to seriously consider a new career in real estate and enrolled in a real estate course. I think it was only for the love of his family that he made this difficult decision. Only a person who cherished his wife and adored his children as much as he did could give up his life's vocation and begin a totally new career – and do so without regretting his decision for a moment. He had made up his mind, and he never once said he was unhappy with his decision or complained about the sacrifice he had had to make for his family.

In the fall of 1970, almost a year after we moved to Toronto, the Rosh Pina Synagogue called Orland to ask him to come to Winnipeg to discuss returning as their cantor. He very much wanted to go back and talk to them, and this time I went with him as an adult, a person with experience who could advise him, no longer the shy naive girl he married all those years ago. Our visit proved healing, and if we had any earlier ill feelings towards our previous employers, they were all washed away. The congregation made Orland a very generous offer that they hoped he would not be able to refuse. We told them we would have to think about it.

I remember that we spoke very little about the offer on our flight back to Toronto. When we landed at the airport, we held hands, squeezing tight, and turned to each other.

"At last, we are home," we whispered in unison.

My life as a cantor's wife was over, but when I think back now to those years in Winnipeg, I have great memories of that time in my life. I only wish I had had a greater understanding at the time for people's idiosyncrasies because I could have been happier instead of being angry and hypercritical with people I did not understand. I had very little admiration or tolerance then for what money can get you nor any idea what it takes to be a successful business person. I am grateful that I have been able to change this judgemental aspect of my character and that now I take every person for what he or she is, rather than trying to force them into a mould of the person I think they should be. I can relax now, secure in my place in the Canadian mosaic. It did not come easily to me to change, but I now take pride in the person I have become, outgoing and not easily intimidated, no matter where I am or with whom.

Even though we decided not to return to Rosh Pina, Orland continued singing as a cantor during our first few years in Toronto, freelancing at different synagogues outside Toronto for their High Holiday services. He loved being a cantor, and this was an opportunity for him both to keep up with his music and to make some extra money on top of selling real estate. Because these engagements were all out of town, the girls and I always accompanied him. Eventually, though, Orland gave up these temporary engagements. The synagogues paid for our family to travel with him, but it was very difficult for Orland to adjust to the travelling and to shift from his day-to-day real-estate-agent mindset to a cantorial one. Moreover, just serving in a congregation for the High Holidays never gave him the opportunity to "connect" with the congregation or to get to know them as he would have liked to. It wasn't easy for the girls and me either to always be away from home for the holidays.

Even when he stopped singing professionally, he continued to listen to his favourite operas and cantorial pieces and practised his repertoire every day throughout his life. He wanted to make sure this beautiful art he so cherished was preserved so he made arrangements to leave all his music, his life's work, to the Cantors Institute in Israel. On one of our visits to Israel, he finalized his agreement with the Institute, and I made sure this agreement was promptly and properly honoured according to his wishes after his untimely death.

I had been at my Girl Friday job for perhaps six or seven weeks when I saw another newspaper ad that said that Montreal Interglass Corporation, a company selling Duralex glassware, dinnerware, and gift items, was opening a showroom in Toronto. I knew about this product, which is made of a glass-like material that is virtually unbreakable, because it is popular in Israel, and I had bought a dozen small clear Duralex bowls for myself on my trip there in 1968. The company was looking for a salesman who could travel and sell their product. At the time, I did not even know whether there was such a thing as a "travelling saleswoman," but I answered the ad anyway, signing my letter "O. Verrall." They wanted to interview me and asked me to come to the 1970 Hardware Show, which was then on in Toronto, to meet with the president, who was in from Montreal. Here I was, thirty-three years old, a former cantor's wife accustomed to dressing modestly in long skirts at a time when everyone else was wearing mini-skirts. Besides, I was almost entirely inexperienced in business, to say nothing of being a little anxious about the kind of impression I would make. But life was making me a go-getter, and what I did know was that I wanted this job very badly. What I didn't know, but soon found out at the show, was that the president of the company, Thomas D. Spitzer, was a Hungarian about my age and a devout Jew. Would this be a good sign or a bad one, I wondered.

When I got to the show, I went to the Duralex booth and watched one of their demonstrations. Duralex glasses were stacked in a pyramid on a long, narrow table, and someone was throwing baseballs at them. When the glasses fell down, they did not break, and even if they crumbled occasionally, they did so in such a way that the user wouldn't be cut. I watched the demonstration and said to myself, "That's easy. I can do that."

When I met with the president, I could imagine him saying to himself, "Who is she? She has no experience." But I mentioned that I knew about the product and even owned some pieces, and I was so full of enthusiasm that he took a chance and hired me on the spot. He told me I would have to travel in the city and around Ontario and sell the product to wholesalers and buyers for large chain stores. He offered me an excellent salary, a car, and a map that I knew would come in very handy since I didn't know the city, let alone the province, and would probably get lost a lot in the beginning. He said someone would train me for a little while and then I would be on my own. Even though I felt rather badly about leaving my first job so soon, I was very excited about this new opportunity and couldn't pass it up. I told my new boss I couldn't start right away because I would need to give a week's notice at my present job, and we were both fine with that. I was to work successfully and happily at M.I.C. for thirteen years, leaving only because Orland asked me to join him in selling real estate.

Now our little family could begin to breathe a little easier. We had one excellent, steady salary coming in plus the added bonus of a second car. I took to business like a fish to water. Orland sometimes resented the fact that I was often taken advantage of: working hard all day and then having to be on the telephone, sometimes until four in the morning, discussing upcoming shows, only to have to be back on the road or in the office at nine o'clock. But I didn't mind. Nothing was too hard for me. I took care of my home and family, cooked, baked cheese buns, made *gefilte* fish, and still had time to prepare for Shabbat every week and for holidays. Looking back, I don't know how I had the energy to keep it up, but I did. Happiness has always given me boundless energy, and I was very happy. I loved every minute of work and felt that I was truly contributing to the company.

In return, the company made me feel important, and I earned some great rewards, including bonuses and trips.

Thank God my mother was living with us, though, because that meant I didn't have to worry about the children when I was away on the road during the day or if I was going to be late for dinner. I always made sure, however, that I was there for my children every night to talk to them and discuss their day at school. I could see my mother beginning to change from the person I had known as a child. She was now able to demonstrate her affection openly by hugging and kissing. She could give my children all the love they needed, perhaps more easily than she had been able to give it to me when I was a child. As a grandmother, she fulfilled herself, and she began to feel that Toronto was her home. She made friends and settled into life as a Canadian, even becoming a snowbird and going to Florida for a few weeks in January every year.

Orland, too, soon found success in his new career. He was very good at selling real estate, winning prize after prize and always being the number one salesman. His excellent knowledge of English, French, Italian, German, and Yiddish came in very useful in his work, and because he was charming and had a very easy-going, accommodating outlook on things, many doors opened to him. Whenever I asked him if he liked what he was doing, he would always say that he had to love everything. "That is life," he would say. "If you love life, you are happy. If you like what you are doing, you are happier." Yes, finally we had all settled down, life was good, and time was flying. Before we turned around, the children were teenagers.

In May 1971, Judy turned twelve and wanted a *bat mitzvah*. We celebrated her special day with a dinner at home for family and for some friends who came in from Winnipeg for the occasion (although sadly, Pali and Zsuzsi couldn't make it). Afterwards, Judy had a slumber party for her many girlfriends. Both Judy and Lesley were very popular in their early teenage years, and many Saturday nights I served as their chauffeur, driving them to and picking them up from *bar* and *bat mitzvah* parties and celebrations. Neither Judy nor Lesley was particularly happy about their strict eleven o'clock (and later midnight) pick-up time, and sometimes I wondered where the other parents were and whether I was the only one who seemed to care about a proper upbringing for daughters.

As for life in Toronto, I loved everything about it. I had missed the sophistication of Budapest when I lived in Winnipeg, and now I revelled in the big city atmosphere of Toronto. Finally, I told myself, I had awoken from a long sleep. In Winnipeg, there had been very little cultural life at the time we lived there, and the long hard winters gave the city a quiet small-town atmosphere. Toronto offered theatre, music and art – all the things I had loved when I lived in Budapest. Orland and I both worked very hard and loved every moment of it. Our children made lots of friends, and our home was always open to them, day and night, for lunch and supper and even sleepovers. We attended our synagogue of choice, and Shabbat and holiday celebrations were occasions to look forward to and to spend with family and friends of our own choosing.

We became reacquainted with our friends Ethel and Israel Stercz from Winnipeg, who lived nearby. Israel had also been a cantor, and he and Orland spent many a Saturday afternoon after Sabbath services talking about music. Ethel and I would go for long walks, talking about our favourite subjects and sharing our problems. I even ran across some old friends from my schooldays in Budapest. One day when we had taken the girls to buy shoes, I saw a young boy, perhaps six or seven years old, being scolded in Hungarian by his parents for running around. For some reason, the father looked very familiar, although I just couldn't place him. Then it struck me – the father was none other than Tibi Klein, a man I had met in Budapest when I was a sixteen-year-old modelling children's dresses for Central Dress Designing and Planning Industry. We became friends after I graduated and was assigned to work at the same place as he did. He was engaged to be married at the time. Tibi, his wife,

Ilonka, and I are still friends today and often get together to compare grandchildren stories.

During these first few years in Toronto, my mother became very anxious for us to own our own home, and she enlisted Orland as her partner to go and look at houses. As I had papered and painted the walls, made the drapes, and furnished our apartment, I had grown to love our current home and was very comfortable and at peace there. I had everything I needed and wasn't particularly interested in moving to something bigger and "nicer." The children were settled, and we had many close friends in a neighbourhood that was filled with newcomers. People were always welcome at our home, and it was a constant open house where people could come for the evening or stay over. New Year's Eve was always a special time, and we threw some wonderful parties. I didn't really want to move. But my mother wouldn't let go of the idea, and when she got home from Florida in 1973, she and Orland began looking in earnest for a house to purchase, taking me to see any that they liked. Finally that March, they found one they loved, and I gave my blessing. Moving day would be June 1, and my mother was thrilled.

Before we knew it, April had rolled around and it was time to prepare for Passover. The day of the first *seder*, my mother and I had both been working hard since early morning, when around eleven o'clock she suddenly sat down and called me to come and sit down beside her on the sofa. I knew her well enough to see that there was something very wrong with her.

"Please take me to the hospital," she said. She had been complaining since January about pain in her shoulders and about feeling tired and run down, but not even the best specialists had been able to come up with a reason for her pain or her exhaustion. Now I felt it was serious. "I'm sorry," she said, "to leave you with all this work, but I just can't go on any longer." I helped her dress to go out. Then with all the tenderness and outward optimism I could muster, even though my stomach was churning from fear and anxiety, I drove her to the hospital and stayed with her until she was comfortably settled in. Then in her usual no-nonsense way, she sent me home to prepare the first *seder* for my family.

We had to celebrate that Passover without my mother, who remained in the hospital for two weeks while she underwent extensive tests. In the meantime, we went on with our lives, and I continued to work travelling around Ontario. My mother was readmitted to the hospital in May for further tests. The day my mother's results came back was a particularly beautiful day in early May, as I recall, a day that gave no hint of the pain that was to come. I was driving from Toronto to St. Catharines, a drive I particularly loved. The fruit trees were covered with spring blossoms, which reminded me of candy floss. I smiled as I imagined the trees being decorated by hand, the sweet pink and white cotton candy being applied one blossom at a time, and I breathed in the sweet aroma through my open car window as I drove. Eventually, I turned into a plaza on the mountain in Hamilton to make some business calls, relax over a cup of coffee, and call home to see if there was any news yet from the hospital.

The news was shattering. My mother had advanced cancer, and there was little the doctors could do for her. Right there at a table in the food court, I broke down. As I sat weeping, a salesman I hardly knew sat beside me and tried to comfort me by telling me how he had lost his wife to cancer. I appreciated his kindness, but it was very little comfort to me at that time. He offered to drive me back to Toronto, but I pulled myself together and drove home alone. This was not a time for me to wallow in my own pain or give in to my own feelings. My mother needed me and I had to carry on. I had to be strong – for my mother, for my family, for myself.

When my mother was discharged from the hospital, we started packing, getting ready for the move to our new home. On the day of our move, my mother became very weak, and we drove her back to the hospital, which again admitted her. As we moved into our beautiful house, we prayed silently for her return, and the first thing we did was to prepare a bedroom for her. Our prayers were answered this time, and she did return home from that short hospital stay. She kissed every *mezuzah*, crying from both happiness and exhaustion. She settled into her room and thanked God that He had let her live to see the day we had our own home.

Over the next months, I set about making our home beautiful, picking up bargains on my many business trips in and out of town, putting up new wallpaper, and generally turning the house into a warm, inviting home. Soon our house became my pride and joy. Whenever my mother felt a little stronger, she would come shopping with me to help me make decisions about the things I wanted to buy. On one such trip, we both fell in love with a solid rosewood wall unit, three metres long. At that time, very few people in Canada were buying this type of furniture, but we loved it because it reminded us of the furniture we had had in Hungary before the war. She insisted on buying me the unit out of her savings as a gift for our new home. I still cherish this piece of furniture both as the last gift my beloved mother gave to me and because it brings back to me the joys and beauty of our mother–daughter relationship and reminds me of my happy early childhood.

My mother was in and out of hospital over the next weeks. Each time she came home, she would thank God for letting her enjoy our home just a little longer. As the weather became warmer, she would sit outside in the back yard, enjoying the warm weather and the flowers she so loved. But soon, her visits to the hospital became more frequent, and she had to remain there longer and longer. I was with her constantly, making her as comfortable as possible, gently massaging her, telling her good news, cooking for her, and feeding her. But she had no appetite and would blame my cooking. Many of the lunches I made for her went down the toilet along with my tears. I was too naive and distraught to realize it was her condition and *not* my cooking that kept her from eating, reproaching myself for not being a "good" daughter and becoming very frustrated. My brothers

– even Pali from Winnipeg – came frequently to visit her, but even they couldn't reassure me that I was doing the best I possibly could for her.

In July, my mother's hip broke as she was just lying in bed, and the pain became unbearable. The attending doctors told us she had to have an operation, even though she would probably have very little chance of surviving. I just prayed she wouldn't suffer. The day of the operation, her former G.P., Dr. A. Blau, who was retired at that point, came to the hospital early in the morning and sat with me, holding my hand through the long hours of her operation. I am still amazed and overwhelmed by his kindness to me and still feel grateful to him. After the operation, Zsoka and Sanyi Mandel, friends of Manyi and Peter, came and waited for me in the hospital lobby until midnight to make sure I got home safely. Their kindness, too, has stayed with me as an example of how far friends would go, and it moved and comforted me.

My mother survived the operation, and we hired a private nurse for two nights so I could go home to rest, although most of the time I refused to leave her side. As I sat with her, we never talked of illness or dying. She did not want to; she was so afraid of cancer because some friends of hers had died from it. She often spoke of her own mother, though, whom she had loved with utter devotion. She told me that when her mother died, she had closed her eyes with kisses, and I knew that soon it would be my turn to do the same thing with my mother. But most of the time, I simply sat by her bedside, telling her about the girls and Orland and talking of other everyday things. We celebrated my birthday that year at her bedside, and as we hugged and kissed, I tried to describe my feelings for her and how proud I was to have her as a mother. I could not possibly imagine at that time how much I would miss her, but I felt that I was finally coming of age. I knew that soon I would have to learn to mother myself.

One morning towards the end of July, I arrived at the hospital and found my mother's bed empty. Fortunately, a nurse came into the room before I had a breakdown, thinking that my mother had passed away. The nurse told me my *aχ en draga Anyukam* (my dear Mother) was very near the end and had been moved into her own room, closer to the nursing station. *Anyuka* (Mother) looked shrunken but peaceful and alert when I came into the room, a room that was full of sunlight even though the blinds were drawn. She was such a lady, in deeds as well as looks, and I thought of how much courage and strength she had shown during her difficult life, especially the horrendous years of the war. I kissed her, my wet cheek rubbing against hers, and she wiped the tears off my face. For the last time, she asked me to help her write a letter to her cousin in Israel, whom she had visited twice after my father, who had never made it to Israel, passed away. It was only then, while she was dictating that letter, that she expressed some of what she felt about her illness and dying in a way meant for me as she could not tell me these feelings of hers directly. As she spoke haltingly and I sat writing, we both knew that these were her departing words. She became more and more tired and paused often to renew her strength. I held her hand, kissing it, and moistened her dry mouth with wet swabs. Then she continued to dictate and I to write until I finished the letter in the late afternoon.

My mother died July 25, 1973. She was seventy-one years old and I was thirty-seven. When the time came for us to part, the parting was gentle and peaceful, but it left a deep scar on me. As I kissed her eyes closed, I prayed I had contributed some pleasure to her life. I recalled her story about how they rang the church bells in our little Hungarian town when I was born. I had always tried to live up to the expectations of being born the girl, the princess, whom she had longed for after giving birth to three sons. *Aχ en Anyukam legnayob orome* (My mother's greatest pleasure) came from my marrying a *chaχχan* (cantor) who was a loving and caring "fourth son" and not just a son-in-law to her and my giving her two beautiful granddaughters to love and help raise.

I am only sorry that my mother and father had to be buried in different cities and that they who had always been together in life were parted in death. I wanted to take the remains of both of them to Israel, but my brothers each wanted to have at least one parent they could go and visit. We did not want to take my mother to Winnipeg or make the decision for her that Winnipeg was to be her resting place. So my brothers and I discussed it, and I went along with their wishes to bury her in Toronto.

The Toronto Hungarian-Jewish newspaper, *Menorah*, ran a beautiful death notice for my mother, which read (translated):

> Szarvas city's once-celebrated beauty, Barsony Mariska, closed her eyes forever this last week in Toronto. She lived to be seventy-one years. Great numbers of friends, relatives, and family members came to the Bathurst Lawn Cemetery to pay their last respects to her memory. The ceremony was very moving and an outstanding farewell speech was given by Dr. Zagon Rabbi, which summed up her outstanding qualities in life. It felt so real, it was as if she was there amongst us. Her sons, Dr. Peter Barsony, Paul Barsony, and Tibor Barsony; her daughter, Olga; her son-in-law and daughters-in-law and her seven grandchildren will miss her and in their grief, we feel with them and turn to them with consolation.

Here I was again, facing another huge adjustment, my mother's death leaving a huge missing piece in my life. I cannot remember anything from the time I closed her eyes until Passover the next year. I do not even remember the funeral or sitting *shiva* (the seven-day period of ritual mourning). I spent the next twelve months as a zombie, completely blanking the entire year from my mind. I believe that my mother's death was one of the greatest traumas of my life, and my family and friends told me later that they feared I was going to have a nervous breakdown. But I didn't have the breakdown – at least not then. My collapse was to come upon me very slowly, only manifesting after several more great tragedies in my life.

By the time Passover rolled around the following April, I knew that I just couldn't handle preparing for it and insisted that we take our children to Israel instead. I packed up all my mother's elegant clothes and took them to Israel to donate to charity. It was the best thing I could have done, and it gave me a certain degree of closure and some peace. But my biggest step to healing came one night in July about a year after her death. I got up in the middle of the night when everyone was sleeping because I decided that I would have to try and bake a cake, something I hadn't been able to do since my mother died because it reminded me of what she had always said – "Why? Do you expect me to die?" – when I would ask her for her recipes. I cried and cried, finally starting to grieve for her and my great loss, but I managed to bake my first cake since she had passed away.

Today in my seventh decade of life, I am only now becoming conscious of why Passover has always been so difficult for me as an adult. I've always followed the observances of the holiday just as I learned them from my mother. Preparing for Passover takes a great deal of work, but it would not be so hard if it weren't for what the holiday signifies for me. My first memories of Passover as a child in Szarvas before the war are happy ones with my family joyously gathered together in a house filled with the delectable aromas of my mother's cooking and baking. But then during Passover in 1944, our family was wrenched from our home and taken to the ghetto. Tall, scary men in uniforms came to our house, took away my doll, and ordered us to leave. After the war, when we should have been permitted to try and heal ourselves and put our lives together again, the world around me was hostile and dangerous. That first Passover after the war when my friend Ilona did not come to our *seder* because her parents did not want her to associate with Jews was a shock and a tremendous disappointment to me. And then almost thirty years later, my mother's illness came to spoil our joy as we prepared for Passover together in Toronto. I dread this Festival of Deliverance, as Passover is also known, and, try as I might, I become mentally and physically more and more paralyzed as the *seders* draw near. Year after year, the pattern has repeated itself, but nevertheless, even though I don't want to make Passover, I still do so, if only for my children and grandchildren.

I am grateful to my mother, to both my parents, for teaching me all the special Jewish traditions that make up my life and the lives of my children and grandchildren. Every year, bit by bit, I tell them about my early childhood and about the happy and difficult experiences of my life. Through these younger generations, my mother will live on, and her values and traditions will live on as well. Her life will remain within me; it will never leave me. We are part of each other forever, and it continues on with my daughters, never-ending, in a circle of unconditional love.

CHAPTER 10

Strength, Courage, and Faith

All life's loves, small and great, / Are treasured in my love of you, / In my love of all of you. – "Harken, O My People!" *Sabbath and Festival Prayer Book*

After my mother died, my children missed her terribly. I, too, felt a great emptiness that couldn't be filled. In addition to the loss, my life became more difficult because I had to take over the entire management of our household – shopping, cooking, and cleaning this bigger house we now had – while I still worked full-time. I have often thought that our lives were much better in the old basement apartment. Now that I had a beautiful house and garden, I had very little time to enjoy it. Still, life has to go on, and we settled back into the everyday events of it – the good, the ordinary, and the bad.

As hard as I tried to be a good mother, I felt something was missing. My children were entering their critical teenage years, and they desperately needed a full-time mother. It wasn't a question of love; I loved them with all my heart. I was their playmate as long as they needed one and then a confidante and friend later on. I gave them everything even before they asked for it. I dreamed their lives even before they were living them. But was that all that was required to be a good mother? I was raising them from instinct, shaping and shielding their every thought and step lest it lead to pain or disappointment, mapping out for them each perfect step to what I thought would be their happiness. But the way I mothered them also meant that I didn't allow them to develop on their own. As far as Orland was concerned, as loving and caring a father as he was, he was from the old school – strict and critical. We were what is now commonly called a dysfunctional family. We most certainly did not know how to communicate effectively.

Judy and Lesley strained against our loving leash, but they could not voice their unhappiness without getting into constant fights with their father. I was brought up not to fight, and conflict scared me. I was not used to it nor any good at it, and I looked for ways to prevent confrontations between the girls and Orland. I began covering up for them to keep the peace with my husband. But I lost, and all of us walked on eggs around each other, unable to have any open discussions about anything that mattered. We could not talk plainly about the girls' futures, their partners, religion, or even their growing up as women. I was giving my daughters my tainted, narrow, old-country view of sex that I had learned from my own mother, while at the same time trying to be a modern mom. As for them, the girls began growing apart from me. They helped very little around the house and stopped sharing their lives with me. I would have sold my soul to keep our friendship open and alive, and I craved intimacy and closeness with them especially since I was still hurting over the loss of my own mother.

Materially, we gave our teenage girls everything we were able to. We took them on holidays almost every summer. In 1976, we drove as a family to the Catskills and from there to Montreal where we had tickets for the Olympics, a bonus from my employer. We took the girls to Israel, to Hawaii, and to Disney World. I think, though, that I was more excited by Cinderella's Castle than they were, although I tried to hide it. The thwarted child in me never got enough of being a child. I did not know then that it was "normal" to feel that way; I was afraid of criticism and ashamed to show my emotions openly.

Our daughters had lots of friends, and because I always encouraged them to bring their friends home, the house was always full of young people, something that I cherished. When Judy finished high school, she went to Israel on her own for three months, and when Lesley graduated, she went backpacking with two girlfriends to Europe and Israel. Little did we know then that the things we gave them and did for them could not sugar-coat all the criticism and judgment we were pouring on them. The resentment they felt but couldn't voice was to take a heavy toll later on.

When Judy finished her BA with honours, she planned to go on in the field of psychology, specializing in working with mentally challenged children. We had always instilled in both of our children a love of education so we were delighted. Both Orland and I thought it was an excellent choice for her, and we were very proud. Lesley was finishing high school at the same time, and her goal was to become a dietician. We felt so lucky to have two such extraordinary, capable, healthy, talented children and were so very proud to attend both their graduations. For me, seeing my children excel at school had an added dimension because it reminded me of how much I had wanted to go to university and how the Communists had barred me from achieving my dreams.

Orland and I continued to work hard. After I had worked at Montreal Interglass Corporation for thirteen years, Orland asked me to give up my job and join him in real estate. House sales were booming, and he felt we would make a good team and do well together. I loved my job at M.I.C. and hated real estate, but I switched and we did do well together, raising groans among the other agents when we came up with our joint working name: "a pair of overalls" (O. Verralls).

Once I started working with Orland, I was usually at an open house almost every Sunday afternoon from two to four o'clock. One Sunday, I was sitting in a well-built, clean, back-split in a very nice area of Toronto. It was the kind of house that showed well, but on this particular afternoon, there were not many visitors. As I was sitting dreamily by myself, idly contemplating why so few people had showed up, I was interrupted by the chimes of the doorbell. It was Judy and her boyfriend, Michael. They walked in, hand in hand, their faces bursting with exciting news to tell.

Judy and Michael had been friends for about a year, and during that spring and summer, their relationship seemed to have progressed to a more intimate phase. Orland and I had not really taken much notice of their budding relationship, or perhaps we just hadn't wanted to acknowledge the seriousness of what was happening between them. Both of them were still young and had a long way to go before they completed their studies. We both also had our misgivings about Michael. Good-looking and extremely intelligent, he was well brought up, having been raised in the Caribbean where both of his parents still lived. But I had a mother's sense that he was not the right boy for my daughter. He was very laid back, and I sensed a lack in him of wanting to better himself.

As Judy and Michael approached me, they asked if they could talk to me about something. "Mrs. Verrall," Michael started, "I would like to tell you that I love your daughter, Judy, very dearly, and that we have decided, Judy and I, that we would like to get married."

I think that the words "atomic bomb" would have registered more clearly on my mind than the words "get married." Here was my first daughter planning to get married. She was only twenty-two years old, and I had envisioned a golden future for her. Since she was born, I had fantasized about and anticipated how it would be. Now I was faced with a different reality. My face must have shown the shock I was feeling, but Michael went right on talking, not taking much notice of my changed expression.

"We plan to get married a year from now and have an August wedding. Both of us want our parents' blessings." As he spoke, he rocked from leg to leg, and I could tell he was very nervous. Questions kept whirling around in my head. What kind of life would they have together? Would he be able to make a living? But I forced myself to listen and to speak calmly and sensibly to them.

"How about your studies?" I asked, my fears jumping ahead of their answers, question after question popping into my head.

"We both want to drop out of school," Judy said, "and get jobs." My heart skipped a beat. Judy had been working part-time at Bell Canada since she was eighteen, and I guessed she had already asked for a full-time job there. She quickly confirmed my fears.

I asked them both to come to dinner that night to talk to Orland. Ever since Judy was a baby, she had been able to twist me around her little finger, sometimes against my better judgment. But Orland was different. He was a more conventional father, and the dinner conversation that night was a disaster. When he heard what Judy and Michael were planning, he did not try to hide his true feelings, nor did he mince words with them. He told them that they had no idea what they were doing and that he was absolutely against them getting married.

Over the next few weeks and many more discussions with Judy and Michael, my heart began to soften. Somehow I managed to convince Orland to accept the marriage, and unhappily and with great misgivings, we began to make arrangements for a wedding to take place the following August. To celebrate their engagement, we threw a large, catered cocktail party at our home for our closest friends and family. Ironically, this affair would turn out to be the last completely happy occasion we would celebrate together as a family. Fate had plans for us.

I am often held hostage by my own fears, which paralyze me for hours or days at a time. It is a cause of great unhappiness in my life. Every once in a while, I am able to surface, desperately trying to concentrate and count my blessings, but my body, mind, and spirit usually do not want to co-operate. All three seem totally bankrupt, and even though I put up a great fight and try to appreciate that I have the capacity in my life to be content and grateful, I am unable to. Perhaps all the tragedy and loss I have suffered in my life has made me unable to trust my own abilities, to believe in myself. This next period of my life would challenge me as no other ever had.

The beginning of May 1984 delivered the first of many fatal blows to come in the next few years. Peter's wife, Manyi, had been feeling ill for a month, but suddenly, the pain had become intolerable. She was admitted to hospital and had an exploratory operation on May 5, her sixtieth birthday. It was then that we learned that she had pancreatic cancer, that she had had it for a while, and that it was rapidly taking over her beautiful mind, heart, and body. She was released from the hospital with a cruel diagnosis of three to six months to live.

Manyi and I had known each other since we were children. When she and Peter were dating in Szarvas, she had lived on the same property as my friend Kati, and I often stayed over at Kati's so we could watch her and Peter from the window and catch them kissing. My dear Manyi would offer me gifts to get out of their way, and we developed a very close relationship very early on. I had loved her even more dearly ever since she became my sister-in-law in 1950. She was a very warm person and had become the loving centre of our family. Because I was so close to her and because of my natural tendencies to be a caregiver, I made sure that I spent as much time as I could with her. It was no wonder that I wanted to help her in any way I could and spend every last moment of her life with her. Indeed, I cherished our friendship until the day she died.

At the end of June while I was still distressed by Manyi's situation, an even greater tragedy hit. Orland pulled me aside one morning and showed me how severely he was bleeding when he urinated. It scared me, but he was not a complainer so I had to push him to meet with his doctor at St. Michael's Hospital. Orland would not let me come with him; he said he truly believed it was a minor thing so he didn't want me to worry. He told me to go to the office, and we would meet there as usual. As soon as he left, though, I called his doctor, who reassured me that my husband was as healthy as a person could be and not to panic, to wait at home and he would call me.

By the time the doctor called, Orland was on the operating table with one of the best surgeons in the city operating on him. The doctor apologized to me and said that there had been no time to waste. It was critical that Orland be operated on immediately even if it meant they had to get my consent over the telephone. It did not take me very long to drive to the hospital, but by the time I got there and was speaking to the surgeon, Orland was already in the recovery room. The doctor explained to me that they had had to remove my husband's left kidney, which was totally riddled with cancer. But, he reassured me, the cancer was contained in that one kidney only, and Orland would be totally fine with only one kidney for many years to come.

Now I had two patients. Of course, Orland's health was my priority, and I knew that Manyi's brother, Gyuri, had come from Hungary to be with her and she would have lots of people around her to take care of her. Orland came through the surgery very well. His stamina and dedication to total recovery was amazing, and he even told me he was looking forward to dancing with me at Judy and Michael's wedding. But it felt as if my world was in a shambles, with Manyi dying, Orland just having come through a very serious and difficult cancer operation, Lesley still off in Europe, and Judy having bridal showers. The wedding suddenly took on new importance. The whole family would be reunited by then, I told myself, with Orland's family coming from Israel as well. Soon we would have cause to celebrate. Could I dare to hope?

A few weeks later, I got a call from Judy. She was in the emergency room of another hospital. She and Michael had been about to get on a bus at the university when a car swerved in front of the bus, forcing it up on the sidewalk. The bus hit both of them. They were fine, she reassured me, and just needed a ride home. I rushed to the hospital, not knowing what to think. Judy was shaken up but not bruised or hurt. Michael was in worse shape. He was limping badly, his pants were torn, and he had bruises everywhere.

Judy's accident transported me back to Budapest that day in December 1953 when Jeno and I were hit by a jeep full of drunken Russian soldiers. My marriage to Jeno had lasted only twenty-four hours and had had very painful consequences. Judy's life and my own seemed to be running on dangerously parallel courses. Was "someone" trying to tell me something? There was far too much similarity in the circumstances. First her rush to marry this boy who was not right for her and now the accident. I had never spoken to my children about my marriage to Jeno because just the thought of it drove me close to insanity. Even now, frightened as I was for her happiness, I could not tell Judy how what was happening to her seemed to eerily mirror my own experiences. My already frail mental health was cracking, and my mind was running in aimless circles, my heart assailed with helpless feelings of unspecified guilt. But Judy and Michael were fine, I told myself. Be grateful and count your blessings.

Lesley came home from Europe while Orland was still in the hospital but just in time for the bridal party dress fittings. For some reason, though, she never wanted to come for her fitting. My concentration was scattered in so many directions that I didn't notice that my little girl was visibly and rapidly losing weight. By the end of July, she had gone from a size ten to a size seven, and it was then that I noticed a strange pattern to her eating. I didn't think too much of it at the time, but we couldn't figure out what was wrong with her. Was she in love? On drugs? Pregnant?

In July, Manyi had a setback and suffered a stroke on the right side of her brain. The slightest movement required her to exert great effort, and her speech became unintelligible. She was moved to a palliative care facility. It was the first time in my life I had heard the term "palliative care." It would not be the last.

Six weeks before Judy's wedding, I brought Orland home from the hospital. He had lost a little weight but otherwise did not look too bad. I picked him up on a Friday morning, and he asked me to drive him over to see Manyi. When we came in, there were other visitors in the room, but Orland and Manyi fell on each other's necks, hugging and kissing. But all this emotion tired Manyi out. She asked everyone to leave but requested I come back later.

I took Orland home, tucked him into bed, made sure he was comfortable, and rushed back to Manyi around five o'clock. In the short time I was gone, she had taken a turn for the worse, and I found her in terrible distress. To make matters worse, she had soiled her bed. She was struggling to clean herself, too ashamed to ask for help. Since I seemed to be the only one who could understand her gestures and mutterings and was the only one she permitted to touch her, I had come right on time. I gently cleaned her and made her as comfortable as I could. When I was finished, she seized my arm, kissing every place she could reach a thousand times, mumbling blessings for me repeatedly. Her face expressed so much love for me that she looked like a heavenly angel as I sat on her bed, putting my face close to hers. It was so hard to leave and I really didn't want to. I had stayed with her many nights before, but with Orland just out of the hospital, I had to go home. I had prepared an *Erev* Shabbat dinner to welcome him home, cooked all of his favourite foods, and set a festive table for Shabbat. We were all together, happy to be a family again, and I so wanted to believe this would be a new beginning for us all. As I left, Manyi looked at me and said, "Pray for me."

On Saturday morning, Orland insisted on going to synagogue, so of course I went with him. That evening, July 21, 1984, at around ten o'clock, I got a call from Peter that Manyi had passed away. She left a great vacuum behind because she had touched so many people. Her son-in-law made a beautiful eulogy at her funeral and spoke these meaningful words: "My mother-in-law's house was the place I first learned the true meaning and essence of love…."

With Manyi gone and Orland out of the hospital, I was spending more time at home, and it was then that I became more acutely aware of Lesley's peculiar eating habits, pushing food around on her plate to make it look as if she were eating and then running to the bathroom right after every meal. I did some research and realized that she had an eating disorder. As I probed deeper, I discovered that it had started in Israel. I wish I had never had to find out what anorexia and bulimia were and what they can do to a person, but among so many other dreadful things I was learning, I was now finding out about that, too. With very little energy to carry on, I started running on empty.

Plans for the wedding were proceeding with every little detail according to Judy's excellent but very demanding taste. Even the plans for the honeymoon were in place. The newlyweds were going to Spain, but they would not be leaving till a week after the wedding because Michael's parents would still be in Toronto and the children wanted to spend a few days with them. As for me, I couldn't even find a dress for the wedding and didn't actually have one until the last minute, but that was hardly the main issue. The Friday before the wedding, I had forty-two people at our table for dinner, including our ultra-orthodox guests from Israel. Help came from all my dear and cherished friends who shopped, cooked, and just listened to my aching heart's cries for Manyi.

The wedding photographer we hired agreed to come to our house in person with his crew on the morning of the wedding. That meant I had to prepare food and other conveniences for all the people who would congregate at our house for the wedding pictures: our immediate family; my brothers and their families; Michael's parents, brother, and sister; Orland's family; and all the bridal attendants. Still, things went along smoothly that Sunday. Lesley looked thin but pretty, and Orland was handsome in his tuxedo. When I looked at Judy in her wedding gown, I dared to feel elated.

After all the commotion of the photography session, everyone else drove off to the Shaarei Shomayim Synagogue, leaving Judy and me alone together in the house. "Behold the moment," I said to her as I noticed that the house was empty except for the two of us. On the spur of the moment, I plucked up my courage and asked my daughter to come with me to the airport and disappear. There was still time, I told her, to change her mind. At that moment, I believe Judy was tempted. Perhaps reality had begun to sink in. However, the wedding did take place that August 26, 1984, and Judy walked down the aisle looking like the prettiest bride I had ever seen. As far as the guests could tell, it was a fairy tale wedding. But to me, everything from the ceremony on was like a dream. Maybe the champagne helped, as did those tiny white pills, prescription tranquillizers that I had been taking "as required" ever since my mother died.

I only wish I could say here that Judy and Michael lived happily ever after. But the day after the wedding, they came to thank Orland's family for coming to the wedding and to say goodbye. When it came time for them to go, Judy did not want to go home with Michael. I have never seen her break down and cry the way she did that day. "What have I done, Mom?" she said. "I don't want to go back." But she did go back.

By October of the following year, Judy told us that their marriage was falling apart and they were planning to separate. Michael had finally taken a job in Montreal, but Judy was staying in Toronto and continuing to work here. By this time, Lesley's anorexia was getting more and more out of hand. She was studying at the University of Guelph, and I drove there frequently, hoping to help her through this hard time. To make matters worse, Orland did not quite understand the nature of her illness, and what's more, did not even believe there was such an illness. As far as he was concerned, this might not be normal behaviour, but it certainly was not a sickness. He just ignored it and was very uncooperative with us. At the end of her first year at Guelph, on the advice of her doctor who thought it would be better for her to be closer to home but living on her own, Lesley returned to Toronto, moved into a bachelor apartment, and began attending York University to obtain her MBA.

Orland, meanwhile, was seeing his oncologist every six months for a check-up, and each time the doctor reassured him that the cancer was in remission, telling him, "You're in better health than I am." I, on the other hand, was searching frantically for some way to help Lesley. I had devoted myself to learning as much as I could about anorexia and bulimia, and I joined a support group, looking for answers. It was agony for me because there was so little knowledge about this illness at that time, but what I did know was that many young girls died of this disease or struggled with it throughout their entire lives. I was desperate and decided to take Lesley back to Israel where the anorexia had started, thinking that it might help her take her mind off whatever had brought it on. We were in Israel for three months, and of course, the doctors who had told me that the trip wouldn't help were right. Lesley would eventually have to embark on a long and painful recovery that would include hospitalization.

During Christmas vacation that year, Judy went to visit Michael in Montreal, hoping to give their marriage one last chance. When she came back in January, I could tell within a few days that she was pregnant. She discussed the situation with Michael, and they decided to have the child. Michael came back to Toronto, and Judy worked very hard until the baby was due, carrying on even through that next very hot summer.

Judy was expecting her baby in September, and as her due date approached, we decided to have some work done in the house in case she had a son and we needed to make a *brith milah*, or circumcision ceremony. The house was in chaos, Lesley was ill, and Judy was expecting her baby in a few weeks when I received a call from Hungary. Zsofi had stomach cancer and had been operated on. Most of her stomach had been removed and the doctors were doing all they could for her, but the prognosis wasn't good. They suggested that I come and see her.

My family had continued to be close to Zsofi and Miklos after we came to Canada, and even after my father and mother passed away, we had brought Zsofi and Miklos to Canada several times and helped them financially as much as we could. For my fiftieth birthday, Orland's gift to me was to bring Zsofi and Miklos to Israel and meet them there. It was their first trip to Israel, and it made me feel so good to do that for them. Zsofi had been a second mother to me and had given me comfort when I most needed it as a child. Now she needed me. I left everything and went to Hungary.

The situation in the hospitals in Hungary was appalling. I was devastated by the condition of the beds, the bedding, and the care that patients were given there. I had to try whatever I could to help her and secretly began using American dollars to buy better treatment for Zsofi from the doctors and nurses. Of course, with Hungary still under Communist rule, I had to be careful. I could not, and would not, think about what might happen if I were caught. I was a Canadian citizen, but I had no doubt I would be thrown straight into jail.

I did whatever I could to make Zsofi more comfortable and to give her something to smile about. I bought her a beautiful doll, and the irony wasn't lost on me. Now she was the child and I the loving caregiver. Every day, I stayed with her at the hospital from early morning until late at night, and we laughed and recalled stories from my childhood as she held my hands and caressed them. I fed her ice cream, chocolate, and whatever I could get at that time in Budapest. At night, when I left the hospital, I spent time with Miklos and listened to his hopes for Zsofi's recovery. As he spoke, I suddenly saw how vulnerable he was, just another scared child fearing for the worst. But Judy's due date was fast approaching, and the day came far too soon when I had to say goodbye to both of them. I've always hated goodbyes, starting from the time my family was forced to leave Szarvas during the war. Now here was yet another goodbye, this time to my beloved Zsofi. I think my hatred of saying goodbye will stay with me for the rest of my life.

I came back from Hungary just before Rosh Hashanah, and our first grandson, Jared, was born by Caesarean section on September 16, 1987. Both Orland and I were standing outside the delivery room when he was born. As Michael and the nurses pushed Judy into the recovery room, no one stopped to tell us Judy had had a boy, but when we found out, we were both speechless at the great miracle that had occurred. Jared's *brith milah* was held on the day after Rosh Hashanah on the Fast of Gedalia. In the morning, we had the service at the synagogue and then threw a dinner celebration for him in the evening with the entire family in attendance.

Unfortunately, Orland would have only two years before his cancer recurred to get to know his grandson and to enjoy his new role as a grandfather. Even though he was in and out of the hospital for the next few years and couldn't spend too much time with Jared, I am grateful for the bond they were able to forge. As for me, Jared was just what I needed. There is no feeling in the world that can compare to being a grandmother.

My beloved Zsofi passed away on October 5, 1987. I continued to keep in close touch with Miklos, and my brothers and I often brought him to Toronto to visit with us. When he could no longer take care of himself, we put him in a home for the aged in Szeged, and when he died on June 20, 1994, my brother Tibi went back to Hungary to arrange his funeral. Later on, Tibi went back a second time to put up a tombstone for him. I think my brothers and I treated both Zsofi and Miklos as my father would have wanted.

To Orland's and my delight, Judy and Jared moved in with us for the first three months after the baby was born. Judy was breast-feeding and Jared was colicky. "Grandma" helped, and Michael came for dinners and then left. At the end of January, Judy and Jared moved back home, but things with Michael did not improve. A few months later, they decided to officially separate, and Michael moved out for good. Still, Judy insisted that Jared know and be close to his father, and she has maintained a relationship with Michael and his parents solely for Jared's benefit.

Over the next two years, however, I did not have time to cry over spilt milk. Lesley needed constant help and a great deal of time and patience to overcome her distressing illness. And I never gave up. Judy was working full-time and needed help with her son. When Jared was two and started nursery school, I would pick him up from school every day and bring him home to my house where Judy would join us later for dinner. In spite of all the hardship, I enjoyed watching Judy and her baby and loved seeing the interaction between mother and son. Even more important, the time I got to spend alone with Jared was very dear to me. These were the most precious moments in my life, and I concentrated on the joy my grandson gave me.

But fate reached in again. By April 1989, Orland's cancer had recurred, worse than before. He needed one operation after another. He was a great fighter, and I fought with him. We were determined to beat this monster. Then our friends Israel and Ethel Stercz told us about an alternative cancer treatment program called Gerson Therapy, which was offered in Mexico. We had met Israel and Ethel when we lived in Winnipeg and had forged a lifelong friendship with them. Ethel was like a sister to me, and Orland and Yisrual (as we called him) were both cantors and shared an unusual closeness. After the Sterczes left Winnipeg, they moved to Montreal and then to Toronto, settling here a few years before we did. When we arrived, we rekindled our friendship with them. We always listened to each other and helped each other as much as we could. Ethel had had a very grim and difficult life and then became ill with rheumatoid arthritis. No conventional medication seemed to help her, so she turned to alternative therapies and homeopathic healing. She had never tried Gerson Therapy but had heard about it and suggested that it might work for Orland. I checked into it and we agreed to try it. After all, we had nothing to lose.

Gerson Therapy is based on a book by Max Gerson, MD, called *A Cancer Therapy – Result of Fifty Cases*, and as soon as we heard about it, Orland wanted to go to Tijuana, Mexico, where the hospital was located. We flew to Los Angeles and were transported by a old small pick-up truck to the facility, which was housed in a Tijuana motel. As soon as we arrived and rested up, we had an orientation lecture about the treatments and schedules, our introduction to a program that was to become the focus of our lives for the next three years. Orland began the strict diet of organic fruits and vegetables that the clinic advocated, believing strongly in the program's ability to cure him. Although I had my doubts that this would help Orland, I had given him my solemn oath to try it for his sake, and I did my utmost to assure him that he would be well and live a long life. In the evenings, I would walk in the enclosed courtyard, praying to God to give me strength to believe and to carry out this very difficult regimen. My dearly beloved husband deserved this and more. And a miracle happened. I can testify that he got stronger, and I am positive that the Gerson diet and the other complementary treatments extended his life. I could not ask for more.

I bought an eighty-pound juicer that I carried back from California to accommodate the diet. Orland had to drink thirteen ten-ounce glasses of freshly squeezed juice daily, so each week I washed and prepared fifty pounds of carrots for carrot juice as well as huge amounts of vegetables for the green leaf juice; both juices also contained apples. Organic produce was very hard to obtain in those years so I was lucky to be able to get it, and I kept it in an extra fridge in our basement kitchen for a week at a time.

The making of the freshly squeezed juices every day was a lengthy procedure. First I had to grind the carrots and the apples, using an attachment that filled a large, strong cotton bag with the ground contents. Then the cotton bag had to be folded in three, very carefully, and placed under the heavy press, which in turn squeezed the juice into a container. The pressure on the cotton bag was very great because it had to be pressed until the pulp was completely dry. If the procedure was hurried and the press came down too quickly, the bag would break at the seams and explode, splashing its contents all over my white kitchen from floor to ceiling to appliances to counters to doors to me. The first time this happened, I sat down on the floor, looked around at my splattered white kitchen, and didn't know whether to laugh or cry. As I set about frantically cleaning up, my tears wouldn't come. So there I was, bespeckled with carrot juice and pulp, laughing hysterically as I went about cleaning up as best I could before the mess dried permanently. Then I calmly prepared the next juice, focussing my energy on the struggle of keeping up.

Everything in our lives became geared to cleansing Orland's body, including enemas with freshly made coffee, which I administered to him several times each day in bed, tucking a green garbage bag under him so he could eliminate right there since he was sometimes having difficulty walking or even standing up by this time. The liver injections he was taking were not allowed into Canada, but I succeeded in getting them, along with many other medications, from the United States and Europe. We went through many doctors until we found one who would help us obtain some other supplies, like needles, that we needed. I also learned to give Orland the injections myself, determined to hold onto him for as long as I could. While I cannot mention this doctor's name, he is always in my prayers for what he did for us and the kindness he showed us.

I went twenty-four hours a day, day in and day out, with very little rest or sleep. I was desperately fighting, doing things I had never even dreamed of. I started leaving notes in health food stores and asking the clinic in Mexico for names of patients in Toronto. I found five more people who were in the same or similar circumstances as we were, and we formed a support group. I never had time or wanted to feel sorry for myself. Finding out as much as I could about the cancer and sharing it with the others in the group was a challenge and became a way of life for me. One by one, everyone in that group was losing their loved ones, and the scream of an ambulance siren became a nightmare for me. I had begun crying in the shower, the only time and place I seemed to have to myself, when Lesley became ill, and now it became a routine.

Orland spent the next three years in and out of hospital. Most of the time, I kept him on the strict Gerson diet, adhering religiously twenty-four hours a day to every aspect of what was prescribed. Orland's belief never left him, and he continued to think he would get well. Many times, he asked for his sister and brother in Israel. I begged them to come, but for their own reasons, they did not feel they could make the trip. I did not want to tell Orland the truth, so I said that I wanted to go to Israel. Without his knowledge, I purchased two first-class tickets and took him to see his family again, just in time for his nephew's wedding. I have pictures of Orland dancing at that wedding, even though afterwards I had to hold him up while he urinated because his knees buckled and he would have collapsed. He didn't want me to tell his brother and sister what he was going through, but it was obvious to anyone who looked at him.

Even though Orland carried on with his diet, medications, and enemas while we were away, the toxins in his body had built up again by the time we returned from Israel, and he wanted to go back to Mexico for another round of treatment. He believed in what the clinic there was doing even though I was having some doubts by then, but it was not for me to say no. Within a few days, we arranged for our second trip. We were in Mexico for only a short time before he became paralyzed from the waist down. I would not allow him to be operated on in Mexico and had to call his brother, Jack, to come and help me bring him home to Toronto. I still don't know how we managed it. Lesley arranged for an ambulance to wait for us at the airport. We arrived in Toronto at six in the morning, and the ambulance took us straight to the emergency operating room of St. Michael's Hospital where the neurosurgeon was waiting for us.

He told us that Orland would need two surgeries but that we would have to wait and see how the first one went before he could attempt the second. The operations, on two different vertebrae, were to relieve pressure on his lower body. While Orland underwent the first operation, I fell into an exhausted sleep in the waiting room with Peter, Tibi, Marika, and my daughters surrounding me. Orland came through that difficult and serious operation, and the surgeon ordered the second to be done within forty-eight hours. Between the two operations, Orland had two incisions that almost completely girdled his body above and below the waist. I believe that even though the doctors here had ridiculed it, everything we had done in Mexico had strengthened Orland's body, and that is why he was able to withstand those two horrific operations and recover relatively quickly from them.

I stayed with Orland around the clock, coming home from the hospital only to prepare his food, medication, and enemas, which I administered to him twice a week or more without the knowledge of the doctors or nurses for fear of being thrown out of the hospital. I think that because the neurosurgeon was such a great doctor and a wonderful person they all turned a blind eye to what we were doing. I can never thank that doctor and all the staff of St. Michael's Hospital enough for what they did for us.

I believe that Orland fought so hard and went through all those surgeries and treatments because he loved us so much and because of his trust in the Almighty. He became stronger, and to his great happiness, he was soon ready to leave the hospital. He went from the hospital to the Baycrest Centre Rehabilitation Unit for three months for physiotherapy and recuperation, and being in such a Jewish atmosphere did him a lot of good. It just so happened that a great rabbi was also at Baycrest at that time and had the room next to Orland's. When men and boys from his *yeshivah* (orthodox religious school) came to visit the rabbi, he sent them over to wish my husband a speedy recovery as well. That meant a great deal to Orland.

Several times during that summer of 1992, Orland was readmitted to the hospital, but he always came home again. One morning, however, during the long holiday weekend in August, he got up, felt dizzy, and fell against our dining room table. He looked like an Auschwitz survivor by then, and I was sure he had broken his shoulder. I couldn't lift him and phoned frantically for help, but I couldn't reach a doctor. Finally, a nurse came, and together we got Orland into bed. She said that in her opinion nothing was broken, that he should just lie quietly and rest. But he was in terrible pain. I phoned Mount Sinai Hospital and was put in touch with the palliative care unit. They sent an ambulance and told us that someone would be waiting for us when we got there.

Unfortunately, the ambulance took us to Branson, the nearest hospital, not Mount Sinai. It took a whole day before they transferred us to Mount Sinai, but fortunately, there was a bone specialist on duty at Branson who eventually put a bandage around Orland's broken shoulder to make it more secure and to lessen the pain. When we got to the Mount Sinai, they removed these special bindings against my better judgment and tried to operate on his shoulder. But they couldn't do much for him. He was to live for three more weeks in great suffering.

The morphine they gave him kept him hallucinating as I sat by his bed day and night, not moving my eyes from him. He spoke very little and slept a great deal. On Thursday, August 20, he was strong enough to talk on the telephone to his brother, Jack, who was visiting their birthplace in Czechoslovakia with his family. The following day, Orland was alert and asked me to bring him a decent *Erev* Shabbat meal of his favourite veal stew. I went home to prepare his dinner, and when I came back that afternoon with the food, I found Lesley there talking to her father. She was working at Mount Sinai at the time and often came up to visit Orland. I was happy that father and daughter had finally come to an understanding with each other. Orland ate well after being such a long time on his special diet, and that night

I asked a nurse if I could remain overnight since the bed next to his was empty. They graciously allowed me to stay. During the night, I noticed that his coughing was getting worse and worse, and I was afraid he might have caught pneumonia. Each time the nurses came in, I helped them change him carefully so as not to hurt him, and we made him as comfortable as possible.

His breakfast arrived before seven o'clock on Saturday morning, and I noticed a glass of juice on his tray. He seemed to be sleeping deeply and breathing normally so I went to the bathroom and washed myself. Then I washed his face, bent over him whispering, "*Shabbat shalom*," and kissed him. He was on intravenous, and I knew he couldn't swallow the juice so I took the glass from the tray, said, "*L'chaim*" ("To life," a Jewish toast), and drank it. Tears ran down my face, and I had to turn my head away for just a moment. When I looked back, Orland's eyes were vacant. Life, as we know it, had left him.

This being Shabbat morning, there wasn't an Orthodox Jew around, and I didn't know what to do. I wanted everything to be religiously correct for Orland, as he would have wanted it, but couldn't find anyone to ask. So many times while he was ill, I had asked our religious doctor and our rabbi what to do if Orland died, what the proper procedures were according to our laws and my husband's wishes. No one would tell me. They had all said not to ask such questions until it happened.

Now, in a panic, I called my children and Tibi, and they all came at once. I asked my children if they wished to go in for a moment to say goodbye, and they did. Finally, a doctor came and removed all the needles and covered Orland's face. The hospital allowed Orland to stay in his room the whole day instead of taking him to the morgue, until we could notify the funeral home. The hospital staff opened the windows in Orland's room and laid him out on the floor, and we sat with him until ten o'clock that night and recited *tehilim* (psalms said for the dead), my brother close to his room and the three of us further away since women are not allowed to be in the room with a body. After Shabbat was over, his body was removed to the funeral home.

We laid him to rest on Sunday, August 23, 1992, and his brother, Jack, and sister-in-law, Estelle, managed to make it back from Europe at the very last minute in time for the funeral. As for me, the rug seemed to have been pulled out from under me. I had a feeling of complete emotional collapse. Thanks to the wonderful Jewish tradition of *shiva*, I had nothing to do but sit while a stream of kind visitors kept me feeling comforted and at peace from early morning until late at night. Every morning, there were early prayers, then talk, talk, and more talk until the evening prayers. This routine kept me from thinking too much, and I could not even cry. The feeling of loneliness would take a while to set in.

The next Friday, we got up from *shiva*, and my loving sisters-in-law, Estelle and Marika, prepared Shabbat dinner for us. I went to pick up my grandson, Jared, from kindergarten, which was a short, pleasant walk away, and then we all gathered around the dinner table to welcome Shabbat. Suddenly, five-year-old Jared stood up on a chair, turned to his mother and said, "Mommy, now that *Zaidy* (Grandfather) is in heaven, I am the only man in this house. Don't worry, I want to take care of you." He proceeded to make a *kiddush* (blessing) over the wine and the *bracha* (blessing) over the special braided *challah* as we all watched in wonder and held back the tears. As he finished, we all said, "Amen."

I was shaken to the core. I didn't know how to go forward from there. At first, I just felt a terrible tiredness and relief that my beloved Orland was not suffering anymore. My children didn't leave my side for a whole year, and my grandson was always there with me, too. I will never know how in the course of those five short years that he knew his grandfather, Jared could absorb so much from him. He always loved going to the Beth Jacob synagogue with Orland, and after Orland's passing, he insisted on being taken to his *Zaidy's* synagogue. For years afterwards, Jared would quote things to me that

Orland had said. Often, when I would pick him up from school and bring him home, he would ask me, "Do you have *Zaidy's* favourite record?"

"I don't know which one you mean," I would answer. Then he would go and pick up some tapes that had indeed been my husband's very favourites.

Out of respect, I go to the cemetery to visit Orland, but I have never truly felt that he is there. His *neshoma*, his soul, is with me constantly. Orland was a warm and loving person, and he left me much to remember. His soul and my memories of him are part of me, not touchable or visible, but ever-present. I only wish he could have lived to see Lesley give birth to our second grandson, Justin, and I wish we could have grown old together. He lived by his beliefs and fought on during his great illness with strength, courage, and faith. That is how he lived, and that is what he left behind for us, along with his adoration for all his women – Judy, Lesley, and me – and his caring, his giving, his honest straightforwardness. Fourteen years after his passing, I miss him more and more, and I cannot wait to lie next to him again.

CHAPTER 11

Life Must Go On

God grant me the serenity to accept the things I cannot change, the
courage to change the things I can, and the wisdom to know the difference.
– Alcoholics Anonymous

Over the years, I've accumulated little mementos, given to me
by people whom I have loved, that have become part of my daily
life. Most of these people have passed away now, leaving behind
an emptiness, and, as I grow older, I have become more and more
grateful for these small gifts that give my changing life an added sense
of permanence. Until I settled in Canada, I never allowed myself to
accumulate memorabilia because I did not want to become attached
to any material things. I had lost so much when I was a child and
young person that I feared becoming connected again to things that I
might lose or that might be taken from me. I did not have the energy
to grieve for things that were replaceable. But in the last few years,
I have lost so many dear people who have gone to their eternal rest,
leaving me craving their gentle touches. I miss them all, and each of
the articles they gave me brings warmth to my heart, allowing me to
relive a faded memory from the past.

I do not need a memento, however, to remember every single
moment of sitting beside Orland's sickbed, watching people around
me go on with their everyday lives and feeling that my whole world
had stopped turning. Once he was gone, I did not want to see life
going on at its usual, crazy speed. Especially in the days after sitting
shiva, I desperately hungered for solitude, and in my anger, remorse,

and just plain exhaustion, I created a bubble around myself so I would not have to deal with the urgings of my family and close friends to "get on with life." My brother Tibi, who thought I might be co-dependent and needed help, urged me to go and see a doctor who was a close friend of his. I had no idea what Tibi was talking about, but I appreciated that someone cared. I knew that I could no longer carry on so I willingly went for help. I had been taking very small doses of a prescription tranquilizer on and off to calm my nerves since my mother passed away, and the doctor decided I had an addiction. He told me that before he could decide what was really wrong with me, I would have to come off the medication. I agreed with him. It would do me good to be off all medication. I felt helpless and very vulnerable and would gladly have gone anywhere to get some help or relief from my physical and mental agony. That was why I was being shipped off to the St. Joseph's Hospital Chemical Dependency Unit in St. Paul, Minnesota, at that time one of the top addiction rehabilitation centres in North America.

I sat in Toronto's Pearson International Airport feeling unreal, like a Picasso portrait with its warped images that haunt us. I would have liked to be invisible. It was the beginning of December 1992, more than three months after my husband died, and I was falling apart emotionally. His death had left me shaken and empty, like a house after an earthquake. As I sat waiting for my flight, I heard my name being called on the loudspeaker, telling me to report to the U.S. immigration office. My heart was thumping at twice its usual rate, my throat was dry, and I was finding it very hard to swallow. What was happening? I thought. Were they trying to remind me, here of all places, that I had to report to the authorities, to deal with formalities, Nazi soldiers, or Communist government officials, the way I used to in my former life? "No," I told myself, trying to keep calm, "this is a free world. I am here of my own free will."

I opened the office door, and what I saw did not appease my anxiety. U.S. officials were questioning some very shady-looking people, and the conversations were anything but quiet or polite. I announced myself and was told to wait my turn. I sat down. But my plane was due to take off in just one hour, and as time ticked by, I politely inquired what would happen if I missed my plane. Rather offhandedly, I felt, I was told that in that case I would just simply have to get on another flight. I felt humiliated, and my mind was filled with distrust and questions. Why hadn't I been told this would happen? I felt helpless, ashamed of being treated this way at my age. I deserved better, I told myself. Couldn't they see I was well-dressed? Wasn't honesty written all over my face?

I did not know at that time what would become crystal clear to me later on. I had been labelled a drug addict, and no matter what walk of life I came from, in the eyes of U.S. officials I belonged to that particular group of individuals and was getting the kind of treatment that comes with the territory. My turn finally came, and I was interrogated about drugs of all kinds. I was extremely anxious about whether they believed in my ignorance about such things or whether they thought I was faking it, but it soon became obvious that I really did not know anything about any kind of drugs. Once the paperwork was completed, the officers thoroughly checked my small suitcase and then, to my horror, body-searched me. By this time, I was so numb I didn't care what was happening. I was sure I had signed away my rights to be part of decent society and now belonged to the underworld. Once again, as during the war, I felt like a lamb being led to the slaughter. I had no lawyer, nobody to ask what my rights were or if they were being violated. Finally, they let me go, just in time to make my flight.

I arrived at the Minneapolis-St. Paul airport around supper time and was picked up by a minivan and driven to the detox centre, which was part of a large hospital complex. After a very short, preliminary questioning, I was taken down a corridor to the end room. There was no one around except the night staff as I entered a room furnished with only one chair, a chest of drawers, and an unmade hospital bed.

Suddenly, I felt cold and shaky and realized that I was not only scared but hungry; I had eaten nothing since breakfast. Eventually, a young, kind-looking nurse came into the room to check me in. Appearances were deceiving. She turned my suitcase out onto the bare floor and then took everything apart in her search for drugs. My nail file, scissors, even my hair dryer, were confiscated in case I intended to harm myself. She asked question after question, interrogating me thoroughly and sternly. There is no place for sympathy or empathy here, I told myself as I answered the questions quietly and looked at my belongings on the floor. She gave me strict instructions about how I was to behave and then left me alone to pick up and put away my possessions. I retrieved my things, put on a warm sweat suit, and stretched out, mentally and physically exhausted, on the bare mattress. My eyes burning with tears and unanswered questions still racing through my mind, I saw the strong beam from the nurse's flashlight as she made her nightly rounds.

At six o'clock roll call the next morning, I was greeted more civilly. A nurse took my blood pressure, temperature, and other vital signs. As I walked around, I became aware of other people, in and out of their rooms and in the showers. After breakfast, I had to register with a myriad of doctors, nurses, social workers, and different group leaders who assigned me to various different group therapy workshops. I was becoming more used to my surroundings by now and was actually looking forward to meeting other people.

The first night, I discovered, had been a kind of initiation test where the staff treated you harshly to see if you were serious about wanting help. Now that I had "passed the test," I was given a room of my own with a sink and toilet as well as fresh bedding and warm blankets for I was constantly cold and shivering. As the days passed, I also felt disoriented and exhausted because even though I was being slowly weaned off my habit with diminishing doses of the drug, I found coming off my medication a nightmare and could not sleep for eight straight nights after I arrived.

Food, too, became an issue for me. Although there was also a small kitchen on our floor with all kinds of treats, we addicts ate our meals together in a communal cafeteria. But regular meals were problematic for me: I was uncomfortable asking for kosher food. I was ashamed to say I was Jewish because I was an addict and Jews weren't "supposed" to have addictions (or so I had been led to believe). On the other hand, I didn't want to eat in my room and be different either. I had lost about sixteen pounds during Orland's illness and was by this time very thin. Then a young girl who worked in the cafeteria came to my aid. She had noticed I was not eating much and started to ask me questions. I was touched by the sincerity and concern she showed me and told her about my dietary concerns. From that time on, she prepared all kinds of vegetarian dishes for me and showed genuine interest in my stories of my former life in Hungary.

Luckily, I make friends easily and met people from all walks of life: lawyers, doctors, teachers, nurses, spoiled brats, and even some hard-core drug addicts who had been brought to the clinic from jail. I was getting an excellent education in drug-related sicknesses, alcoholism, and other addictions. I learned how easy it is to get hooked by an addiction but fail to realize that addiction is a chronic sickness that one cannot just walk away from. Breaking an addiction is a lifetime struggle and maintaining the addiction-free life a lifestyle adjustment.

My days became a jumble of activity, and time took on a new dimension. From the wake-up knock on my door at five-thirty in the morning till seven in the evening, my day was filled with individual and group therapy sessions, lectures, films, even swimming as relaxation therapy. We addicts were also given responsibilities: carrying out morning wake-up call, keeping the kitchen clean, and keeping general order. Evenings were free, and we could go for a walk in the park on the hospital grounds as long as we were accompanied by another addict and didn't venture into the clearly marked restricted areas. And to while away sleepless nights, there was the smoking room, where intelligent conversation flourished and debates raged on, some nights until our wake-up call at five-thirty the next morning. Catholics, Jews, believers, agnostics – all of us arguing for our rights and beliefs. The masks came off. We shed tears. We connected with each other.

The clinic also gave me two "firsts" in my life. It was here that I met my first mentor, a woman psychiatrist, who urged me to write a book; I promised her I would. And part of my therapy involved participating in a grief group, and it was in this group that I was taught for the first time in my life *how* to grieve.

I made friends with people who couldn't read or write. I listened to them and found out how beautiful people can be beneath their outward appearances. I became more aware of human suffering. I shed some of my old beliefs and became more tolerant and part of a group. I got to know myself better, and I made lasting friendships. We were all sick people, and that was our common denominator. I came to feel sorry for those of us there – whether rich or poor, black or white, educated or simply streetwise – who could not be reached: those who cheated, who smuggled in drugs and got thrown out of the program when they were caught using them. I truly hoped that they would come to understand their addiction and return for the help they so badly needed. But most of the addicts in the clinic were good people who had simply ended up on the wrong side of the road, many because of some very sad beginnings.

By the time Christmas arrived, everyone who had been in rehab for twenty-one days, except for the very sick, was being discharged. I, too, was being sent home after only nineteen days there, but I did not want to go. Chaos awaited me outside. How would I cope with the outside world? I had told almost no one where I was going when I left; only my children and brothers knew. Everything was so well organized here at the clinic, and here I knew my place. How would I practise what I had learned here – the new language, new behaviours? But I said my goodbyes, took the self-help books and spiritual readings I had encountered during my time there with me as ammunition against my old habits, and set out to rediscover my old world. The problem was that most people I knew – even my closest friends and relatives – still thought of addiction as a weakness that I was too weak to control. I'm sure they sincerely believed that I had a choice, that I should have been able to help myself through sheer willpower. But I knew differently – that my addiction was a sickness – and although it had taken a rather drastic wake-up call for me to think of it as such, I was now taking my first baby steps towards recovery, and I wasn't going to let anyone stop me.

When I returned from the addiction rehab centre, I went to see my doctor who put me in a recovery group in Toronto. I joined a chemical dependency group and attended frequent meetings. As with any of the addiction recovery groups, all of which are based on the Alcoholics Anonymous model, anything said in our group stayed there. The words from the oath we spoke at every meeting were very valuable to me, too: "God give me the serenity to accept the things I cannot change and the courage to change the things I can."

I volunteered to work at the Branson Hospital, and it felt so good to help people. I even went to a Holocaust survivors recovery group. I joined a grief counselling group run by the Canadian Jewish Family Services for people who had lost a life-partner and found we were all, more or less, in the same headspace and had a lot in common. (There was also a second similar group for younger individuals who had lost a child or a parent, and my daughter Lesley joined this one.) Our group tried to organize on our own and socialize among ourselves, but we failed. We could not commit to any relationship; we were not reliable because of our pain.

In April 1993, following Jewish tradition, we put the headstone up on my husband's grave. Afterwards, my brother-in-law, Jack, and his wife, Estelle, took me back with them to Vancouver for a rest, and from there we drove to California. It was a very relaxing, beautiful holiday, and I found I was mesmerized by the beautiful scenery, especially along the Pacific Coast Highway, with its cliff-hanging turns overlooking the ocean. Every tree, every monument and bridge, every glimpse of the sea healed me a tiny bit more. In San Francisco and Los Angeles, we visited with some distant cousins of Orland's who had come from Russia and whom I had never met before. It felt good to be with them and to listen as they and Jack reminisced about their childhood with Orland. As they talked, Orland once again came alive for me as I learned things about his past that I had never known before.

But finally the vacation ended, and I had to come home and live in my empty house. I was not frightened to be there alone, just lonely. I read a lot about recovery and healthy lifestyles. At the Ontario Institute for Studies in Education, I attended a course on transformation of the mind, a theory related to Buddhism, which was led by a Tibetan monk, and we practised yoga relaxation at the end of each session. I also started to read all of Elie Wiesel's books. I learned a lot, and Elie Wiesel became my inspiration. His words gave me courage and motivation to write even though I still carried the Nazi stigma inside me that I was inadequate and not quite "normal." In August 1994, I attended the first International Conference of Holocaust Child Survivors and Second Generation in Montreal with my younger daughter, Lesley. Through that experience, we forged a stronger relationship based on our new understanding of the problems both of survivors and the next generation. That conference made me fully aware for the first time that I was indeed a child survivor. Afterwards, I wrote a letter to the *Canadian Jewish News* about the conference, urging all survivors to record their experiences and join me in leaving our memories to our children and grandchildren.

Orland had made the Jewish holidays a significant and wonderful experience in our home, and with him now gone, they had become torture for me. As Rosh Hashanah approached, I began to feel restless again and could not find peace. My children tried their best to help, to give me meaningful things to do to occupy my time. Judy, divorced and working, needed help with her son, and it was good for me mentally to have a purpose so I looked after my grandson, Jared, picking him up after school and making dinner for him, Judy, and myself. He was everything to me. Nevertheless, I could feel the old depression setting in, and after two years with the recovery group my doctor had put me in after I returned from St. Paul, I left them. I felt "grouped out." I then started to go to a hypnotherapist. At first, I felt good but soon began to realize we were not getting anywhere.

This time, the doctor treating me for addiction sent me to North Bay to another addiction centre that specialized mainly in co-dependency. For two weeks in the fall of 1994, four women, a delightful young man who wrote music, and I learned through videos, role-playing games, and discussions what co-dependency was all about and how not to get locked into it again. We became a family sharing many secrets, sometimes even physically digging holes to symbolically bury them. Before long, I began to feel I was back on the right track. I was given my first cuddly teddy bear with whom I slept. I loved him. I also began journaling, and it helped to relieve my mind. And I began to learn how to relax better. Then I went home to start the harder part – to put into action what I had learned.

I was fine for a short while, but before long, I began to experience physical pain in every muscle of my body. I could not sleep so I would take hot baths, day and night. Finally, I started going to a psychiatrist once a week. I felt frightened and did not know how to express myself. But we became great friends and went for walks and talked instead of sitting in his office. The walking and talking did nothing for the physical pain, however, which was becoming increasingly unbearable. I felt I was coming to the end of my rope. My psychiatrist suggested mood-altering drugs – Prozac and its brothers and sisters – and I began to try them. But I started losing weight rapidly from these medications and became disoriented. I was on a high, but my physical pain was still agonizing. Soon I was back on tranquilizers, the same "tranks" I had weaned myself off of in St. Paul. Guilt. Shame. I blamed myself for everything. I was a bad mother. I was a nobody, totally useless, an addict. The physical pain never stopped; it was a symptom of my poor mental health. I wanted to get off all medications desperately and tried again.

This time I was sent to the Homewood Health Centre in Guelph, Ontario. In February 1995, my brother Peter took me there, and while I appreciated his willingness to drive me, I felt we could not connect. He is an excellent psychiatrist and I look up to him, but I could not tell how he felt about me and was afraid to ask. I felt so utterly vulnerable and did not want to be preached at or judged. When we got to the centre, we kissed goodbye, and the silence between us spoke to me of the fragility of our relationship, of how sorry we both were, and indeed, of how strong our love was for each other.

This treatment centre was set up as part of a large hospital on unbelievably beautiful grounds. I was welcomed sternly but not in as discouraging a way as I had been in St. Paul and was assigned a room I would share with another patient. After a physical examination, I again began the process of being weaned off pills. The daily schedule here was very strict and busy. We had very little time to ourselves, and I had trouble keeping up the pace with all the younger addicts. Everything was geared to recovery. Mornings began with roll-call exercises and a walk on the beautiful grounds. Then we had breakfast cafeteria-style. After breakfast came morning group check-ins, questions, assignments, problem-solving. Then we were off to group therapy. Everyone got their turn in these small and very intense groups. We even had homework as well as having to attend evening meetings of the dependency group for our addiction.

Most of the time I felt groggy and disoriented, but I am a fighter and didn't want to give up. The first few days in any rehab centre, called drying-out time, are the worst. You can get discouraged and opt out or get depressed and be in total denial. I got so depressed in Guelph that, by the Friday of the first week, I could not stop crying, and the doctor wanted to send me home. I packed my few belongings, but I knew that if I left there, I would have nowhere to go. This was the first time in my life I seriously considered committing suicide. It is one thing to just think about suicide in theory and quite another to have a plan, and I had come up with a specific plan for ending my own life. I became terrified that in a mental blackout or in a moment of complete despair, I might execute my plan, but thanks to the nurses who alerted the doctor and the doctor who stayed and talked to me for long hours, I pulled through.

The physical pain, meanwhile, was ever-present, and I had heart problems as well as bleeding hemorrhoids so bad that two or three towels would be soaked with blood before I could crawl to the nursing station for help. Even during the worst times, however, I was allowed only ten minutes rest with my feet up on pillows and an ice pack on my behind before being sent off to my group. It was that kind of toughness that finally brought me some results – that toughness plus the group therapy where we all slowly began to share our stories, the emotionally and psychologically stronger patients encouraging the others. We became a big family, a family where I was the huggy one, and everyone needs a hug.

After being in rehab for two weeks, patients were permitted to go home for the weekend, as long as we submitted a written plan for the weekend and had it approved by the doctor. The following Friday, my family picked me up. I was told to make sure I allowed for leisure time, attended any weekend meeting of my chemical dependency group, exercised, and ate proper meals. On Sunday afternoon, Marika had the honour of bringing me back. Although we are sisters-in-law and have been friends since we were fourteen, I still felt like an evil stepsister causing all sorts of problems for the family because I was ashamed that I was still an addict.

Visitors were also allowed to come to the centre on certain days, and my daughters came to see me then, which meant a lot to me. All this family help gave me encouragement to get well. I had also decided this time not keep my addiction a secret. The first time I went for treatment, I had lied to almost everyone and said that I was going to Vancouver. But now I was proud to be on the road to recovery, and I needed all the help I could get from my family and friends, and in turn, their participation in my treatment helped them understand a little better what my illness was all about.

Each time in the centre that I walked out of my room into the corridor, I was greeted by a very large painting showing a beautiful morning sun shining through the trees and bearing the simple inscription "Believe." A person could not help but gaze at that picture until it became imprinted on his or her mind. That picture did not say what to believe or whom to believe in, but it helped me learn to believe in myself and in a higher power. I became, or started on the road to becoming, a very spiritual person. I met people from all over Canada from all walks of life – highly educated people, professionals, working people. I learned a lot and realized that I was just one of many Jewish people who needed help. I was not ashamed of being Jewish or an addict any more. By now I had met many Jewish addicts and knew of many Jewish help groups. The dining room at the centre provided a variety of tasty vegetarian and fish choices so I could easily follow the kosher dietary laws. I spent Purim there, but I was not alone and felt at home with the other Jews there who were also celebrating the holiday. I was allowed to visit my family just before Purim, and I returned to the centre with lots of Purim treats that we all shared.

I was discharged and came home from Guelph hopeful, even if somewhat still apprehensive. I attended five meetings a week for recovering addicts where I'd like to believe I became an example for the many youngsters whose mothers were addicts and in denial. These young men and women needed all the help and understanding I or anyone could give them, and I tried to help wherever possible.

I took a walk every morning, snow or rain, with my girlfriend Agi, who came to my house early every day so we could walk and talk together for an hour before she went to work. She would come again during her lunch break, and we repeated our walk. God bless her; she kept me sane. Agi and I have known each other for fifty years. We have a common background and went to high school together in Budapest where we shared clothes and many ideas. During the 1956 revolution, however, we lost track of each other. She came to Canada, living first in Montreal, where she got married and had a daughter, and then moving to Toronto. While I was still living in Winnipeg, Marika called me to say that she had run into Agi again on a Toronto bus, so after I moved to Toronto, Agi and I revived our friendship. Now we both have two grandsons and live a short block away from each other. We carry on our friendship where we left off. We need each other, and Agi has always been there for me through rough times, never hesitating to help.

When I left Homewood, I worked hard to use all the tools I picked up there. I read from my daily meditation book every morning, practised relaxation techniques, and began to believe that I really was getting better. I wrote my favourite sayings down in large letters on sheets of paper and hung them all over the house. It helped! The slogans I picked up at the different help groups, such as "The only way to grow is to let go," run through my mind even today.

I knew I was searching for answers, so I just let myself follow my instincts. As I explored the world and myself, I became even more spiritual and my belief in myself became stronger. I had never questioned the existence of God, but somewhere along the way, I had shed my childish belief in a punishing or rewarding Almighty. I was coming to understand that the answer is within each one of us, that we have to help ourselves, and if we listen, we can hear that "still, small voice" within and know that God is with us and guiding us to find our own answers. I was finally finding *my* own answers, and I held onto them. I was also learning that any rewards for being a good person would not come directly from God but rather from the feeling of satisfaction I gained from doing good to others.

But no matter how my spiritual self was progressing, the physical pain – tremors, muscle pain, headaches, total fatigue – was always present. Plus now I was having anxiety attacks. I tried to keep busy, but nothing seemed to help. I needed desperately to sleep. Then came the inevitable – what I had been fighting for three years – I had a breakdown. At the end of 1995, three years after Orland's death, I checked myself into the Mount Sinai psychiatric ward. Peter came with me, and after contacting my doctor, the hospital admitted me. New questions. New pills. Within a few days, however, I was allowed total freedom to go out for walks and return home during the day. But I couldn't face being alone in a large, empty house and never went home at all.

While I was at Mount Sinai, I made friends with most of the other patients who had the same privileges I did, and we often played cards together. As the new medication kicked in, the physical pain went away. But during therapy, it became clear that my problems were war-related and caused by early childhood trauma that I had never dealt with. The doctor called it shell-shock. Not being able to discuss my wartime experiences even with my family, I had spent most of my life feeling alone. I desperately missed Orland, who had been my rock of support, and I was just plain scared of life. I had financial worries, too, and I found that my will to live was eroding away.

My daughters were very understanding. We had family sessions, and finally I began to feel that the most important people in my life were coming to accept and understand my illness and no longer thought of depression as something that is self-induced. Even my mah-jong group came in to spend time with me. By the time I was discharged from Mount Sinai, I had been cleared of my addictions even though it was evident I would need ongoing therapy. One of the first things I did was enrol in a two-year program on co-dependency at George Brown College where I earned a group leadership certificate. When I finished the program, I had an offer to run a group at the Baycrest Centre, but I just wasn't ready for that.

Nevertheless, as the years without Orland passed, I felt I was still just hanging on. Working in real estate became impossible for me, and I put my licence on hold, thinking I might go back to it, although I never did in the end. I had no patience to watch television or to listen to music, something Orland and I had loved to do, and I had a minimal social life because it irritated me to be with couples. "Why me?" I would think to myself when I was with them.

Around that time, too, I began to realize that no matter what I did, coming home to a large, empty house triggered anxiety in me, so I sold our family home and moved to a condominium. In this new environment, at least I could see and hear people around me and could join in their activities if I chose to. I continued to keep up with the Jewish traditions I loved and didn't drive on Shabbat or holy days. My children lived nearby, and we all joined a conservative synagogue within walking distance of my home. Going to synagogue for High Holiday services with my children and Jared beside me helped me tolerate the loneliness even though I could hear my husband singing in my mind as I sat and desperately tried to concentrate on the prayers and the here-and-now.

That winter of 1996, in celebration of my sixtieth birthday, I used some of my savings plus money left by Orland to take Judy, Jared, and Lesley to Mexico. But it felt strange and sadly unbelievable to be back in Mexico without my husband at my side to enjoy it with us.

The next fall, I registered at York University for a course on the history of Canadian Jews with Professor Irving Abella, whom I had heard speaking on other occasions and had enjoyed very much. I was becoming more interested in what was going on in the world and attended current affairs and other lectures to learn about politics. I began to read all kinds of books, magazines, and newspapers, and volunteered at the Jewish Book Fair and the Hadassah Bazaar. In the course of my pursuit to better understand myself, I read books by Abba Eban, Elie Wiesel, Marik Halter, Martin Gray, and numerous others, and was lucky enough to meet all of them in person at various times. I also joined a support group for gays and lesbians because I wanted to learn about homosexuality to help my friends and family who were having a hard time understanding and dealing with it.

Towards the end of 1998, I also joined a grief group of widows and widowers who had been meeting weekly for about a year before I joined. There were between eight and fifteen of us in the group but only one man. They briefed me on what had been happening, and after a couple of meetings, we, along with Dr. Ed Pekas, the psychiatrist who led the group, decided it would be a good idea to form a Jewish social group for adults fifty-five and over. Perhaps, we thought, the Canadian Jewish Congress or one of the synagogues in the Toronto area would accommodate us and help us since there was no such group in our community.

I was very enthusiastic about the idea and took charge. When I undertake something, I will go to any length to make it happen, so I made appointments with the Canadian Jewish Congress, the Bathurst Jewish Centre, the *Canadian Jewish News*, and some synagogues to discuss our proposal. At first, no one was interested so I decided to take our one male member with me. Perhaps the presence of a man would give us a more professional air; it didn't. It wasn't until an article appeared about us in the *Canadian Jewish News* that we started to make some headway. We gave our group a name, *B'Yachad* (Hebrew for together), and I had some cards printed up for myself so I could look more professional. Then Beth Tzedec Congregation, a conservative synagogue, called me to set up a meeting with their rabbi, Rabbi Roy D. Tanenbaum. I was delighted. Three months of hard work and effort were finally paying off. Our group met with Rabbi Tanenbaum, who was a great help to us in every way. Now we had a place to meet, refreshments provided by the synagogue's caterers at a reduced fee, and preparation and clean-up help. We became organized. We scheduled events, delegated responsibilities, and appointed a secretary and a treasurer. When the notice for our first meeting appeared in the *Canadian Jewish News*, my phone didn't stop ringing.

At the same time I was planning Lesley's wedding, and we ran around together at this extremely happy time for her. I open-heartedly welcomed Ian, her fiancé, into our family, and our two families got on famously together. I knew Ian's mother, Helena Isenberg, very well from when she joined the *B'Yachad* leadership group, and Ian had two lovely sisters who were both married with small children. Helena and I became very close as the two of us attended to the wedding details. Since both of us were widows, though, we sometimes had to pause to deal with our memories and feelings, although it was a blessing for both of us that we had each other to lean on during those instances.

The first time I saw Lesley in her wedding gown, her beauty revived the old heartache and my eyes filled with tears. If only her father could have seen her. The wedding took place at the Beth Shalom Synagogue, and everything was outstanding. Ian had a large family, but there were few guests on our side. However, my family was there, and Jack and Estelle represented Orland's family. Jack and I walked down the aisle together and gave Lesley away. After the wedding, Mr. and the new Mrs. Isenberg set off for their honeymoon, and shortly after they returned, we learned that there was to be a little addition to the family. "Oh, dear Lord," I asked, " is this possible?" I had been so afraid that Lesley's old eating disorder, which she had by now recovered from, would make it impossible for her to become pregnant. Now my happiness and gratitude were boundless.

Our opening meeting of *B'Ychad* in the spring of 1999 was a great success with over 150 people in attendance. We handed out questionnaires and asked people to provide their names, addresses, professions, and contact information. We solicited program suggestions to give us an idea of what topics people were interested in, and we called for volunteers. I had been delegated, with my still-heavy Hungarian accent, to deliver the opening speech. My children and some of my friends were there that night. I am usually my own worst critic and never give myself credit for anything, but I looked into their faces and was thrilled to see how proud they were of me.

I felt so honoured to welcome everyone and to speak to the crowd. Here is part of the speech I delivered on that wonderful evening:

Honoured *Rebbitzen* and Rabbi Tanenbaum, ladies and gentlemen, and my dearest co-workers. My name is Olga Verrall, and I was given the privilege to welcome you to the opening session of our newly formed group, *B'Yachad*, meaning "together."

Being a widow for seven years myself inspired me to start this group for other singles between the ages of fifty-five and seventy, which is not adequately addressed in Toronto's community. I thank you and I am overwhelmed and encouraged by your heart-warming interest. We have a common need to help and support each other. From here on, you are no longer alone! My hopes and plans are that this place would become our second home and all of us will become a nurturing extended family to each other.

We were left without partners, and I am positive that they wish us to continue with our life. We will never forget them, just try to fill the loneliness and emptiness they left behind. Our cup is half full, not half empty, for those wonderful years our partners devoted to us, and we are thankful to God for giving it to us! We are here to socialize, support, and form smaller compatible groups to listen to each other's needs. Listening is a form of art....

As it is written in Genesis, Chapter 2, I quote: "And the Lord God said: It is not good that the man should be alone; I will make a helpmate for him." "*Ezer kenegdo.*" From the beginning of *Beresheit*, man was not meant to be alone....

In conclusion, I quote from Rabbi Hillel: "*Im ein ahnee lee, me lee, v'eem loh achshav, aymatay?*" "If I am not for myself who will be for me and if not now, when?"

May this day be a new beginning for all of us *B'Yachad* – together.

Shalom!

After that first meeting, we expanded our leadership group to fourteen and held bi-weekly meetings, first at the synagogue and then taking turns in our homes. We managed to get great speakers, some who spoke to us for no fee and others who asked for a small remuneration, and were booked ahead to the end of the year. We scheduled lectures ranging from current events to networking, a concert of popular songs, and a night of interactive games. But unfortunately, after that glorious opening session, the turnouts for events started to drop, and our spirits fell. I was well aware that we were on the right track, but we needed some professional guidance. These organizations take devotion and hard work, but no matter how many times I arranged for a capable person to meet with us and point us in the right direction, there was some difficulty getting our leadership group to commit. By the fall, Lesley was expecting, and I asked my group to let someone else take over, but no one would believe that I actually wanted to leave. I was devastated to think that I might be breaking up the group, but I needed a leave of absence. I officially resigned in December at our last program of that year, and we announced the closing of *B'Yachad*. Not one person volunteered to carry on without me.

For the little girl from Szarvas with no formal higher education, making this group a reality was a great achievement. I was very happy and proud that I could bring this adventure to fruition, and I got a lot out of it mentally and spiritually. In addition, being so totally involved and committed to its success kept me busy and brought some sanity and purpose back into my life.

Unfortunately, Lesley and Ian soon began having problems adjusting to married life. Sadly, I was not surprised. "Olga," I said to myself, "haven't you learned yet?" I was disappointed and unhappy not only for Lesley and Ian but also for myself. After all I had gone through, I thought, here was yet more pain to come to terms with, even though deep down I knew that these hard lessons in life were making me a more understanding and caring person. Lesley and Ian were constantly fighting. On top of that, the baby was due on December 31, 1999, a day the media were saying would herald disaster. Lesley was very uncomfortable carrying the baby, so the doctor suggested a Caesarean section and scheduled Lesley to be induced on December 19.

In the hospital, she had a room with a single bed all to herself, and I was with her when they gave her the epidural in the early evening. Then the doctor became so busy that we did not see her again until the next morning. I lay next to Lesley in her bed, caressing and kissing her, holding her tight through the night. Her water broke at two in the morning, and I went yelling for help. No doctor in sight, only nurses. Then at six o'clock, her doctor walked in, looking well rested. She saw the state Lesley was in and sent me out of the room, but I refused to leave until I saw the head start to appear. Then I left and less than thirty minutes later I was called back for my first look at my second grandson, Justin Isenberg-Verrall. At that point, Ian came and could not restrain his tears of happiness as he held his newborn son in his arms.

With trembling hands and voice, I congratulated the new mother, hugged her, and gave her a million kisses. Then I went outside and spoke to Orland. "You got your name bestowed upon the luckiest little gift from heaven," I told him. "Thank you is not enough. This is the greatest miracle so far in my life." As soon as Lesley was comfortable in her room with her son beside her, I went home. Silently I prayed all day. Only I know to whom I prayed and for what. The ones who know don't need telling, and the ones who don't know, well, they don't need to know.

When mother and son came home, I moved in with them to help out. Actually, it was more for myself than for them because I didn't want to miss a single Justin-smile or -cry. The baby was adorable and I was once again in love. I could not get enough of him. We had the customary *brith milah* (circumcision ceremony) when Justin was eight days old, and it was a truly joyous event because we were so grateful for the health of both mother and baby. Then Ian disappeared when Justin was only ten days old. The marriage continued on a trial basis for more than another year, and then Lesley and Ian began the long journey to divorce, which lasted until Justin was four-and-a-half years old.

When Lesley had to go back to work, she hired a nanny whom I would oversee, and over the course of the following years, I have been spending a great deal of time with Justin. I cannot express in words what he means to me. I cherish the times we are together as I see him grow and develop. I hope that all the love I show him will remain with him forever. It is that love that encourages me to write this book, hard as it is for me to do. I have a great need to leave a living testimonial to all of my closest, dearest family so that they may read about my inner thoughts, to know what I feel and what I have experienced, to be aware of things that might otherwise never be spoken between us or known by them.

In life, there are always changes from bitterness to happiness and back again. At the same time it had become obvious that Lesley and Ian couldn't remain married, Judy announced that after years of struggling alone, she had rekindled a relationship with an old school mate and they were planning to get married at the end of June 2000. I was delighted with my daughter's choice. Mel is a very outgoing, huggable person who brought much fun and love with him to our family. Judy and Mel arranged their own wedding, and I joyfully walked down the aisle with six-month-old Justin in my arms and almost thirteen-year-old Jared by my side. I had a lot to be grateful for.

Soon after the wedding, Judy announced that she wanted to celebrate Jared's *bar mitzvah* in Israel, so that August, Judy, Mel, Michael (Jared's birth father), Jared, and I went to Israel with a small *bar mitzvah* group. The day of the *bar* and *bat mitzvah* celebrations (girls celebrate *bat mitzvahs*), we started out at four in the morning from the Dead Sea to Masada, the hilltop fort that was the site of a last heroic stand of the Jews against the Romans in 70 CE. As we arrived, the sun was just starting to rise, shining across the stillness of the Dead Sea and mirroring our joy and excitement with its glorious arrival. The rabbi who delivered the sermon was excellent, and I am sure his words will stay with all the children for their lifetimes. The *bar mitzvah* boys and *bat mitzvah* girls outshone even the sun with their collective reading of the Torah, and the chanting of their portions was like a pledge of faith echoing the heroic determination of our ancestors.

During the ceremony, my mind wandered back to the last time I had been at Masada. Orland, may he rest in peace, and I were there on October 13, 1988, for Israel's fortieth anniversary. There had been a great celebration that night, and the Israel Philharmonic Orchestra conducted by Zubin Mehta had given a concert on the hilltop. Afterwards, I had been privileged to shake hands with people such as Gregory Peck, Yves Montand, and Martin Gray, author of *For Those I Loved*, one of the saddest and most moving books I have ever read. What a splendid night that had been, with Masada lit up to showcase the bandshell and the audience's hearts beating in unison to Mahler's Symphony No. 2, all of us making our pledge to the heroic people who had fought for our land. Being there had given me strength.

One of our stops on the *bar/bat mitzvah* tour was at Mizpe Hayamim, a spa at Rosh Pina overlooking the Sea of Galilee and a place for me of beauty, harmony, tranquillity, and serene pleasure. On the way there, I was looking forward to resting and sorting out my memories of the wonderful trip that was coming to an end. My husband's *yahrtzeit* (anniversary of a person's death) was approaching, and I was anxious about how I would feel lighting the memorial candle for him. I soon realized that fate must have meant me to come to Mizpe Hayamim. In front of the building were several stag statues crafted from wire – Svarvas, where I was born, is "stag" in English. And what better place to honour my Orland (of blessed memory), who had been a cantor at the Rosh Pina Synagogue in Winnipeg, Canada, than in the town of Rosh Pina in Israel?

After leaving Rosh Pina, we continued our tour. The *bar/bat mitzvah* celebration dinner took place on the last night before the group was to leave Israel for Toronto. Some of Orland's younger generation of relatives came to join us at the Hilton Tel Aviv Hotel. It couldn't have been more wonderful. Afterwards, Judy and Mel left for Greece for a two-week vacation while Michael remained in Israel for a few more days and Jared and I flew back to Toronto.

When I returned from Israel, I again took up my quest to better my life. In the spring of 2001, I decided to go with some friends to a B'nai Brith summer camp for seniors in the Laurentians in Quebec. After months of planning and great excitement, we set off: three *bubbies* (grandmothers) and two *zaidies* (grandfathers) in one car with me driving. We all had to cut down on our supplies to accommodate everyone, but that did not dampen our spirits in the least. I was a first-time camper, and there was a glow in my heart. I felt like a kid, never having had the good fortune as a child to really be a child. At the same time, I felt like a very grateful adult who now knew how to appreciate things in life. During our eight-hour drive, we shared comradeship, laughter, wrong turns, and regular 'pee-pee' stops before we finally arrived at our destination.

I was overwhelmed by the warm reception we received, and while I was tired from the drive, nothing could have kept me in my clean, comfortable room. Those who had been there before ran around excitedly showing the rest of us everything at once, and I was caught up in their enthusiasm and pride. At dinner that evening, there were eight of us sitting around the table. We were in the "fifty-five and over" category and from different parts of the world, but we had a great deal in common, particularly our Jewish culture and heritage. Many of us were Holocaust survivors who had suffered a great deal and were living day by day, praying for a few more healthy years to be with our children, grandchildren, and great-grandchildren. All of us were gathered together for relaxation and fun.

The seniors' Camp Vatikim is in the middle of the B'nai Brith children's camp located near a large, dense forest on a lake in the Laurentians. While we were there, the weather was bright and sunny, and our days were filled with activities specially planned for both mind and body by a terrific, caring staff. In the cool evenings, talented people entertained us, and we were all moved by the beautiful music under the clear, star-bright sky. Soon we were all at ease with each other, putting our worries, pains, and shyness aside. As for myself, I was so grateful at my age to be among people of my culture, to share with them every little Jewish symbol that means so much to them and to me. It was an experience that brought me great joy.

Nevertheless, of all the things I have done and experienced in the last few years, it was on our trip to Israel for Jared's *bar mitzvah* that one of the most significant events of my life took place. It was at the Mizpe Hayamim spa in Rosh Pina that I began to thread together my life, piece by piece. At the drug rehab clinic in St. Paul, a seed had been planted by the woman psychiatrist, and now, at last, it was taking root. I made up my mind to start writing this book and to call it *Missing Pieces* for all my loved ones who have departed as well as for all those who perished in the Holocaust, forever becoming missing pieces in my life. The morning after I lit Orland's *yahrzeit* candle, I found a peaceful room overlooking the Sea of Galilee and began to write as fast as my hand could move, allowing my fifty years of pent-up feelings to dictate what to put down on paper. Once I believed I could write this book in memory of my late husband, it became the most important thing in my life to see it in print. If I could do that, I could say that I had accomplished one of my dreams.

I am seating in a room called 'For relaxation'
it is 9 a.m. and the sun is already high over
the lower gallile & the beautifull sea of
Galill. It is so quiet here that I can hear
my own heart beat & it is racing. My love
for Israel & it's people is beyond comp-
rehention since I live in Toronto.
I rationalize, that it is my children &
grandchildren & of course the remien-
der of my family - I am here. with my
chilren on the occasion of my grandson Jakov Barnitzvah. I haven't been
here for since '89 when I brought
my husband who was very ill with
cancer to say goodby to his family
1 brother (who also died since than) and
1 sister who is a Salmarer and we
very seldom see eye to eye, but I ad-
mier the way they live, the naches they
receive from their hard work, Their very
large family was all killed, but for a
small handfull, and they are devoting
them self to replacing the dead, giving a
name of each child who they bring to
this world (and by new chara they have a
lot names of their lost Mother, Father, sisters
brothers, cousins, nices, nephews and so on ..)
I was here 10 times in the last 35 years

הרמוניה, יופי, שלוה והנאה צלולה HARMONY BEAUTY TRANQUILITY AND SERENE PLESURE מצפה הימים ח.ד. 27, ראש פינה 12000 ■ 06-5999555 .פקס ■ 06-6999666 .טל ■ 12000 ח.ד. 27,
■ MIZPE HAYAMIM ■ p.o.b. 27. Rosh-Pina 12000, Israel ■ Tel. 972-6-6999666 ■ Fax. 972-6-6999555 ■
■ E-Mail: Info@mizpe-hayamim.com ■ Internet Site: http://www.mizpe-hayamim.com ■

First thoughts for what would become *Missing Pieces*,
written at Mizpe Hayamim, 2000.

CHAPTER 12

Return to Hungary

Purge your soul from angry passion;/That is the inheritance of fools.
— "Words of Wisdom," *Sabbath and Festival Prayer Book*

At sixty-six years of age, I was returning to Hungary, my birthplace. I never dreamed that I would ever go back to my roots, especially with my daughters. But in November 2002, I saw an ad in the *Canadian Jewish News* saying that Breakthrough Films and Television Inc., a Toronto-based documentary film company, was looking for mothers and daughters who would like to take a "once in a lifetime journey into the past." Here was my chance to show my children where I came from. It was an opportunity I couldn't pass up. I realized the wish to do this had been buried in my subconscious for a long time.

I got in touch with Leslie Cote, the producer, and she told me that she would need about three to four hours to talk with the girls and me. It was only at this point that I called Judy and Lesley to tell them about it, and they agreed to meet with Ms. Cote. At that first meeting, we were questioned and filmed separately, and then my daughters and I sat down to talk. It was then that I first became aware that Judy would not go to any of the Holocaust sites, only to Budapest and Szarvas. My daughters told me that they have always been ashamed of me and my accent and of whatever little they knew about my past. I broke down and cried bitterly, but once I had regained my composure, I felt thankful that all the dirty laundry had finally been aired. "All the more reason," I told them, "to go. Thank you for telling me now. It is not too late."

Olga (centre), Lesley (left), and Judy (right).
Photo © 2003 by Deborah Samuel.

As I began preparing for the trip back to Hungary, I barely knew
what to think. I had been back to Hungary twice since we emigrated
and thought I had no wish ever to return again. I hated the Hungarians.
The first time I went back to Hungary was in August 1978. Many
people had been returning to Hungary for some years by then, some
because they still had family there and others for sentimental reasons.

My girlfriend Kati (not the Kati of my childhood but a friend I had met as an adult in Winnipeg after we both immigrated to Canada), approached me and asked if I would go back for a visit with her. Our life partners had no interest in accompanying us, and so in August we set out on our own, first to London for the Queen's Jubilee and then on to Hungary for a week.

We were flying Malev Airlines, the national Hungarian airline, and the trip was a disaster. After "mechanical problems" held us up in London's Heathrow Airport for ten hours, we endured a very long and boring flight from London to Budapest in a ramshackle plane with practically no passenger services. We arrived at the Ferihegyi Airport, which still looked the way it had in the 1950s when I used to travel by plane on assignment for the Central Dress Designing and Planning Industry. I disembarked from the plane into a terminal full of soldiers, thoroughly frightened by them, afraid to even look around. I knew that regime and what they were capable of. The customs officers turned our luggage inside out, and when we were finally allowed to go, they told us we had to register at the local police station within twenty-four hours and then every day while we stayed in Hungary. Nothing had changed; we still had to watch what we did and said.

Gyuri, Manyi's brother, picked us up at the airport and drove us to Zsofi and Miklos's apartment. Kati had originally come from a small town called Bekescshaba, and we asked my friends Juli and Jancsi to drive us to our hometowns, only a few kilometres apart. Although both of them had good jobs, the pay was low, so Juli and her husband still lived in the same apartment in Budapest where they had lived with Juli's aunt when they got married in 1956. Nothing had changed. In Szarvas, I found our old house and was able to go in. It still looked the way it did when we left. A couple with their ten-year-old daughter and the wife's mother were living there. Only the grandmother was at home when I knocked. She was exceptionally pleasant to me, making coffee while we talked and insisting on sending me home with some gifts. But I felt nothing for the house itself – no attachment, no sorrow – as if it had never been my home at all. When it was time to leave Szarvas, I tried to buy some souvenirs to take back with me, but the shop shelves were bare and there was nothing to buy.

At the airport check-in, all the customs workers were young men wearing army uniforms. This put me off immediately. When they checked my luggage, they asked me if I was taking Hungarian currency back with me, and I foolishly cracked a joke. I said that I didn't have a "stinking penny," which used to be a popular saying in Hungary. Unfortunately, the young soldiers didn't understand the joke and searched me. I had a hard time getting to my plane on time, and it was only once I was finally seated and buckled in that I finally felt safe. With a great deal of anger, I suppressed all my feelings for my Hungarian heritage. The next time I was to go back would be when Zsofi was dying in 1987, a painful time for me. Most of my ties to Hungary were gone, and I had no desire to ever go back.

But now the thought of returning to Hungary generated a strange emotion in me. There are some things in my heritage I am very proud of. There are very famous Hungarian writers and composers whom I cherish but never dared to talk about. The country itself is very beautiful, and I was looking forward to seeing it again. Now I would go back fifty-nine years to when I was an innocent child of seven. I would go back to look for that little girl and that wonderful family that existed in Szarvas before the war. And, most importantly, I would be able to do it with my daughters. I needed to go back, I realized, to put all my anger and resentment behind me. Then I could come back to Toronto and officially – and finally – declare it my home.

Until we were actually preparing to go, however, I hadn't realized that I had never discussed my childhood home very much with my children. As with the Holocaust, it was just something I didn't talk about. When my family came to Canada, we had too many things to do and did not want to look back. Then when I got married and had children, I didn't have time for introspection and explanations. I just wanted to get on with my life and make a success of it.

Now that it had come about that I could go back with Judy and Lesley, I felt I had another chance. It was like a gift I'd been given. I could take my daughters back to see where I came from, to fill in the blanks for them, to put the missing pieces of my life together. Now they could see for themselves the real, true "me," the person I had never been able to show them or put into words for them before. When we started to discuss the trip, many things came up that hurt me very much. I had never realized how important it would have been to talk to them about my history and my home, to help them visualize life in Hungary back in the forties and fifties, to show them that even with outhouses and no indoor plumbing, we had still been "civilized."

Judy does not show her feelings easily and was very much against coming and being filmed. But I hoped this trip would clear up some of the mystery for both of them.

In the end, unfortunately, Lesley was not able to come. Her bitter divorce was dragging on and on. It was ironic that her husband, Ian, had waited until now, some three years after their separation, to agree to the divorce. Perhaps, though, it was better that I go with only one daughter at a time. It would be a much more difficult trip if both girls were there with me. Travelling with Judy alone would give us both an opportunity for some important mother–daughter bonding. But I hope to go back one day with Lesley, too, as well as someday with my grandsons.

When the film company phoned to confirm that we would be going, I tried not to show any excitement, worried that the trip might still not come about. I didn't tell anyone I was going to Hungary until perhaps a week before we were actually leaving, afraid that their opinions or views about the trip would conflict with my own feelings. Then I had a dinner at my house and told Tibi and Marika and Peter and his companion, Clari. At that dinner, I found out so many things from my brothers that I had never heard before in my life. Everyone just opened up about their experiences and feelings, about how they felt about me and our parents and what we had all gone through together.

Judy and I were taking separate flights, and her arrival two days after me would give me some much-needed time to be alone to become acclimatized. As soon as I arrived at Terminal 3 at Toronto's Pearson International Airport for the night flight, I could see how much the Hungarian national airline, Malev Airlines, had changed. The staff wore lovely uniforms with little scarves, and everyone, starting at the ticket counter, was very courteous, pleasant, and helpful, even wrapping my suitcase in plastic so it wouldn't scratch. The Communist regime had not been conducive to such a relaxed atmosphere and such European courtesy. On the flight, I began to see that things must have improved in Hungary. The last time I had flown with Malev was to see Zsofi. On that flight from Frankfurt to Budapest, they had served only salami sandwiches, and there had only been one toilet on the plane with a door that was constantly swinging open, allowing unpleasant smells to waft through the cabin. That plane had been in such disrepair that I had been more than a little concerned about landing. This time, the flight attendants were very cordial, constantly coming over to ask if there was anything I needed. The food was excellent, we could drink as much champagne or wine as we wanted, and there were films and beautiful music on the intercom all through the night.

During the last weeks before the trip, I had felt very strong negative as well as positive forces pulling at me. How, I asked myself, could I love Hungarian music, literature, and films so much and still feel so much animosity towards the Hungarian people? As a child, I had memorized so many poems and read so many of Hungary's great writers, and yet I always thought of Hungary as a dark, evil force. Now, in February 2003, I was sitting on a plane, relaxed and ready to admit to myself that, yes, perhaps it was possible to love a person but to not love certain things about him or her. In the same way, I reasoned, a person could love a country for many different reasons yet hate its people who betrayed her and were responsible for so much of her childhood suffering. Once I came to this realization, I was able to calm down and thoroughly enjoy a very pleasant flight to Budapest. I conversed with my fellow passengers, listened to delightful music, and became increasingly excited as I anticipated what would happen when I arrived.

Budapest's Ferihegyi Airport had changed and now looks like any other airport in a big European city. When a porter came up to me and asked if he could help me with my bags, I had no problem letting him. The terminal was very attractive and airy, and I noticed that they were in the process of putting up more buildings. The airport is almost an hour's drive from Budapest so I took a bus to my hotel. Tired from my sleepless night flight, I spent my time on the bus looking around and noticing how the signs and advertisements were just like the ones in Toronto, some even in English. That was something I had never seen before. When I arrived at my hotel, the Helia, I was greeted with a very warm, Hungarian welcome that made me feel special and right at home, although since I spoke the language, they didn't know what more they could do for me. The hotel itself was very beautiful and had a spa and hot springs treatment centre in it. Breakfast was included, and the buffet was wonderful and the food delicious.

I met all kinds of people during my first two days alone in Budapest. I felt free to speak with the many people who were at the hotel on conventions. There was a gentleman from Belgium with whom I had breakfast one morning and two ladies from Germany and one from England whom I befriended. I met a Jewish man who was there for a lingerie manufacturers' convention, who told me that some Hungarian businessmen were finding it very difficult to adjust to the transition from Communism to a free country; everyone had been so suppressed that they had no idea of how to conduct business as free enterprise.

As soon as I was settled into the hotel, I phoned my old girlfriend Juli, who got in touch with another friend of ours, Zsuzsa (not to be confused with my sister-in-law Zsuzsi), whom I hadn't seen for forty-seven years and who lived just a few blocks from my hotel. Within an hour, they were both there. We talked as if we had parted only yesterday. This visit with my school friends touched me deeply as we reminisced about our Sunday picnics in the mountains, the swimming pool on Margit Isle where we used to go swimming, the cafes where we would sit and talk and eat mouth-watering pastries. Juli and Zsuzsa arranged for me to meet with more of my old schoolmates whom I hadn't seen for so many years, and we all gathered in a very beautiful coffee house, just one of many in Budapest. Some of my friends were Jewish, although none of us had been too anxious to discuss religion while we were in school. Now I found I needed to ask questions. I wanted to know about their beliefs, their work experiences, money, religion, and so many other personal things.

It was a great reunion. Certainly our years of being apart would need more time to overcome, but I felt no strangeness, and there was a genuine warmth and interest in each other's lives. In general, though, I felt like a tourist, even though I spoke the language, knew where I was going, and was able to take the bus and the underground. Once the filming started, that sense of being a stranger would intensify as the camera, always beside me, interfered with my feelings. I experienced something like culture shock, too, as I walked around Budapest. There were the theatres, the opera house, the architecture. How could I have forgotten that Budapest was so beautiful? I remembered how ugly and run-down I thought it was when we first came there from Szarvas in 1949, but truly it is a picturesque and charming city. Why, I asked myself, should I be ashamed to have come from Budapest, from Hungary? There was nothing to be ashamed of. My parents had been too attached to Hungary and could not believe that their neighbours and friends would betray them the way they did during and after the Holocaust. I could not and would not ever forgive that betrayal. But the country itself was dear to me. I think Budapest can easily take its place among the great cities of Europe, and I loved every moment I was there.

When Judy arrived, we started filming. I waited for her at the airport with flowers, and although she tried to hide her tears, I could see she was moved by finally being in my country of birth. The schedule was that we would do the Budapest part first and then move on to Szarvas because there had been a big snowstorm and the crew did not feel it was safe to drive or even take the train to Szarvas at that point. Among other things, they filmed Judy unpacking the three-ply toilet paper she had brought because she remembered my story of our outhouse in Szarvas and the old cut-up newspapers we used for toilet paper. Nothing like that for my Canadian-born daughter!

In Budapest, we visited the apartment building where my family had lived when we first arrived from Szarvas, and my heart was in my throat as we approached it. As we rang for the superintendent, I remembered our life there and how difficult it had been in that small, shared apartment. The Communists had big ears and harsh punishments, and we had to watch every word we spoke. When the super came to the door, I explained to him what we were doing there, and he was kind enough to let me ring the people who lived in our apartment now. They were very nice, and without hesitation invited us in to look around the apartment my parents, Pali, Zsuzsi, and I had shared with another couple. Now an elderly mother and her daughter lived there alone.

Many things, of course, had changed since we had lived there, but the building was still in good shape, and Judy loved the ten-foot-high ceilings. There was now electric heating, and some of the beautiful blue tiles on the wood-burning fireplace were missing. I showed Judy where I used to sleep when I was a young, mischievous teenager. Even though the current residents had some of their own furniture in the apartment, I found our dining room cabinet still standing there with our knick-knacks in it, almost exactly as we had left it so many years ago. Then I noticed a painting that had been ours on the wall. I was stunned to see it there, and my first reaction was to ask them to sell it to me. But then Judy asked me how I felt to see it there, and I realized that I really didn't want anything from my former life. My parents could have stayed behind in Budapest with all the furniture and paintings, but they didn't. They risked their lives to flee Hungary with their children. That was worth more to me than all the material things we had left behind. I just wanted to take some photographs of the apartment and the furniture.

At four o'clock, we thanked the people, and for the last time closed the door to my old apartment and the life I had lived there. As we drove to the train station with all the heavy film equipment, I talked about how my parents and I had walked at four in the morning to that very train station on our last day in Budapest. Then the lot of us visited the Hauer Cukraszda, the famous coffee shop from my childhood that had just reopened a few days before we arrived. I explained that this was where I had run across the road the first time I had ever visited Budapest with my parents and talked about how my father had spanked me for scaring him half to death. From there, we visited my schools, both the gymnasium and the fashion college. Unfortunately, they would not let us inside the college because it was a Sunday, and we could not go back because we were leaving Budapest the next day. Even though I didn't get to go inside, it was still a good feeling to be able to identify those places meaningful to me and say, "Yes, I was here."

I felt my Jewishness very strongly in Budapest. In general, I found the people very open and not at all reluctant to answer my questions freely. If I thought the person I was speaking to might be Jewish, I simply went ahead and asked. One of the few exceptions I recall to this openness occurred while we were visiting our old apartment: Our Hungarian translator took me aside and confessed, very quietly, almost surreptitiously, in Hungarian, that he was Jewish. I wondered at the time why some people were still covering up, but I never got a chance to ask him.

I also wanted very much to visit the Jewish areas of Budapest, and we all drove around to see them. I went to the big supermarkets and was amazed to find they all have small, kosher sections. I went to the magnificent Dohany Temple, and that synagogue just took my breath away. I sat down in the very room where I had been confirmed at fifteen and remembered how all the girls had come, all dressed beautifully and each carrying a flower, on Shavuot to receive their certificates. I was told the temple still has a similar ceremony today. It amazed me that I didn't have to hide when I went to speak to the Jewish shopkeepers across from the synagogue to ask them about the Jewish community in Budapest.

My time with Judy was wonderful and a great revelation for both of us. I loved watching her reactions to everything that was happening. She even told me she would like to bring the whole family back here again because she never knew I came from such a beautiful and charming city. She was very impressed with the food in the restaurants and how elegantly it was served and said it was just the way I made it at home. We had our evenings to ourselves, and we went shopping, of course, and had lovely dinners together. It was during these dinners that we talked of our feelings. The camera had put her under pressure as well, and it was hard for her to be totally honest when it was running. We joked a lot and even wanted to have our hands tattooed: Buda for me and Pest (playing on the pun) for her. One night, I took her to the place where I had been hit by the jeep full of drunken Russian soldiers. That club is now a very expensive gambling casino, and we had an costly but delicious dinner there along with a great heart-to-heart talk. I was very happy that by this time I had learned how to love unconditionally, something that has made a great difference in all our lives.

The next day we set out for Szarvas. The drive took close to three hours because of the bad winter driving conditions. I had never seen so much snow in Hungary. The road was lined on both sides with trees that had snow piled two or three inches high on their branches, creating a fairyland where the trees themselves seemed somehow to be welcoming me and talking to me. It was a perfect, grand entrance.

When we arrived and I saw the sign SZARVAS just before the bridge over the Koros River, it shook me up more than I had anticipated. I felt both old sorrow and fear as I recalled the past. Just inside the town, we stopped for lunch at a restaurant known for its delicious fish soup. Across from the restaurant, on the other side of the river, are two castles, one large and one smaller, built very close to the water. These castles, which had been part of the landscape long before I was born, are now part of a campground organized by the World Jewish Congress, where some 2000 Jewish children come every year from all over the world. Even though I still cannot visualize Jewish children walking around in Szarvas, I would love to actually see those child-campers walking proudly as Jews on the streets of that small town, not bent like the willow trees on the banks of the river, shamed and forced to wear the yellow star as I was because I was a Jew.

Szarvas had changed a lot since we lived there, even since I last visited in 1978. Now all the streets and walkways were paved, and condominiums and town houses were going up all over. The main street was full of pastry shops, and there were hotels, restaurants, and stores selling everything from souvenirs to cell phones. Szarvas used to be nothing but a small farming village, but now it had been transformed into a spa and the kind of place you would come for vacation. Of course, there was the beautiful Koros River, and I would have loved to see Szarvas in the summer and swum across the river as we used to do as children.

It was time to go and see my old home. I had been back to Hungary in 1987 when Zsofi was dying, but my brothers and other people I knew had been back to Hungary and Szarvas more recently. They told me approximately where the house was but warned that the houses had been renumbered since we had lived there. The street is long, and the camera crew and I walked up and down in three feet of snow trying to find my house. As we walked, I told Judy that the road, which is now paved so that cars can go on it, used to be a dirt road when I lived there and that I used to travel it in a horse-drawn buggy.

We stopped at the corner of the street, and I pointed out the corner house where the Zionist organization had been located when we came back from the Holocaust. I remembered how that organization had saved my life and kept me sane. Now that building is a pub; Hungarian people drink a lot. We went in to see if anyone could help us find my house, but when I asked about it, they got scared and turned away. I suppose that the film crew with their cameras and mikes might have looked very official, so I told them we were not there to frighten them. I told them I used to live there and was trying to find somebody who might know where my family, the Bergers and the Scheiners, used to live. Maybe someone remembered my grandfather's bakery. They told me that there were no people there by that name. Yes, Jews used to live there, they said, and there had been a bakery, but they had no idea where the Berger/Scheiner house would be. I walked out and encountered a young couple coming home from church and asked them, too. They told me they had lived in Szarvas for only a couple of years. As soon as I mentioned Jews, the man became rude to me. I told him that I was Jewish and that I just wanted him to know we were not people-eaters and no harm would come to him if he talked to me. It was ironic that for the first time since I had come back to Hungary on this trip I would encounter anti-Jewish remarks here in Szarvas. That encounter did little to help me relax, and it put a damper on my stay in the town.

But as hard as I tried, I couldn't seem to find our house. Some of the group gave up and went back to the warm car. Only I and one cameraman continued on relentlessly, walking for another two-and-a-half hours in that cold, my disappointment captured on film. When I crossed the road for the third time, I walked up and down the street and finally recognized our house. It was not where everyone had told me to look, but I just knew it was the right place, even though it looked different, all run down and dirty, with one of the windows in the front of the house made into a door and the part of the house that had been our gorgeous dining room turned into a flower store.

I fetched Judy and the film crew, and I knocked on the door until a man came to the window. He looked scared. I told him that I had been born in that house and explained everything to him about the film company that was with me. I said we would like to come in to see the house and that the film crew would like to film everything and show it on television in Canada. He absolutely refused. He said he couldn't because the police would come and question them, that the police were probably watching even as we spoke. Perhaps his family had suffered under Communism and still feared the old system. I told him that those days were gone, but if he was afraid, to direct me to the police station and I would be happy to go there and bring a policeman back to advise him that he had their permission to let us in. I told him I had a book about Szarvas that was written in 1936 that very few people were even aware of and that my father's and grandfather's names were in it. I added that I would show him the book where their names were underlined.

He went to talk to his wife, who in a little while came to the window.

"I know you." I said to her.

"No, you don't know me," she answered.

I told her I had been there in 1978, and a lady who looked exactly like her had let me in and had given me coffee and even a gift to take back with me. That lady had told me she was a grandmother and that her granddaughter was away at school.

"That was my mother," this woman told me. "She passed away twenty years ago."

My story about her grandmother must have triggered something in the woman because she relented, and she and her husband opened the door and let us in even though they still seemed a bit scared about everything and did not welcome any questions. I entered first and stepped into their kitchen. The house was not at all the same as I remembered it, even from my visit in 1978. They had boarded up our open veranda on both sides. The sunroom with its windows on three sides, where we would eat in the summer, was still there, but the beautiful rose garden that had been in front of it was gone. Now they were raising pigs in the area where the outhouse had been. Beyond the garden was the well where my father would lower the cantaloupe or watermelon in a bucket on Fridays so it would be cool and we could have it for Shabbat dinner. I remembered how I would come and help him and how he would always be afraid I would fall in. I couldn't take a picture of the well; I couldn't hold the camera steady enough in my hands.

It was almost as if my mother were standing there right beside me, I felt her presence so strongly. I saw a vision of her in her blue dress with the very small, beige polka dots on it, buttoned all the way down the front. I remembered the day she was doing a final walk-around to make sure that our house was ready for Shavuot and I told her I got my period. Now all the windows were covered with newspaper although I didn't ask why. I turned to my daughter and she saw that I was crying. She told me she was very happy for me but that she could not feel the same things I did. And I understood as she wrapped her arms around me.

I had bought a Cabbage Patch doll some time before in Toronto and had brought her with me. I wanted to replay for the film crew what had happened to me when the Nazis had taken my doll, Pani, away – how I had wanted them to shoot me or give me my doll back. I had the doll in the car, but I now found I just couldn't re-enact what had happened to me. It was as if that Cabbage Patch doll didn't belong here. The pain of my old loss was so sharp, as if the incident with Pani had happened only yesterday, that my anger and anguish rushed back to almost suffocate me. It felt to me like loving a child and then losing him or her – you cannot replace that child with another one. I had lost something all those years ago, and that loss was still hurting me. I had lost not only my beloved Pani, but also my dignity, childish as it was, and my faith in the goodness of humanity. Even worse, I lost my faith in my parents, that they could protect my child vulnerability from any outside threats. My whole world had come tumbling down that day, and the smallest thing still triggers my anxiety and depression and leaves me helpless and paralyzed with fear.

Later after we left the house and walked around the corner to see where the synagogue and the Jewish school had stood, I really felt pain. I showed them the exact buildings where the Hungarian Iron Cross soldiers had stripped us and searched us, trying to find gold, and I told them how violated I had felt, a child of seven. Later that year, the Hungarians had burned the synagogue to the ground. Now there were other buildings on that piece of land, with an apartment building and car garages standing on that shame-filled site. The film crew asked me to go to the spot and walk around there, but I couldn't and I refused. I wasn't ready to do that. I just couldn't go back there.

By then it was already six thirty in the evening, and I was exhausted. We had to go back to the hotel. I couldn't come down to eat dinner that night and simply ordered tea to drink in my room. There were so many feelings in me that I couldn't sort out and come to terms with. The next day, everyone told me that they had heard me crying upstairs but didn't know what to do – to come up or to leave me alone. I would have appreciated someone to hug me, but I had my doll for comfort, and in the long run, perhaps it was good that I had that time to myself and had let all those poisonous memories come out. In the end, I felt almost nothing for the place where I was born. I couldn't relate to it anymore even though it was my birthplace.

It was actually a relief to realize that I had absolutely no roots left in Szarvas. Those roots had all been torn up. My roots were in Canada now. Even my parents are buried in Canada. From now on, if I ever come back to Hungary, it will be as a tourist. I will not be coming "home." I have come to understand that there is no real going back, no "homecoming" without a home. We have to go forward, and I *am* going forward.

The next day, we came back to the house to film some more in daylight, and to my surprise, Manyi's brother, Gyuri, had found out that I was there. A car pulled up beside us and he got out. He lives in Budapest but was visiting some of his wife's relatives and had come to show us around. It was a great help to have him there because my memories were so tangled up with emotions. Later, we went with him to the Jewish cemetery. Because there was so much snow, we did not attempt to go in, but with Gyuri's help, we did venture far enough in for me to see a memorial monument that had been erected with the names of Jews from Szarvas who had been murdered in the Holocaust inscribed on it. As I stood there and read the names, I was amazed that almost everyone in my father's entire family, who didn't even live in Szarvas, had been killed by the Nazis. No one had ever talked about what had happened to my relatives. When we came back from the Holocaust, we didn't know who had survived and who hadn't; some people just never came back. It was very painful for me to stand there and read their names.

After we left the cemetery, Gyuri took us back to his relatives. They were celebrating the hostess's fiftieth birthday party and welcomed us eight complete strangers warmly, feeding us a feast with drinks to warm us and cheer us up. I could not thank them enough, and the whole film crew said that this was the highlight of their tour.

Although Judy left for Canada right after the filming finished, I stayed on in Budapest for a few more days to spend some more time with my friends. This was great fun because when the film crew had been there, I had to always watch where and how I stepped and what I was feeling in front of the camera, knowing that it all could end up on television. Now I was free to be myself, and my friends showed me around the city very proudly. We went to the opera, and I was very impressed with how elegantly people still dressed for the occasion.

Still, I could hardly wait to come back to Toronto and be at home. I am very happy to have had such a wonderful experience in Budapest and to hear from my daughter Judy that she would like to go back. I know this is a big thing for Judy because she has told me that, even now in her late forties, she often wakes up in the night and feels like she is being hunted by the police or soldiers. I don't know why she has this nightmare; she refuses to talk about it. She hates to see me hurt and feels guilty and scared that what happened to me could happen again. I had never talked to my children about the Holocaust when they were small so I don't know how she knew to feel those things. As far as my younger daughter, Lesley, is concerned, I have promised to take her to Hungary when she is ready. With the Almighty's help, I will be able to do that.

On my flight home, I thought about what I had just experienced in Hungary and what had changed in me. I think I stopped hating the Hungarians. I realized there are bad and good people everywhere. I had wanted to meet ordinary people, to try to understand how a person can be transformed from a human being into a beast. I have learned in my quest to know myself over the past few years that there iş good and beauty in every person and that if we can talk, if we can connect with people and *really* get to know them, perhaps we can begin to eradicate hatred from the world.

I can say now that I have lived a full life, even though my vision has sometimes been blurred by hatred and pain. I have always loved children, and God knows, I love my two daughters. Now that I am a grandmother, I can relive my own childhood through my grandsons and be a child again. Life, I have learned, is the greatest miracle. You just put one foot in front of the other, and one day, you arrive at your destination. I am here and I am leaving a living testimonial to my family – and to you, my reader – of my trials, tribulations, and growth as I go towards my twilight years.

LEGACIES SHARED SERIES

Janice Dickin, series editor
ISSN 1498-2358

The Legacies Shared series preserves the many personal histories and experiences of pioneer and immigrant life that may have disappeared or have been overlooked. The purpose of this series is to create, save, and publish voices from the heartland of the continent that might otherwise be lost to the public discourse. The manuscripts may take the form of memoirs, letters, photographs, art work, recipes or maps, works of fiction or poetry, archival documents, even oral history.

Memories, Dreams, Nightmares: Memoirs of a Holocaust Survivor Jack Weiss ·
No. 13

The Honourable Member for Vegreville: The Memoirs and Diary of Anthony Hlynka, MP Anthony Hlynka, translated by Oleh Gerus · No. 14

The Letters of Margaret Butcher: Missionary-Imperialism on the North Pacific Coast Margaret Butcher, edited by Mary Ellen Kelm · No. 15

The First Dutch Settlement in Alberta: Letters from the Pioneer Years, 1903-14 edited by Donald Sinnema · No. 16

Suitable for the Wilds: Letters from Northern Alberta, 1929-31 Mary Percy Jackson edited by Janice Dickin · No. 17

A Voice of Her Own edited by Thelma Poirier, Doris Bircham, JoAnn Jones-Hole, Patricia Slade and Susan Vogelaar · No. 18

What's All This Got to Do with the Price of 2 x 4's? Michael Apsey · No. 19

Zhorna: Material Culture of the Ukrainian Pioneers Roman Fodchuk · No. 20

Behind the Man: John Laurie, Ruth Gorman, and the Indian Vote in Canada Ruth Gorman, edited by Frits Pannekoek · No. 21

Missing Pieces: My Life as a Child Survivor of the Holocaust Olga Verrall · No. 22